Minority Populations in Canadian Second Language Education

NEW PERSPECTIVES ON LANGUAGE AND EDUCATION

Series Editor: Professor Viv Edwards, *University of Reading, Reading, Great Britain*
Series Advisor: Professor Allan Luke, *Queensland University of Technology, Brisbane, Australia*

Two decades of research and development in language and literacy education have yielded a broad, multidisciplinary focus. Yet education systems face constant economic and technological change, with attendant issues of identity and power, community and culture. This series will feature critical and interpretive, disciplinary and multidisciplinary perspectives on teaching and learning, language and literacy in new times.

Full details of all the books in this series and of all our other publications can be found on http://www.multilingual-matters.com, or by writing to Multilingual Matters, St Nicholas House, 31-34 High Street, Bristol BS1 2AW, UK.

Minority Populations in Canadian Second Language Education

Edited by
Katy Arnett and Callie Mady

MULTILINGUAL MATTERS
Bristol • Buffalo • Toronto

Library of Congress Cataloging in Publication Data
A catalog record for this book is available from the Library of Congress.
Minority Populations in Canadian Second Language Education/Edited by Katy Arnett and Callie Mady.
New Perspectives on Language and Education: 32.
Includes bibliographical references and index.
1. Language and languages—Study and teaching—Canada. 2. Second language acquisition—Study and teaching—Canada. 3. Multicultural education—Canada. 4. Linguistic minorities—Canada. 5. Education, Bilingual—Canada. I. Arnett, Katy. II. Mady, Callie.
P57.C3M56 2013
418.0071'071–dc23 2013022859

British Library Cataloguing in Publication Data
A catalogue entry for this book is available from the British Library.

ISBN-13: 978-1-78309-030-3 (hbk)
ISBN-13: 978-1-78309-029-7 (pbk)

Multilingual Matters
UK: St Nicholas House, 31-34 High Street, Bristol BS1 2AW, UK.
USA: UTP, 2250 Military Road, Tonawanda, NY 14150, USA.
Canada: UTP, 5201 Dufferin Street, North York, Ontario M3H 5T8, Canada.

Copyright © 2013 Katy Arnett, Callie Mady and the authors of individual chapters.

All rights reserved. No part of this work may be reproduced in any form or by any means without permission in writing from the publisher.

The policy of Multilingual Matters/Channel View Publications is to use papers that are natural, renewable and recyclable products, made from wood grown in sustainable forests. In the manufacturing process of our books, and to further support our policy, preference is given to printers that have FSC and PEFC Chain of Custody certification. The FSC and/or PEFC logos will appear on those books where full certification has been granted to the printer concerned.

Typeset by Deanta Global Publishing Services Limited.
Printed and bound in Great Britain by Short Run Press Ltd.

Contents

Contributors   vii

Introduction: Broadening the Lens of Second Language Education in Canada: Minority Populations in Canadian Second Language Education   xi
Katy Arnett and Callie Mady

Part 1: French as an Additional Language: Immigrants' Learning of French in English-dominant Canada

1 Adding Languages, Adding Benefits: Immigrant Students' Attitudes Toward and Performance in FSOL Programs in Canada   3
Callie Mady

2 Learning French in British Columbia: English as Additional Language Learner and Parent Perspectives   22
Wendy Carr

3 French is Hard: An English Language Learner's Experience in Core French   38
Jordana F. Garbati

Part 2: Heritage Language and Culture Maintenance for Immigrants and Their Families

4 Fostering Heritage Languages and Diasporic Identities: The Role of Grassroots Initiatives in Alberta and British Columbia   55
Martin Guardado and Ava Becker

5 Self, Identity and Motivation in the Development and Maintenance of German as a Heritage Language   71
Kimberly A. Noels

6 Learning Chinese as a Heritage Language 87
Patricia A. Duff and Duanduan Li

Part 3: Individuals with Disabilities and Second Language Study

7 The Genesis and Perpetuation of Exemptions and Transfers from French Second Language Programs for Students with Diverse Learning Needs: A Preliminary Examination and Their Link to Inclusion 103
Katy Arnett

8 Reading Without Borders: At-Risk Students Transitioning from L1 to L2 in French Immersion 118
Renée Bourgoin and Joseph Dicks

9 The Writing Processes of a Grade 7 French Immersion Student with Asperger Syndrome 135
Josée Le Bouthillier

Part 4: The Revival, Maintenance and Growth of Aboriginal Languages in Canada

10 A Fair Country? Consideration of Canada's Debt to Indigenous Language Renewal 153
Donna-Lee Smith, Josephine Peck and Donald Taylor

11 First Nations, Métis and Inuit K-12 Language Programming: What Works? 169
Carmen Gillies and Marie Battiste

12 How Have Aboriginal North Americans Responded to Writing Systems in Their Own Languages? 184
Barbara Burnaby

Conclusion: Additional Conceptions of Second Language Education in Canada 199
Callie Mady and Katy Arnett

Index 201

Contributors

Katy Arnett is an Associate Professor of Educational Studies at St Mary's College of Maryland, USA, and was a Fulbright Scholar during 2012–2013, based at the Second Language Research Institute of Canada at the University of New Brunswick. She teaches undergraduate and graduate courses on second language education, special education and instructional methods. Her research explores the experiences of students with more specialized learning needs in second language learning settings, with particular attention to students with disabilities and newcomer students learning the language of the new community.

Marie Battiste is a Mi'kmaw educator from Potlotek First Nations, Nova Scotia, and Full Professor in the College of Education at the University of Saskatchewan. Her research interests are in initiating institutional change in the decolonization of education, in particular the humanities, language and social justice, and post-colonial educational approaches that recognize and affirm the political and cultural diversity of Canada.

Ava Becker is a doctoral student in the TESL program at the University of British Columbia and she holds an MA in Applied Linguistics from the University of Alberta. Over the past few years, she has conducted two studies on Spanish heritage language development in Edmonton and has presented her findings at teacher, graduate and international conferences. Her research interests include language and culture development in refugee contexts.

Renée Bourgoin is a doctoral candidate at the University of New Brunswick. Her current area of research centers on teaching and intervention strategies needed to support struggling readers in French immersion. Renée is also a part-time instructor at the Second Language Research Institute of Canada within the University of New Brunswick's Faculty of Education. She is also a member of the Institute's research team on exemplary literacy and teaching practices.

Barbara Burnaby has been involved in Aboriginal language education for nearly 40 years and has also worked in contexts supporting the learning of English as a foreign and second language. She co-developed Ontario's Native Language Instructors Training Program and school policy on Native languages, as well as developing Language Arts for Native children, teacher training in ESL and ESL assessment for adult immigrants. Most recently, she taught at Memorial University of Newfoundland. She volunteers full-time now with refugees in Newfoundland.

Wendy Carr teaches graduate and undergraduate courses in the Department of Language and Literacy Education at the University of British Columbia. She has been a teacher and teacher educator for over 30 years and played a leadership role in British Columbia's implementation of Intensive French, including conducting research, since its inception in the province in 2004.

Joseph Dicks is Director of the Second Language Research Institute of Canada and a professor in the Faculty of Education at the University of New Brunswick, Canada, where he teaches undergraduate and graduate courses in assessment and bilingual education. His research focuses on literacy and assessment in second language programs. He is also the author and series editor of textbooks for French second language programs.

Patricia Duff is Professor of Language and Literacy Education (TESL and Modern Language Education) at the University of British Columbia. With co-author Duanduan Li, she currently co-directs the Centre for Research in Chinese Language and Literacy Education. Their joint SSHRC-funded research examines language socialization in both English and Chinese language education contexts.

Jordana Garbati is a PhD candidate in the Faculty of Education at The University of Western Ontario. Her current research examines teachers' perceptions of inclusion of English language learners in French as a second language programs. She has received funding from the Ontario Graduate Scholarship and the Social Sciences and Humanities Research Council of Canada. Jordana has taught at the elementary, secondary and post-secondary levels in English and French in Ontario, France and Switzerland.

Carmen Gillies is of Métis, Norwegian and Chinese ancestry and is from Saskatoon, Saskatchewan. She is a PhD candidate at the University of Saskatchewan, Department of Educational Foundations and a Senior Research Assistant with the Aboriginal Education Research Centre. Her areas of research include critical race theories of education, Indigenous education, Métis epistemologies, mixed-race studies and violence prevention.

Martin Guardado is an Associate Professor of Applied Linguistics and the Academic Director of the English Language Program at the University of Alberta. He obtained his PhD from the Department of Language and Literacy Education at the University of British Columbia. His research interests include second language socialization in home, school and community settings, heritage languages, diasporic identities, and technology and second language education. His work has appeared in several peer-reviewed journals and edited books.

Josée Le Bouthillier is in her third year of a PhD program in Education at the University of New Brunswick in Fredericton. Her research interests are French immersion programs, literacy, more specifically writing and at-risk students. Josée taught for many years at the middle-school level and also at the university level in the area of second language methodology.

Duanduan Li is Associate Professor of Chinese Applied Linguistics at the University of British Columbia, where she served as Director of the Chinese language program for nine years. With co-author Patricia Duff, she currently co-directs the Centre for Research in Chinese Language and Literacy Education. Their joint Social Sciences and Humanities Research Council of Canada (SSHRC)-funded research examines language socialization in both English and Chinese language education contexts.

Callie Mady is an Associate Professor at Nipissing University in the Schulich School of Education, North Bay, ON, Canada. She holds a PhD from the Ontario Institute for Studies in Education (OISE) of the University of Toronto with a focus on second language education. Her research interests include French as a second language education and multilingual language acquisition. In particular, her research focuses on minority populations in those areas – immigrants and students with learning difficulties.

Kimberly A. Noels is a professor in the Social and Cultural Psychology area of the Department of Psychology and an adjunct professor in the Department of Educational Psychology at the University of Alberta, Canada. She studies the psychology of language and communication processes, with a focus on intercultural communication. Her current research program concerns the contextual and temporal dynamics of experiences of self-determined motivation, language use and ethnic identity.

Josephine Peck is an Elder in the Cape Breton Mi'kmaq community of Wagmatcook, speaking both Mi'kmaq and English fluently. A former teacher and principal, she is in high demand to teach her heritage language at both the community and university levels.

Donna-Lee Smith, Faculty of Education McGill University, has been an instructor for over 20 years in the Office of First Nations and Inuit Education (OFNIE) – teaching in communities throughout Nunavut, Nunavik, Quebec and Nova Scotia. She served as Director of OFNIE for six years, overseeing the delivery of teacher-training programs for the Innu, Inuit and Cree nations. Her areas of research and interest include literacy – a longitudinal look at the status of the Mi'kmaq language in Cape Breton; and children's literature – a series of workshops with teachers who wrote and illustrated storybooks in Innu, Inuktitut and Mi'kmaq.

Donald Taylor, Professor in the Faculty of Psychology at McGill University, is author/co-author of over 200 articles and author/editor of six books. He has received international recognition for his work on Inuit language retention and the impact of heritage language learning on self-esteem.

Introduction: Broadening the Lens of Second Language Education in Canada: Minority Populations in Canadian Second Language Education

Katy Arnett and Callie Mady

In 1972, the Canadian second language education system received worldwide attention when the results of the 'St Lambert Experiment' were published, chronicling the development and initial years of a French immersion program in Quebec for Anglophone children (Lambert & Tucker, 1972). Using French as the language of instruction for nearly all aspects of the school day, the teachers in St Lambert were not only able to help their Anglophone students learn their subjects, but also develop proficiencies in the target language. In the 40 years hence, immersion programming has been touted as 'the great Canadian success story' (Hayden, 1988) having been identified as not only the best way to learn French in Canada (Genesee, 2007; Lazuruk, 2007), but also the program model for successful second language learning in general. Such a positive reputation is perhaps, in part, due to corresponding positive academic results from various research studies (e.g. Genesee, 1987, 2004; Lambert & Tucker, 1972; Swain & Lapkin, 1982; Turnbull *et al.*, 2001). Without a doubt, the innovation and success of French immersion programming earned global respect for Canada's efforts to promote its official language bilingualism within a multicultural context.

Over this same 40-year period, shifts in the Canadian landscape have facilitated the development of new understandings in other areas of second language learning. These new knowledge bases have often been overshadowed by the successes of French immersion, but in light of the world's continued expectations of multilingual skills, the increased determination to revive and sustain our different heritages and the changing views about the rights and potential of *all* individuals in society, Canada is once again in the position to offer the world new ideas about second, third and fourth language development. This volume, as the title conveys, is about offering a broader view of Canadian contributions to second language education; French immersion is now just one of many parts of the language education spectrum in this country.

We have sought to offer this broader view through the lens of various minority populations in Canada, as these groups have been typically the most overlooked in considerations of second, additional, or heritage language education. As a country, Canada is working to facilitate and protect the rights of those with less power in society, and while there is still much work to do, gains are starting to emerge in four key areas in language education: newcomers working to develop skills in both of the country's official languages; newcomers' maintenance of their heritage languages and cultures as they integrate into Canadian society; individuals with disabilities or difficulties seeking access to the same opportunities as everyone else; and Aboriginal populations seeking to revive, preserve and promote their Indigenous languages. These are the four sub-themes of this volume.

Newcomers Working to Develop Skills in Canada's Official Languages

Although Canada has always attracted newcomers, in the past, immigrants were most often from countries that shared one of Canada's official languages. More recently, Canada is attracting immigrants whose languages are from non-European language families. The increase in the numbers of, and the diverse origins of these newcomers' home languages have led policy makers and second language teachers to question if and how students who are learning English in 'English'-dominant Canada should learn French. In this sub-section, the contributors focus on trying to move that dialogue further, by considering the performance, motivation and learning experiences of the students in this learning situation.

Callie Mady's chapter opens this section, as she compares newcomer students' attitudes toward the study of French as a second official language (FSOL) with the attitudes of Canadian-born unilingual and multilingual students. Using questionnaire data, interviews and language proficiency assessments, Mady sought to determine how differences in attitudes may also link to differences in performance in French. Her findings revealed that the most positive attitudes and the greatest successes were within the immigrant student sub-group. Multilingual students born in Canada had more positive views than those of unilingual students also born in Canada, but less positive views than those of the immigrant students. The unilingual Canadian-born students also had the lowest scores in French skills. Mady's findings reveal that calls to exempt immigrant students from FSOL programs may be misplaced, as this student population was the most positive and in several areas, the more successful student group. Further, Mady situates these findings in relation to the data trends of Canada's immigrant population to argue that efforts to promote multilingualism in Canada's immigrant population as they integrate into Canadian society may somehow be falling short.

Drawing on data from two different projects, Wendy Carr considers the perspectives of newcomer students and parents in relation to the reason they pursue or encourage the pursuit of proficiency in French. Using interviews and questionnaires, Carr is able to show that the notion of language as 'social capital', as promoted by Bourdieu (1977) in particular, remains at the forefront of the reasons for which newcomer families favor French study in the province of British Columbia. Multilingualism is viewed in a very favorable light by the participants in her research, who convey that developing skills in French, beyond their skills in English, is an important part of the establishment of a Canadian identity. These findings actually mirror some of the reasons for which British Columbia promotes the development of skills in English and French for its newcomers in official policy documents.

Finally, Jordana Garbati's contribution offers a new path in the research, examining temporary residence students in French as a second language (FSL) programs in Canada. Her case study focuses on an international student who is in Canada temporarily, specifically for the purpose of advancing his English skills to be well positioned for post-secondary education. Many provinces of Canada offer such programs for international students, and to date, previous research on English learners in FSL have considered students who are permanent immigrants to Canada. Garbati's research provides insight into the influences and beliefs that may be at work when an international student here to learn English is required to also pursue French study. The notion of 'relevance' is a key focus in the chapter, as it becomes clear that the student and several key stakeholders question the value of FSL study for a temporary resident not intending to remain in Canada after a year. Garbati's study also shines a light on potential gaps in FSL teachers' knowledge bases about how best to support English learners in the French classroom.

Maintenance of Their Heritage Languages and Cultures

The changes in Canada's demographics over the last 40 years have also underscored the importance of providing the means for a multilingual population to maintain their languages of origin/heritage. Although language maintenance for immigrants and their families has remained, for the most part, outside of mainstream education in Canada, the large number of immigrants has illuminated the urgency to enhance the means by which education can support the maintenance of their language of origin.

Martin Guardado and Ava Becker bring together data from several research projects to explore how Spanish-speaking immigrants to Canada have maintained and deepened their linguistic and cultural ties to their communities. Working with immigrants to British Columbia and Alberta in these projects, Guardado and Becker seek to understand how the participants leveraged their membership in grassroots community organizations to shape their linguistic and cultural identities and incorporate their heritages into their life in Canada, with a particular focus on members of the second generation. As immigrant families become established Canadian families, the ideas explored in Guardado and Becker's chapter provide insight into how heritage languages and cultures may come to be viewed within their communities over time, when less knowledge of the culture of the home country is available to its members. They also consider the nature and goals of the community organizations and how their infrastructures come to shape (or not) the views of its members. Overall, the chapter provides important insights into how some newcomers transition between their old lives and cultural roles in their home country and their new existence in Canada.

Kimberly Noels' chapter touches on themes of identity, in her review of research considering the motivations of individuals who have heritage language connections to German. Through the lens of Self-Determination Theory (Deci & Ryan, 1985), Noels contends that motivations to study German for heritage speakers depend on how much they view knowledge and proficiency in the language as critical to their sense of self. Even with the challenge created by a lack of a true census of German heritage language programs throughout Canada, Noels has successfully mined existing research on Canadian students of German to explore the motivational influences for language study. Finding evidence of motivations from the intrinsic to the extrinsic, from the personal to the professional, Noels is also able to consider how the context of the language study experience also comes to play a role in how students of German come to shape their identities. Such insight is helpful in guiding future heritage language programs for German, which is seeing both a decline and aging of its speakers in Canada.

Finally, Patricia Duff and Duanduan Li consider the experiences of heritage language speakers and learners with Chinese backgrounds. Their work begins by outlining some of the challenges with researching Chinese heritage language speakers and communities in Canada, particularly the fact that there are multiple Chinese languages and cultural traditions linked to different communities from the same home country. As part of the chapter, they consider the way in which Chinese language study for individuals with a Chinese heritage has been positioned within Canada, drawing comparisons not only with programs for Francophones and members of Aboriginal communities, but also with the United States, which also has a large population of heritage speakers of Chinese. The review comes to focus on three particular themes within the field: how children are socialized and supported in their study of Chinese through family connections and access to literacy resources; motivation and identity issues for younger learners of Chinese as a heritage language; and needed directions in future professional development and research endeavors.

Individuals with Disabilities and Second Language Study

Over the last 40 years, there has been a slow philosophical shift in how individuals with disabilities and difficulties are viewed within Canadian society, leading up to the past decade where 'inclusion' has been a primary focus. In the same time period, as often as French immersion has been labeled 'successful', it has also been labeled 'elitist', since its student population has most often been characterized by high-achieving students with strong linguistic skills; students not fitting this profile have often been excluded from French immersion study or transferred out of the program upon encountering difficulties. Because French immersion has been 'the' program for FSL study in Canada, the principles and practices that have defined its existence carry a lot of influence over popular beliefs about who should study French at all, regardless of the program.

Currently, students who have been previously excluded or otherwise discouraged from FSL study in Canada are now populating classrooms in larger numbers than ever before because of the aforementioned changing views about disability. However, FSL programs are still wrestling with a legacy of exclusion, born in the French immersion programs. For inclusive teaching to gain widespread support in FSL programs in Canada, the three chapters in this section show that it is imperative that French immersion programs lead the way.

The first chapter outlines the reasons for which FSL programs sought to limit the types of learner profiles that should have access to its programs and explores possible impediments on its path to facilitating inclusion now. Katy Arnett offers an anthropological treatment of various research strands to explain the genesis of exemptions from FSL study requirements or transfers out of FSL programs for students who encountered difficulties. She argues that views about disability and what it means to be 'proficient' in a language have played an important role in the creation of exemptions and transfer policies in Canadian FSL programs, and that FSL programs (particularly French immersion) were initially conforming to practices and ideas that were prevalent elsewhere in the education system. Arnett also draws on interview data from four current stakeholders in FSL education to explore some of the possible reasons for which the practices of excluding students with disabilities and difficulties continue, even though inclusion is currently the expectation. The chapter concludes with ideas about how to facilitate changes in attitude and practice toward individuals with disabilities in FSL study.

Renée Bourgoin and Joseph Dicks collaborate to offer a chapter that explores the nature of reading acquisition of French immersion students, in both their first language (English) and in French. Responding to calls to better identify which students may be at risk for challenges in reading within the context of French immersion (e.g. Genesee *et al.*, 2004), Bourgoin and Dicks endeavor to describe the reading profiles of eight Grade 3 students participating in a larger study. The study followed them from Grade 2 (when they were just enrolled in their English program) through their first year of French immersion (Grade 3), and collected data on their reading skills in both languages. Bourgoin and Dicks confirm that students who had strong reading skills in English kept similar profiles in French immersion, just as students with weaker reading skills in English maintained the same status in French immersion. Further, their research reveals that the students' awareness and use of strategies during reading exercises played a role in the strength of their overall reading skills. They recommend that knowledge of students' reading profiles and awareness of the strategies associated with particular profiles can offer meaningful starting points for developing intervention plans for struggling readers in French immersion programs.

Finally, Josée Le Bouthillier's chapter offers a novel contribution to our understanding of the development of second language writing skills for a student with an autism spectrum disorder in a French immersion context. Though her case study of 'Molly', a Grade 7 student who has been in French immersion since Grade 1, does not offer generalizable findings, it does confirm that much of what has been found in the first language literature about writing development in individuals with Asperger syndrome (a type of autism spectrum disorder) held true for her experiences with 'Molly' in the second language classroom. As has been the case for previous research (e.g. Cummins, 1983), this study offers suggested supports (e.g. use of written cue cards) for facilitating writing skills in students with Asperger syndrome and as such provides an important contribution to the research literature on inclusion within second language contexts. Le Bouthillier's work represents a key step for showing how inclusion can work in a French immersion classroom, which could then influence other FSL programs.

The Revival, Maintenance and Growth of Aboriginal Languages in Canada

Like all countries founded as part of a colonial and colonizing system, Canada's history includes movements to eliminate and/or otherwise restrict the languages of its Aboriginal populations (Kirkness, 1998). Over the course of the past few decades, the federal government has recognized the necessity to support the revitalization of Indigenous language learning/maintenance, leading to various initiatives to develop, maintain and grow Aboriginal language programs. Perhaps more so than any other section in this book, the chapters presented here offer some evidence to contradict the 'flattering image' accorded to Canada over its treatment of multilingualism (Duff, 2007). These chapters will touch on the social, affective and linguistic consequences of Canada's legacy of discrimination against speakers of the Indigenous languages of this region, as the authors seek to craft and expand understandings of Aboriginal languages in the broader context of language study in Canada. The research in this field is still quite minimal when compared to other bodies of research on language education in Canada, but as is evident in the chapters, scholars in the field are savvy in their use of the existing understandings to identify courses of action for reviving the languages.

In the first contribution to this section, Donna-Lee Smith, Josephine Peck and Donald Taylor consider the overall status of and efforts to stabilize Indigenous languages within Canada, with particular attention to the language of Mi'kmaq, which is spoken in the provinces of Atlantic Canada. Their narrative analysis is three-pronged, beginning with a balanced, but impassioned consideration of the damages done to Indigenous languages within Canada and the challenges those realities raise for establishing heritage language immersion programs within Aboriginal communities. Next, their chapter moves on to consider the challenges associated with developing research protocols that are able to simultaneously respect the cultural traditions and values of the Aboriginal communities in which the programs are based, but are consistent with the scholarly expectations. The third section applies the decisions discussed in the previous part of the chapter to explain the results of studies that compare the Mi'kmaq skills of students in an immersion program to those who attended a regular program for Mi'kmaq heritage language development within the community. Their chapter concludes with a discussion of the implications of not moving forward with efforts to preserve and grow the Indigenous languages of Canada.

The collaboration of Carmen Gillies and Marie Battiste provides a more in-depth consideration of the challenges of developing K-12 programs for teaching Aboriginal languages within Aboriginal communities. Drawing on some of what has been learned through the development of French immersion and heritage language programs, they identify five components critical to the development of successful Aboriginal language programs: sustainable funding, community support and influence, language status and prestige, teacher certification and training and Indigenous pedagogy. Their literature review situates these components within the cultural values of the Aboriginal community, providing readers with a concrete example of how culturally relevant programming can be conceptualized for Aboriginal populations.

Finally, Barbara Burnaby tackles the challenge of chronicling written language literacy within Aboriginal language traditions, which is of relevance in the efforts to move Aboriginal language programming forward. Through an anthropological exploration of decades of primary and secondary source documents, Burnaby aims to give a voice to the ways in which Aboriginal communities have sought to define literacies for themselves and respond to challenges from outsiders toward their language traditions. She resists extrapolating the views of Euro-North Americans toward literacy to the Aboriginal context and successfully uncovers 10 overarching perspectives within Aboriginal chronicles about their conceptualizations of literacy, its use among the communities, reasons for its decline and hopes for its revival. As expected, Burnaby's review highlights some of the ways in which Canada has worked to the detriment of its Aboriginal communities, but the concluding remarks of the chapter provide hope for what may be accomplished.

Conclusion

Since the French immersion programs first began almost 50 years ago, the Canadian second language education landscape has changed noticeably as a result of demographic shifts, new philosophies informing education and a recognition of the need to revive the Indigenous cultures and languages that were in this country before French and English settlements. We hope that you will appreciate this broadened conceptualization of second language education from the Canadian context.

References

Bourdieu, P. (1977) *Outline of a Theory of Practice* (R. Nice, trans.). New York: Cambridge University Press.
Cummins, J. (1983) *Bilingualism and Special Education: Issues in Assessment and Pedagogy*. Clevedon: Multilingual Matters.
Deci, E.L. and Ryan, R.M. (1985) *Intrinsic Motivation and Self-Determination in Human Behavior*. New York: Plenum Press.
Duff, P. (2007) Multilingualism in Canadian schools: Myths, realities, and possibilities. *Canadian Journal of Applied Linguistics* 10 (2), 149–163.
Genesee, F. (1987) *Learning Through Two Languages: Studies of Immersion and Bilingual Education*. Rowley, MA: Newbury House.
Genesee, F. (2004) What do we know about bilingual education for majority language students. In T.K. Bhatia and W. Ritchie (eds) *Handbook of Bilingualism and Multiculturalism* (pp. 547–576). Malden, MA: Blackwell.
Genesee, F. (2007) French immersion and at-risk students: A review of research evidence. *The Canadian Modern Language Review/La revue canadienne des langues vivantes* 63 (5), 655–687.
Genesee, F., Paradis, J. and Crago, M. (2004) *Dual Language Development and Disorders: A Handbook on Bilingualism and Second Language Learning*. Baltimore, MD: Brookes Publishing Co.
Hayden, R.H.M. (1988) French immersion drop-outs: Perspectives of parents, students and teachers. *Reading – Canada – Lecture* 6 (4), 222–229.
Kirkness, V. (1998) The critical state of Aboriginal languages in Canada. *Canadian Journal of Native Education* 22 (1), 93–108.
Lambert, W.E. and Tucker, G.R. (1972) *Bilingual Education of Children: The St. Lambert Experiment*. Rowley, MA: Newbury House Publishers.
Lazaruk, W.A. (2007) Linguistic, academic, and cognitive benefits of French immersion. *The Canadian Modern Language Review* 63 (5), 605–628.
Swain, M. and Lapkin, S. (1982) *Evaluating Bilingual Education: A Canadian Case Study*. Clevedon: Multilingual Matters.
Turnbull, M., Lapkin, S. and Hart, D. (2001) Grade 3 immersion students' performance in literacy and mathematics: Province-wide results from Ontario (1998–99). *The Canadian Modern Language Review* 58, 9–26.

Part 1

French as an Additional Language: Immigrants' Learning of French in English-dominant Canada

1 Adding Languages, Adding Benefits: Immigrant Students' Attitudes Toward and Performance in FSOL Programs in Canada

Callie Mady

Officially, Canada is an English/French bilingual country. This official language status affords the population federal services (e.g. federal judicial services) in the official language of their choice and supports the development of official minority communities (i.e. English minority in Quebec and French minorities in the remainder of Canada). These rights are recognized as law in *the Official Languages Act* (Canada, Department of Justice, 1985). Although the Act also seeks to advance the use of English and French (p. 3), Canada remains English-dominant with 68% of the population speaking English only (Statistics Canada, 2011a). Similarly, as it pertains to official language bilingualism, less than 10% of Canadian Anglophones are English/French bilingual in comparison to to 42% of Canadian Francophones (Statistics Canada, 2006a). The aforementioned statistics show Anglophone and Francophone Canadians' tendency to remain unilingual. The seemingly greater resistance on the part of Anglophones to become official language bilingual, in combination with their larger population numbers, highlights the English language dominance of Canada.

Language Education in Canada

Although education is not federally governed, second language education in Canada, for the most part, mirrors federal statistics. In provinces and territories, with the exception of French-dominant Quebec, bilingual New Brunswick and Francophone minority regions, education is English-dominant. In regard to second language learning in the same contexts, three provinces (Ontario, Nova Scotia and Prince Edward Island) mandate the study of French, five provinces/territories (Alberta, Manitoba, Northwest territories, Nunavut and Saskatchewan) have no second language requirement and British Columbia mandates the study of a second language, French being among those offered. A minority of students, therefore, are studying French as a second official language (FSOL). Canadian Parents for French (2011), a national network of volunteers that promotes FSOL learning, reports that, in the aforementioned English-dominant contexts, only approximately 43% of eligible students are studying FSOL.

Adding to the dominance of English in Canada is a lack of focus on immigrants' languages. Absent from federal laws and marginalized, if not also absent, from Canadian education is protection for or formal promotion of immigrants' languages.[1] Federally, the *Canadian Multiculturalism Act* (2003: 4) states that the federal government's policy is to preserve and enhance the use of languages other than English and French. This issue is of particular importance due to the high percentage of the population (21%) who is immigrant (Statistics Canada, 2011a), approximately 6% of whom speak only their language of origin at home (Statistics Canada, 2011b). It is also of urgency due to the potential for language of origin literacy to positively impact immigrants' education (Cummins, 1979). Unlike the *Official Languages Act*, however, the *Canadian Multiculturalism Act* does not go as far as declaring language maintenance a right for immigrant communities. Again, reflecting federal government policy, the majority of provinces and territories offer education in Canada's official languages, relegating language of origin maintenance to hours outside of the school day.

The educational prioritization of English for immigrants is also evident in research that shows that immigrants have at times been denied access to learning FSOL. Research in Ontario (Mady, 2007; Taaffe *et al.*, 1996), where the study of FSOL is obligatory, has shown that immigrants are only sporadically included in FSOL, with administrators occasionally exempting them from the mandatory requirement.

Immigrants' FSOL experiences

The exclusion of immigrants from FSOL study is contrary to research that shows their desire to add FSOL to their linguistic repertoire. National research shows immigrant populations to be more favorable of

English/French bilingualism for Canada than Anglophone respondents (Parkin & Turcotte, 2003). Research with immigrant parents in British Columbia (Dagenais & Berron, 2001) and Ontario (Mady, 2012) also revealed a parental desire for their children to become official language bilingual.

In addition to opposing their desire to become official language bilingual, excluding immigrant students from FSOL learning opportunities is also in contrast to immigrants' ability to meet with success when included. Calman (1988), through FSOL listening tests, determined that immigrant students with less FSOL experience performed on par with their Canadian-born peers. By comparing the FSOL test results of immigrants with those of Canadian-born students, Mady (2007) found that immigrants outperformed their peers although they had studied FSOL for a shorter period of time. Despite immigrants' desire and ability to succeed in learning FSOL in English-dominant Canada, approximately 64% are adopting English as their sole official language (Statistics Canada, 2011b) with only approximately 4% becoming official language bilingual (Statistics Canada, 2006b).

The adoption of English as their sole official language is perhaps due to the lack of opportunities to study FSOL, as determined by administrators who are unaware of immigrants' ability to learn English and FSOL simultaneously. With a view to providing more information on which to make decisions, this chapter presents the results of a more recent study that compared the FSOL achievement of immigrants to that of their Canadian-born Anglophone and bilingual (English and heritage language) peers at the elementary level.

Study Context

This study was conducted in southern Ontario, Canada, in an area that receives the highest amount of immigrants in the world (Ontario, 2001). More precisely, approximately 27% of this area's population is immigrant. In contrast to the situation of prior decades, when immigrants to Canada were almost exclusively European, the majority of this decade's immigrants to southern Ontario come from Asia.

In particular, this study sought to answer the following research questions:

(1) How does immigrant students' achievement in FSOL compare to that of Canadian-born English-speaking students? How does immigrant students' FSOL achievement compare to that of Canadian-born multilingual (CBM) students?

(2) What factors influence the test outcomes (e.g. value placed on learning FSOL, view of progress and nature of/proficiency in dominant languages)?

Methods

This research used a multi-skills test to measure Grade 6 core French students' FSOL achievement and a questionnaire to collect data pertaining to their language-learning attitudes and experiences.[2]

Instruments

Test

A four-skills test – listening, speaking, reading and writing – was used to determine students' FSOL achievement. The test comprised sections of the Diplôme d'études en langue française (DELF, A1, primaire) (Centre international d'études pédagogiques, 2012), which were deemed to be appropriate through pilot testing with the same grade prior to use in the study. All students completed the listening, reading and writing sections. All students in the immigrant (IMM) group also completed the speaking component with a randomly selected sub-group from the Canadian-born unilingual English-speaking (CBU) and CBM groups also completing the speaking tests.

Questionnaire

The questionnaire, created for the purpose of this study, was divided into three sections. The first section contained Likert-scale items pertaining to (a) language anxiety, (b) willingness to communicate in FSOL in class, (c) attitudes toward the FSOL learning situation, (d) integrative (i.e. desire to relate to French Canadians) and (e) Canadian integrative (i.e. importance of French to Canada) motivations, (f) plans to continue to study FSOL and (g) languages in general as well as items on (h) language awareness (as it pertains to prior language knowledge) and (i) strategy use. A principal component analysis was conducted on the corresponding items to create composite variables represented by the (a) to (i) categories. The second section required students to self-assess their English and, where applicable, other language knowledge and use. The last section requested their demographic information.

Interviews

The semi-structured interview protocol consisted of 11 questions. In addition to confirming demographic information and obtaining corresponding details, the questions pertained to questionnaire categories: attitudes toward learning FSOL and the learning situation; motivation to learn FSOL; and integrative and Canadian integrative motivations. The interviews were audio-recorded and transcribed verbatim.

Participants

One hundred and eighty-five students participated in the study by completing the tests and/or questionnaire. Participants were removed if they were English-speaking immigrants, had a romance language background or French immersion experience. The results section, therefore, is based on approximately 164 participants' results. The number of participants varied according to the test component (see Table 1.2 for details) and questionnaire item (see Table 1.4 for details). Of the participants in the IMM group who provided demographic information on the questionnaire (missing 13%), the majority came from south Asia (65.2%) with the remainder of the group coming from Africa (13%), Central Asia (4.3%) and southern Europe (4.3%). Correspondingly, they spoke languages from the following families: Indo-Aryan (65.2%), Afro-Asiatic (4.3%), Austronesian (4.3%), Dravidian (4.3%), Indo-European (4.3%) and Slavic (4.3%). The CBM group had a similar distribution of languages known: Indo-Aryan (56.3%), Afro-Asiatic (4.2%), Austro-Asiatic (4.2%), Austronesian (1.0%), Dravidian (7.3%), Indo-European (10.4%), Indo-Iranian (1.0%), Sino-Tibetan (2.1%) and Slavic (3.1%), with 10% not reporting.

Of the entire group, 35 participants from the CBU group, 68 from the CBM group and 22 from the IMM group were also interviewed.

Results

Test results

ANOVAs were conducted to compare the FSOL test results among the groups. Table 1.1 presents the ANOVA results. Significant differences among the groups were found on Reading 2 scores $F(2, 65) = 4.50$, $p < 0.05$, partial $\eta^2 = 0.03$; Writing 1 scores $F(2, 62) = 5.11$, $p < 0.01$, $\eta^2 = 0.05$; Writing 2 scores $F(2, 53) = 5.14$, $p < 0.01$, $\eta^2 = 0.08$; Speaking 1 scores $F(2, 130) = 10.09$, $p > 0.001$, $\eta^2 = 0.13$; and Speaking 2 scores $F(2, 130) = 6.67$, $p > 0.01$, $\eta^2 = 0.09$, which indicated that repeated statistically significant differences were found when comparing the three language groups. Regarding effect sizes, for η^2 values, small=0.01, medium=0.06 and large=0.14.

Table 1.1 ANOVA results comparing groups' test results

Score	df	F	Partial η^2
Reading 1	2, 53	2.18	0.03
Reading 2	2, 65	4.50*	0.03
Writing 1	2, 62	5.11**	0.05
Writing 2	2, 53	5.14**	0.08
Speaking 1	2, 130	10.09***	0.13
Speaking 2	2, 130	6.67**	0.09

***$p < 0.001$; **$p < 0.01$; *$p < 0.05$ (two-tailed test)

Where differences were noted, Dunnett's C post-hoc tests were conducted and confidence intervals for the differences between the three groups are presented in Table 1.2. With respect to the post-hoc tests in particular, the IMM group has significantly higher mean scores ($M = 4.4$, $SD = 1.08$) compared to the CBM and CBU groups ($M = 3.7$, $SD = 1.50$) and ($M = 3.5$, $SD = 1.50$), respectively, on the Reading 2/5 domain.

Table 1.2 Descriptive statistics and post-hoc tests for each score

Score	Language group	Mean	SD	n	95% Confidence interval CBU	CBM
Reading 1/4	CBU	2.1	1.30	48		
	CBM	2.2	1.03	93		
	IMM	2.8	1.31	23		
Reading 2/5	CBU	3.5	1.50	48		
	CBM	3.7	1.50	93	−0.81 to 0.48	
	IMM	4.4	1.08	23	−1.64 to −0.10*	−1.38 to −0.03*
Writing 1/10	CBU	5.2	1.98	46		
	CBM	5.8	1.58	92	−1.39 to 0.23	
	IMM	6.5	1.24	23	−2.20 to −0.28*	−1.42 to 0.10
Writing 2/15	CBU	7.1	3.41	46		
	CBM	8.6	2.29	92	−2.88 to −0.19*	
	IMM	9.3	2.60	23	−4.05 to 0.40*	−2.17 to 0.78
Speaking 1/5	CBU	1.8	1.25	44		
	CBM	2.5	1.29	66	−1.22 to −0.03*	
	IMM	3.3	1.14	23	−2.18 to −0.68*	−1.51 to −0.10*
Speaking 2/7	CBU	2.7	1.46	44		
	CBM	3.2	1.37	66	−1.16 to 0.18	
	IMM	4.0	1.38	23	−2.22 to −0.42*	−1.66 to 0.00

*$p < 0.05$ (two-tailed test)

The IMM group has significantly higher mean scores ($M = 6.5$, $SD = 1.24$) compared to the CBM group ($M = 5.8$, $SD = 1.58$) and higher but non-significant scores compared to the CBU group ($M = 5.2, SD = 1.98$) on the Writing 1 domain. Similarly, the IMM group has significantly higher mean scores ($M = 9.3$, $SD = 2.60$) compared to the CBM group ($M = 8.6$, $SD = 2.29$) and higher but non-significant scores compared to the CBU group ($M = 7.1, SD = 3.41$) on the Writing 2 domain.

The IMM group has significantly higher mean scores ($M = 3.3, SD = 1.14$) compared to the CBM and CBU groups ($M = 2.5$, $SD = 1.29$ and $M = 1.8$, $SD = 1.25$, respectively) on the Speaking 1 domain. The IMM group has significantly higher mean scores ($M = 4.0, SD = 1.38$) compared to the CBM group ($M = 3.2$, $SD = 1.37$) and higher but non-significant scores compared to the CBU group ($M = 2.7, SD = 1.46$) on the Speaking 2 domain.

Questionnaire results

ANOVAs were also used to compare the questionnaire results among the groups. Table 1.3 presents the significance results for each ANOVA. Significant differences among the groups are identified for all variables except language of origin literacy skills. Regarding effect sizes, η^2 values indicate small=0.01, medium=0.06 and large=0.14. Specifically, significant differences among the groups were found on integrative motivation scores $F(2, 149) = 5.18, p < 0.01$, partial $\eta^2 = 0.07$; Canadian integrative motivation scores $F(2, 151) = 8.82, p < 0.001$, partial $\eta^2 = 0.11$; plans to continue

Table 1.3 ANOVA results comparing groups' attitudes and experiences

Score	df	F	Partial η^2
Integrative motivation	2, 149	5.18**	0.07
Canadian integrative motivation	2, 151	8.82***	0.11
Plans to continue FSOL study	2, 144	7.84**	0.10
Attitude toward FSOL	2, 149	5.77**	0.07
Anxiety	2, 149	10.12***	0.12
Willingness to communicate	2, 54	14.14***	0.18
Language awareness	2, 132	3.56*	0.05
Strategy use	2, 48	8.02**	0.11
Language of origin – oral skills	1, 54	5.83*	0.03
Language of origin – literacy skills	1, 86	0.79	0.01

***$p < 0.001$; **$p < 0.01$; *$p < 0.05$

FSOL study scores $F(2, 144) = 7.84$, $p < 0.01$, partial $\eta^2 = 0.10$; attitude toward FSOL scores $F(2, 149) = 5.77$, $p < 0.01$, $\eta^2 = 0.07$; anxiety scores $F(2, 149) = 10.12$, $p < 0.001$, $\eta^2 = 0.12$; willingness to communicate scores $F(2, 54) = 14.14$, $p < 0.001$, partial $\eta^2 = 0.18$; language awareness scores $F(2, 132) = 3.56$, $p > 0.05$, $\eta^2 = 0.05$; strategy use scores $F(2, 48) = 8.02$, $p > 0.01$, $\eta^2 = 0.11$; and language of origin oral skills scores $F(2, 54) = 5.83$, $p > 0.05$, $\eta^2 = 0.03$.

In general, the following Dunnett's C post-hoc tests given in Table 1.4 identify that the CBU group has the lowest mean score compared to both the CBM and the IMM groups and the IMM group has the highest mean score on most questionnaire categories. More precisely, the IMM group has higher mean scores ($M = 0.23$, $SD = 1.07$; $M = 0.40$, $SD = 0.91$) compared to the CBM ($M = 0.15$, $SD = 0.92$; $M = 0.17$, $SD = 1.00$) and CBU groups ($M = -0.40$, $SD = 1.07$; $M = -0.49$, $SD = 0.95$) on the integrative motivation and Canadian integrative motivation domains, respectively. In addition, the IMM group has significantly higher mean scores ($M = 0.49$, $SD = 0.86$; $M = 0.34$, $SD = 0.84$; $M = 0.47$, $SD = 0.78$; $M = 0.51$, $SD = 0.70$; $M = 0.60$, $SD = 0.75$) compared to the CBU group ($M = -0.44$, $SD = 1.09$; $M = -0.39$, $SD = 0.99$; $M = -0.51$, $SD = 1.04$; $M = -0.65$, $SD = 1.10$; $M = -0.40$, $SD = 1.14$) and higher but non-significant scores compared to the CBM group ($M = 0.14$, $SD = 0.91$; $M = 0.14$, $SD = 0.98$; $M = 0.15$, $SD = 0.94$; $M = 0.21$, $SD = 0.87$; $M = 0.11$, $SD = 0.89$) on the plans to continue FSOL study, the attitude toward FSOL, the anxiety, the willingness to communicate and the strategy use variables, respectively. Conversely, the CBU group has significantly higher mean scores ($M = 0.32$, $SD = 9.38$) compared to the CBM group ($M = -0.17$, $SD = 1.00$) and higher but non-significant scores compared to the IMM group ($M = -0.11$, $SD = 0.94$) on the language awareness domain. No significant differences in attitudes were identified between the CBM and IMM groups.

Interview findings

Interview responses were analyzed and coded within the groups for emergent themes. As they inform the questionnaire findings in the previous section, I report on the participants' attitudes toward FSOL and their Canadian-focused integrative motivation.

Attitudes toward FSOL

When asked why they felt they had to study French, the majority of the responses from the Canadian-born participants (i.e. CBM = 64%; CBU = 67%) centered on the idea that learning French was a useful endeavor.

Table 1.4 Descriptive statistics and post-hoc tests for each score

Score	Language group	Mean	SD	n	95% Confidence interval CBU	CBM
Integrative motivation	CBU	−0.40	1.07	46		
	CBM	0.15	0.92	86	*−0.99 to −0.09	
	IMM	0.23	1.07	20	−1.35 to 0.09	−0.74 to 0.57
Canadian integrative motivation	CBU	−0.49	0.95	45		
	CBM	0.17	1.00	89	−1.09 to −0.24*	
	IMM	0.40	0.91	20	−1.51 to −0.27	−0.81 to 0.34
Plans to Continue FSOL study	CBU	−0.44	1.09	45		
	CBM	0.14	0.91	84	−1.04 to −0.12*	
	IMM	0.49	0.86	18	−1.58 to −0.28*	−0.92 to 0.22
Attitude toward FSOL	CBU	−0.39	0.99	45		
	CBM	0.14	0.98	87	−0.96 to −0.09*	
	IMM	0.34	0.84	20	−1.33 to −0.13*	−0.74 to 0.34
Anxiety	CBU	−0.51	1.04	45		
	CBM	0.15	0.94	87	−1.11 to −0.22*	
	IMM	0.47	0.78	20	−1.56 to −0.40*	−0.82 to 0.19
Willingness to communicate	CBU	−0.65	1.10	43		

(Continued)

Table 1.4 (Continued)

Score	Language group	Mean	SD	n	95% Confidence interval CBU	95% Confidence interval CBM
Language awareness	CBM	0.21	0.87	82	−1.33 to −0.40*	
	IMM	0.51	0.70	20	−1.73 to −0.60*	−0.76 to 0.16
	CBU	0.32	9.38	42		
	CBM	−0.17	1.00	75	0.05 to 0.94*	
	IMM	−0.11	0.94	18	−0.24 to 1.10	−0.69 to 0.57
Strategy use	CBU	−0.40	1.14	42		
	CBM	0.11	0.89	75	−1.01 to −0.02*	
	IMM	0.60	0.75	18	−1.62 to −0.38*	−1.00 to 0.02
Language of origin – oral skills	CBU					
	CBM	−0.11	1.07	70		
	IMM	0.33	0.55	18		
Language of origin – literacy skills	CBU					
	CBM	−0.03	0.99	70		
	IMM	0.21	1.08	18		

*$p < 0.05$

The CBM participants felt that learning French was most useful for getting a job, then for traveling to French-speaking areas (mostly outside of Canada) or increasing their grades in school. By contrast, the majority of the CBU comments centered on the utility of learning French for traveling to French-speaking areas outside of Canada, with fewer comments related to learning French to increase job prospects.

The IMM group's reasons for why they felt they had to study French were split between French being a useful language to learn (34%) (mostly for travel to French-speaking areas within and outside of Canada), and French being the second official language of Canada (34%):

I think it's the...it's like a second, it's the second most important language in Canada. (IMM participant 17)
Like, we're in Canada, French is the second language and there are a lot of French people in Canada, so...you better learn it (IMM participant 13)

Canadian integrative motivation

The participants were asked whether they felt that learning French was part of being Canadian. The three groups diverged somewhat in their response to this question. The large majority of the multilingual groups responded with a positive 'Yes' (i.e. CBM = 81%; IMM = 82%). When explaining their reasoning, both multilingual groups predominantly cited the fact that French was an important part of the Canadian identity, either because it was the second official language or, generally, because it was part of the history of the country:

Yeah, because France was the one that discovered Canada, Jacques Cartier was French. (CBM participant 2)
Yes cause it's the second language of Canada. [Learning] that makes us more Canadian. (CBM participant 11)
Yeah, because it has two official languages, if you know both it's more like you're more of a Canadian. (IMM participant 10)
Yes, mainly because the French were the first people to arrive here. (IMM participant 18)

The CBU group's responses to this question were more mixed in nature – 66% reported that they believed that learning French was part of being Canadian, 20% had mixed feelings and 14% said 'No'. Similar to the other groups, those who responded positively, or who were arguing the 'yes' side of their mixed feelings, reported that the presence of French in Canada and the fact that French was the second official language factored into their belief that learning French is part of being Canadian. Still, uncertainty about the necessity to learn French and the fact that participants have to learn French in school both emerged as factors leading some in the CBU group to doubt whether learning French was part of being Canadian:

> A little bit of it...because we only learn it in school. (CBU participant 9)
> You should be able to learn a little bit of French, but you don't have to learn every single thing. (CBU participant 5)

Factors influencing test results

Multiple linear regression analyses were conducted for each sub-test to identify student groupings, attitudes toward and experiences with French language and education that are statistically significant predictors of FSOL achievement. This approach shows which attitude variables are significant predictors of FSOL achievement while controlling for the grouping variables. It also shows the effect of student grouping variables while controlling for the effect of attitude variables.

Amount of score variance explained by each model

An exploratory approach was used to enter all variables into the model to determine which were the strongest predictors of FSOL achievement. As shown in Table 1.5, all models explained significant amounts of variance, but varied widely in explanatory power. Table 1.5 provides the amount of variance in FSOL achievement measures explained by each predictor that was entered into the model. Specifically, the predictors in this model accounted

Table 1.5 Model significance tests

Dependent variable	R^2	Adjusted R^2	F	Degrees of freedom
Reading 1***	0.15	0.14	9.67	2, 108
Reading 2***	0.30	0.26	8.88	5, 105
Writing 1***	0.28	0.26	10.41	4, 105
Writing 2***	0.55	0.53	25.70	5, 104
Speaking 1***	0.46	0.43	17.10	4, 82
Speaking 2***	0.34	0.32	21.54	2, 84

***$p < 0.001$ (two-tailed test)

for 14% of the variance in Reading 1 scores $F\ (2,\ 108) = 9.67,\ p < 0.001$; 26% of the variance in Reading 2 scores $F\ (5,\ 105) = 8.88,\ p < 0.001$; 26% of the variance in Writing 1 scores $F\ (4,\ 105) = 10.41,\ p < 0.001$; 53% of the variance in Writing 2 scores $F\ (5,\ 104) = 25.70,\ p < 0.001$; 43% of the variance in Speaking 1 scores $F\ (4,\ 82) = 17.10,\ p < 0.001$; and 32% of the variance in Speaking 2 scores $F\ (2,\ 84) = 21.54,\ p < 0.001$.

Predictors of FSOL achievement

One of the research questions asked which French language and education attitudes and experiences predicted FSOL achievement. This explanatory approach added all possible variables that showed the strongest predictors. Table 1.6 reports the regression coefficients for each dependent variable that indicate the relative added value of each significant predictor variable for that dependent variable while controlling for the class that the students were in and their gender.

Membership of the IMM group and being registered in English as a second language (ESL) classes are significant predictors. Being in the IMM group is associated with higher FSOL achievement scores while ESL identification is associated with lower scores. More precisely, being in the IMM group results in a 0.66 point increase in Speaking 1 scores. The ESL predictor decreases FSOL achievement scores resulting in a 0.56 point decrease in Reading 2 scores and a 0.88 point decrease in Writing 2 scores.

French experience and attitudes were also found to impact FSOL achievement measures. Specifically, as the frequency that students speak French in class increases by one point, Reading 2 scores increase by 0.29 points and Writing 2 scores increase by 0.43 points. Additionally, as anxiety levels increase by one point, Writing 1 scores increase by 0.38 points, Speaking 1 scores increase by 0.33 points and Speaking 2 scores increase by 0.72 points. The participants' willingness to communicate in French enhances their Reading 1 score by 0.28 points; use of language learning strategies also provides an advantage – a 0.47 increase in the Reading 2 score. Language awareness, particularly the use of prior language knowledge, however, results in a decrease of 0.29 points in Reading 2.

Discussion

It is important to note that the limited numbers confined the statistical procedures to more basic analyses. In addition, the uneven group numbers are not ideal. The results of this study, therefore, must be considered in light of other research.

Table 1.6 Regression coefficients for student French language attitudes and experiences on each measure of FSOL achievement

	Reading 1/4	Reading 2/5	Writing 1/10	Writing 2/15	Speaking 1/5	Speaking 2/7
Intercept	2.71***	3.34***	5.90***	5.33***	1.87***	3.88***
CBU/CBM						
IMM					0.66*	
ESL		−0.56*		−0.88*		
French with friends						
French in class		0.29*		0.43**		
Integrative motivation						
Integrative Canada						
Motivation to continue with FSOL						
Attitude						
Anxiety			0.38**		0.33**	0.72***
Willingness to communicate	0.28**					
Language awareness		−0.29*				
Strategy use		0.47**				
n	111	111	110	110	87	87
Adjusted R^2	0.14	0.26	0.26	0.53	0.43	0.32

***$p < 0.001$; **$p < 0.01$; *$p < 0.05$ (two-tailed test)

In summary, the CBU group consistently receives the lowest scores on the FSOL tests and expresses the least positive attitudes through the questionnaire. By contrast, the IMM group expresses the most positive attitudes on each category of the questionnaire with the exception of language awareness and through the interviews and significantly outperforms the CBU group on five test components. The CBM group's attitudes as expressed through the questionnaire fall in between those of the other two groups; they outperform the CBU group on three sub-tests. As per the multiple regression analyses, membership in the IMM group, use of French in class, willingness to communicate, anxiety and strategy use are predictors of higher achievement on some test components whereas requiring ESL support and language awareness (the only questionnaire item where the CBU group had higher means) are associated with lower scores on some test sections.

The findings as they correspond to the CBU group suggest that this group may have adopted an 'English is sufficient' approach (Clyne, 2008) to FSOL learning. Support for such a hypothesis can be found in Lapkin et al.'s (2006) research, where the researchers reported on survey results conducted with 1305 FSOL teachers. The FSOL teacher participants indicated that student and parental support of FSOL was limited, detailing that students held negative attitudes toward and had lower achievement in FSOL. Belief that 'English is enough' has also been reported in other English-dominant countries. In his position paper describing the dwindling language-learning opportunities in the United Kingdom for example, Coyle (2010) argues that proficiency in English is insufficient to meet the demands of a multilingual society. This is particularly the case for Anglophones given that the high adoption of English by other bilingual/multilingual communities puts them in an advantaged position to meet multilingual demands, including those of English. Similarly, in his description of sporadic second language learning opportunities in Australia, Clyne (2011) highlights the need for individuals and Australia as a nation to adopt a 'multilingualism as resource' approach to language learning.

The weak performance of the CBU group is further highlighted by the stronger results of the IMM group. Given that the IMM group generally outperforms the other two groups and demonstrates more positive attitudes and experiences toward FSOL provides evidence that these students can be successful at learning FSOL. In fact, FSOL may provide a subject where the participants in the IMM group can excel beyond that of their Canadian-born peers whereas that may not be the case in other subject areas. Taken in light of other research that found learning of FSOL to be of advantage to immigrant students' English (Carr, 2009), these findings suggest that the inclusion of immigrant students in FSOL has positive impacts. In addition to providing English and FSOL learning opportunities, I suggest that supporting students' language(s) of origin/heritage language(s) may not only provide additional language learning support but also help to ensure that languages are being added to individuals' repertoire rather than replacing those already established as is often the case with English replacing their language(s) of origin/heritage language(s). Supporting multiple languages in the curriculum would also prove advantageous to the CBM group which outperforms the CBU group on three of five test components.

In addition to attitudes impacting FSOL learning, of the other potential influential factors, willingness to communicate, strategy use and use of French in class are advantageous to students' FSOL achievement. This last factor, in combination with the negative impact of the language awareness category, which focused exclusively on the use of prior language knowledge, suggests an advantage to placing importance on the use of French. These influential variables suggest that students' use of French increases their FSOL achievement. The positive influence of anxiety also suggests that students are willing to take the risk of using French despite the trepidation it causes. I also note the potential for the test-taking situation to have increased the participants' anxiety (particularly with the speaking components). These results, in combination with the multilingual language acquisition literature, citing the advantages of language awareness (Jessner, 2008; Peyer et al., 2010) and strategy use (Kemp, 2007), suggest that students may benefit from: (a) a French-focused environment that is inclusionary of other languages when the goal to enhance language awareness is explicit; (b) explicit instruction of language-learning strategies; (c) opportunities to use French with their peers; and (d) information on the benefits of speaking French (to balance the anxiety caused).

In addition to offering the above-mentioned learning environment as a means to improve performance, the multilingual groups' enhanced attitudes and FSOL achievement suggest that exposure to languages may increase their willingness to communicate in FSOL and provide them with a conceptualization of languages as resources. Such a conceptualization is supported by other research, through questionnaires and interviews. Mady (2010), for example, found immigrant students to be more motivated than the Canadian-born groups in her study and more confident in their ability to add languages to their linguistic repertoire.

The statistics showing that the majority of immigrants (64%) adopt English as their sole official language in Canada with only a small minority (4%) having knowledge of both official languages suggest that a change occurs from school age to adulthood. Such a change is anticipated where, in the broader social context of English-dominant Ontario, FSOL is not an obligatory subject of study beyond Grade 9 and language(s) of origin/heritage are not provided in the elementary school day, and in the broader context of Canada where language learning/maintenance is not a right protected by the federal government. Although I do not want to suggest that all citizens or all immigrants become official language bilingual, I do suggest that steps can be taken to promote a view of multilingualism as advantageous. For example, instead of encouraging, as is presently the case, the adoption of English as one's only language with limited support for language learning, the provincial government could mandate the study of three languages. As seen in the European mother tongue plus two policy (European Council, 2011), such curriculum offerings not only have the potential to influence a reconceptualization of language learning that judges all language knowledge as a positive resource but also to increase the number of multilingual citizens well equipped to meet the demands of a multilingual, global society.

Notes

(1) Although beyond the scope of this chapter, I note that aboriginal languages are also relegated to a lower position. Please see the chapters on aboriginal language maintenance in this edition.
(2) Core French is the study of FSOL as offered through short daily periods of approximately 40 minutes. In this study, FSOL begins in Grade 4.

References

Calman, R. (1988) *Core French Program Review: Grades 3-8*. Technical Report. North York, ON: North York Board of Education.
Carr, W. (2009) Intensive French in British Columbia: Costs, benefits and connections to Canada's bilingualism ideal. *Canadian Modern Language Review* 65 (5), 787–816.
Canada, Department of Justice (1985) *Official languages act* [R.S. 1985, c. 31 (4th Supp.)], government document, accessed 1 February 2013. http://laws.justice.gc.ca/en/O-3.01/
Canadian Parents for French (2011) *Annual FSOL enrolment in Canada 2006–2011*, accessed 1 February 2013. http://cpf.ca/en/files/CPF-FSOL-Enrolment-Stats.pdf
Centre international d'études pédagogiques (2012) *DELF A1 primaire*. Test online, accessed 1 February 2013. http://www.ciep.fr/delf-prim/docs/livret-candidat-delf-prim-A1/index.htmlDELF-Prim.php
Clyne, M. (2008) The monolingual mindset as an impediment to the development of plurilingual potential in Australia. *Sociolinguistic Studies* 2 (3), 347–365.
Clyne, M. (2011) Three is too many in Australia. In C.L. Hélot and M. Ó Laoire (eds) *Language Policy for the Multilingual Classroom* (pp. 174–187). Bristol: Multilingual Matters.
Council of Europe (2011) *Civil society platform on multilingualism: 2 policy recommendations for the promotion of multilingualism in the European Union*, accessed 1 February 2013. http://ec.europa.eu/languages/pdf/doc5088_en.pdf

Coyle, D. (2010) Language pedagogies revisited: Alternative approaches for integrating language learning, language using and intercultural understanding. In J. Miller, A. Kostogriz and M. Gearon (eds) *Culturally and Linguistically Diverse Classrooms: New Dilemmas for Teachers* (pp. 172–195). Toronto, ON: Multilingual Matters.

Cummins, J. (1979) Linguistic interdependence and the educational development of bilingual children. *Review of Educational Research* 49, 222–251.

Dagenais, D. and Berron, C. (2001) Promoting multilingualism through French immersion and language maintenance in three immigrant families. *Language, Culture and Curriculum* 14 (2), 142–155.

Jessner, U. (2008) A DST model of multilingualism and the role of metalinguistic awareness. *Modern Language Journal* 92 (2), 270–283.

Kemp, C. (2007) Strategic processing in grammar learning: Do multilinguals use more strategies? *International Journal of Multilingualism* 4 (4), 241–261.

Lapkin, S., MacFarlane, A. and Vandergrift, L. (2006) *Teaching French in Canada: FSL Teachers' Perspectives*. Ottawa, ON: Canadian Teachers' Federation.

Mady, C. (2007) The suitability of core French for recently arrived adolescent immigrants to Canada. *Canadian Journal of Applied Linguistics* 10 (2), 177–196.

Mady, C. (2010) Motivation to study core French: Comparing recent immigrants and Canadian-born secondary school students. *Canadian Journal of Education* 33 (3), 564–587.

Mady, C. (2012) Voices of immigrant adults: Perspectives and experiences with French as a second official language in "English-dominant" Canada. *Intercultural Promenades: Journal of Modern Languages and Intercultural Studies* 1 (1), 35–51.

Ontario, Ministry of Finance (2001) *Census 2001 Highlights: Factsheet 5: Immigration to Ontario*, accessed 1 February 2013. http://www.fin.gov.on.ca/en/economy/demographics/census/cenhi5.html

Peyer, E., Kaiser, I. and Berthele, R. (2010) The multilingual reader: Advantages in understanding and decoding German sentence structure when reading German as an L3. *International Journal of Multilingualism* 7 (3), 225–239.

Statistics Canada (2006a) *2006 Census: The Evolving Linguistic Portrait, 2006 Census: Bilingualism*, accessed 1 February 2013. http://www12.statcan.ca/census-recensement/2006/as-sa/97-555/p13-eng.cfm

Statistics Canada (2006b) *English/French bilingualism among Anglophones and allophones, (single mother tongue), Canada, provinces, territories and Canada less Quebec, 1996 to 2006*, accessed 1 February 2013. http://www12.statcan.ca/census-recensement/2006/as-sa/97-555/table/t17-eng.cfm

Statistics Canada (2011a) *Linguistic Characteristics of Canadians*, accessed 1 February 2013. http://www12.statcan.gc.ca/census-recensement/2011/assa/98-314-x/98-314-x2011001-eng.cfm

Statistics Canada (2011b) *Population by knowledge of official languages, age groups (total), percentage distribution (2011), for Canada, provinces and territories*, accessed 1 February 2013. http://www12.statcan.gc.ca/census recensement/2011/dppd/hltfst/lang/Pages/highlight.cfm?TabID=1&Lang=E&Asc=1 PRCode=01&OrderBy=999&View=2&Age=1&tableID=402&queryID=1

Taaffe, R., Maguire, M., and Pringle, I. (1996) The impact of social contexts and educational policy/practice on biliteracy development: Ethnolinguistic minority children in English primary schools in Ottawa and Montreal. *Journal of the CAAL* 18 (2), 85–101.

Student Interview Questions

1. Where were you born?
   a. If not in Canada – how old were you when you came to Canada?
   b. Where did you come from?
2. Which language(s) do you speak?
   HOME LANGUAGE (if more than English and French)
   a. Which language did you learn first?
   b. Do you still use this language? Where?
   c. How do you feel about this language?
   d. Is it important for you to keep using this language? Why?
   OTHER LANGUAGE(S)
   a. Did you learn another language?
   b. Which language?
   c. How did you learn it?
   d. Do you still use this language? Where?
   e. How do you feel about this language?
   f. Is it important for you to keep using this language? Why?
   g. (If an English language learner) How do you feel about learning English?
3. How do you feel about learning French?
4. How do you feel about participating in class? (probes – nervous, confident?)
5. What have been the most difficult things about learning French?
6. What are the easiest things about learning French?
7. Why do you think you have to study French?
8. Do you think it is important for Canadians to learn French? Why/why not?
9. Will you use the French you learned? Where? For what purposes?
10. What does it mean to be Canadian?
11. Is learning French part of being Canadian?

2 Learning French in British Columbia: English as Additional Language Learner and Parent Perspectives

Wendy Carr

Canada's ideal of linguistic duality is based on certain assumptions related to Canadians' collective identity and view of social cohesion. The Official Languages Support Programs' stated outcomes are that 'all Canadians recognize and support linguistic duality' and 'social cohesion in Canada is increased' (Canadian Heritage, 2003: 37). In Prime Minister Chrétien's preface to the Government of Canada's (2003: vii) Action Plan for Official Languages, he notes that, 'the ideal of a bilingual Canada where everyone could benefit from our Anglophone and Francophone heritage seemed ... to be a fundamentally just ideal for our society'. This notion that French and English are important even within a linguistically diverse Canada is reiterated in Statistics Canada's (2012b: 11) analysis of the 2011 census: '[both official languages] exert a strong pull as languages of convergence and integration into Canadian society'. While these outcomes link to the federal government's commitment to recognize French and English as official languages, they provide only a partial view of the Canadian identity. Duff (2007) underscores the limited reach of French/English linguistic duality in Canada, indicating that unilingual English predominates; however, she suggests that new immigrants are among those who do value 'the bilingual norm'. Mady (2007a, 2010, 2012a, 2012b) argues that the learning of French as an additional language by immigrant Canadians serves not only the linguistic duality ideal but is actually valued for reasons that go beyond language, related to citizenship and identity. This chapter highlights two studies in British Columbia that support this view and provide some insights into why the acquisition of French is valued.

Jedwab (2003: 145) refers to a definition of social cohesion adopted by the European Ministers of Education in 2000 as 'an unlimited, multidimensional concept, which seeks to mould society into a coherent—but not homogeneous—whole', adding that the intent is to smooth out differences inherent in diverse populations. He then critiques various efforts to promote social cohesion in Europe and in Canada, noting that not only is the notion vague but also that the related policy initiatives are unrealistic and even inappropriate. Nonetheless, Canadian governmental policies related to promoting linguistic duality within a multicultural country, dating back to the Royal Commission on Bilingualism and Biculturalism (Bilingualism and Biculturalism Commission, 1969), stress the unifying effect of having citizens with diverse origins unified in speaking Canada's official languages while enjoying the right to cultural freedom. In its Social Cohesion Research Workplan, Canadian Heritage (1997: 2) defines social cohesion as 'the ongoing process of developing a community of shared values, shared challenges and equal opportunity within Canada, based on a sense of trust, hope and reciprocity among all Canadians'. If common values and the desire for opportunities can bind groups together in a common purpose, then it seems logical that the acquisition of various assets, including language, can transcend a variety of differences. It is worthy to note, however, that when it pertains to Canadian immigrants, Dagenais et al. (2008) problematize the implications on identity, language and education, noting that social cohesion is neither a static state nor does belonging to the Canadian community mean that immigrants' diverse cultural and linguistic backgrounds are necessarily decreased or assimilated.

This chapter explores two studies in which communities of students and parents sought short-term and long-term benefits related to language learning via a new pedagogical approach. Bourdieu's (1977) notion of cultural capital and its acquisition through competition and/or the expansion of one's networks was useful in analyzing some of the dynamics in the earlier study. A cohesive society, according to Bourdieu and Wacquant (1992: 119), is one that is imbued with social capital, defined as 'the sum of the resources, actual or virtual, that accrue to a group by virtue of possessing a durable network of more or less institutionalized relationships of mutual acquaintance and recognition'. Social capital is an element that, along with economic capital, serves to develop human capital, all three of which are necessary, according to the Organization of Economic Cooperation and Development (OECD, 2001), for sustainable economies, which, in turn, support ongoing human well-being, quality of life and life choices.

Language as an Asset

Bourdieu's (1977) theory of social organization is based in large part on the acquisition of real and symbolic capital. He posits that individuals seek to obtain position and capital in the present and/or in the future as material or symbolic assets, and one's ability to gain this capital is influenced by one's background in the world; however, one has some degree of agency over one's lot in life. Bourdieu maintains that education is a key marketplace in which capital is sought and gained, and that, in spite of the tendency of social hierarchies to be reproduced, it is possible to instigate change through action. The notion that acquisition of symbolic capital can lead to a better life serves to explain why some are motivated to move beyond their present situation, class or geographical location. As mentioned earlier, the OECD (2001) maintains that the pursuit of education for oneself or one's children is a key element in human and social capital.

Norton (2000) applies Bourdieu's view of symbolic capital in considering why students invest in learning a second (or, we might assume, additional) language:

> If learners invest in a second language, they do so with the understanding that they will acquire a wider range of symbolic and material resources that will in turn increase the value of their cultural capital. Learners expect or hope to have a good return on that investment—a return that will give them access to hitherto unattainable resources. (Norton, 2000: 10)

Heller (2001: 47) also suggests that, in a globalized world, languages are now viewed less as symbols of national identity and more as economic commodities, offering opportunities to improve educational and vocational futures with language seen as 'an acquirable technical skill and marketable commodity'.

For new Canadians, seeking an education in French and English can be considered a valuable resource, as seen in Dagenais' (2003) study conducted in the same metropolitan region (Greater Vancouver) as the two studies treated in this chapter. She discovered that families enrolled their children in French second language programs to gain access to powerful official language communities. Dagenais suggests that immigrant parents have their children participate in French as a second language (FSL) programs because they imagine future possibilities for their children not only in Canada and but also across the world: 'As multilinguals, their children's identity can be reframed from offspring of immigrants, whose linguistic resources may be unrecognized in the host country, to transnationals whose capital is marketable elsewhere' (Dagenais, 2003: 281).

Language as a Component of a Canadian Identity

Norton's (2000: 5) proposition that language is 'constitutive of and constituted by a language learner's identity' suggests that acquisition of an additional language enhances one's identity. This identity, according to Norton, is profoundly influenced by education and 'thus an investment in the target language is also an investment in a learner's own identity' (p. 11). Earlier studies (Berron, 1998; Carr, 2007; Dagenais & Moore, 2009; Mady, 2012b; Mady & Carr, 2009) have revealed that choices made by immigrants vis-à-vis their children's education are influenced by the official language status of French in Canada. Berron (1998) studied a small group of Indo-Canadian parents in Surrey, BC, to discover why they enrolled their children in French immersion programs and found that, while instrumental reasons related to French being a valuable asset prevailed, the fact that it was one of Canada's official languages mattered as well. Dagenais and Moore's (2009) study of Chinese immigrant parents in Greater Vancouver, BC, revealed that parents encouraged their children to acquire French and English as additional languages while maintaining the study of their home language in an effort to move from being a minoritized group by participating fully in what it means to be a Canadian citizen, which they perceived to include speaking both official languages.

Overview of the Studies

In this chapter, two sets of data are examined: one related to a study conducted in 2004–2007 (Carr, 2007) in five schools in one urban British Columbia school district (Surrey) and the other in 2012 in two schools in a neighboring urban district (Vancouver). The first study was a longitudinal case study that considered both local and national sociopolitical contexts in which the implementation of a new FSL program took place as well as the perspectives of many stakeholders. The second study comprised a two-year evaluation of the implementation process from multiple perspectives. The common purpose of both studies was an investigation of why parents and their children enrolled in the intensive FSL program.

In both studies, I consider the relationship between language, identity and education and how global and market forces influence individual choices. A responsive evaluation approach (Guba & Lincoln, 1989), involving multiple interviews, focus group meetings and questionnaires, was used to develop understanding in the first study, and a series of questionnaires and interviews was used in the second study. Perspectives are interpreted by applying theories related to investment and identity (Bourdieu, 1977; Bourdieu & Passeron, 1990; Dagenais, 2003; Norton, 2000).

The following research questions were explored in both studies:

(1) Why do students and parents in British Columbia choose to participate in a FSL program?
(2) Why do English as additional language (EAL) learners and their parents choose to participate in the program?
(3) What role, if any, does the federal ideal of official language bilingualism play in parent or student choices, generally and for EAL learners?

The purpose of this chapter is to review and compare data from the recent study with those of the earlier study by comparing the responses of participants in a similar program but in a different location and time period. Of particular interest are the perspectives of EAL learners and their parents. These were explored in greater depth in the more recent study.

Context and Background of the Studies

The first study examined the implementation of a new approach to teaching FSL in a large urban school district in British Columbia (Surrey). It took place at a significant point in the history of national and provincial policy and the field of second language education. The dream of strengthening Canada's linguistic duality was reawakened by the 2003 Action Plan's goal of doubling the proportion of bilingual graduates.[1] Among other challenges issued by the Director General of the Official Languages Branch as he unveiled the comprehensive Action Plan in 2003 was a call to 'do things differently' in second language education. A new program, Intensive French (IF), had been pioneered in Newfoundland and Labrador in the late 1990s (Netten & Germain, 2004a, 2004b), implemented across the country in subsequent years and recognized as part of a possible strategy for meeting the goals in the Action Plan (Canadian Heritage, 2004; Canadian Parents for French, 2005). Adopted as an additional FSL program option in British Columbia in 2004, IF provides a one-year initiation into learning French during which students in Grade 6 spend the first half of the year immersed in French language/literacy activities and the second half of the year following a condensed English curriculum of regular subjects. Students then continue to receive an enriched French learning program. The second study takes place in a neighboring large, urban school district (Vancouver); and, unlike the first study, which took place from the very beginning of the IF program's implementation, the 2012 study takes place two years after the IF program began in one school and three years after it began in a second school.

Both school districts have high populations of EAL students, which is consistent with the general population of the two communities. According to Statistics Canada (2011c), 45% of the population in metropolitan Vancouver reported speaking a non-official language most often at home. Of these, 40% reported speaking a Chinese language (Cantonese [16.0%], Chinese [12.2%][2] and Mandarin [11.8%]), 17.7% (126,000) speak Punjabi, and 6.7% speak Tagalog. In Surrey, 44% reported a non-official language as their mother tongue and 30% reported speaking only that language at home. The most common mother tongues are Punjabi (21%), Tagalog (3%) and Hindi (3%). More people in Surrey speak neither official language (6.4%) than speak both languages (4.6%). In Vancouver, slightly more number of people speak both official languages (10%) than speak neither (8%) (Statistics Canada, 2011a).

In schools where IF is implemented, as in many schools in each district, about half of the students speak home languages other than English. British Columbia's present language education policy embodies a view of second language education rooted in a Canadian context that recognizes linguistic diversity as well as official language duality as indicated in its preamble:

> The Government of British Columbia recognizes that the province is culturally, linguistically and economically diverse. A language policy must reflect this diversity and respond to the needs of the community. The Ministry of Education, Skills and Training encourages all students to develop language skills which will assist them to live and function more effectively in British Columbia's ethno-culturally diverse environment and in a bilingual Canada. (BC Ministry of Education, 1997: 2)

In this citation, as well as the one that follows, there is emphasis on the economic advantage associated with learning languages, official or otherwise (for the community and for the individual):

> In view of the importance of changing economic relations, such as the developing links with Pacific Rim countries, opportunities should be made available to students to learn languages that will prepare them to take a role in future economic development. . . . Learning another language and learning about another culture may give students greater choice when they make career and life plans. (BC Ministry of Education, 1997: 3)

Currently, second language education is mandatory in Grades 5–8 and, while the choice of language is left to individual school boards, French is the default if an alternative is not chosen. The inclusion of EAL students in FSL programs is endorsed by the current language education policy, and exemption is only permitted if the student 'is receiving English as a second language service and unable to demonstrate his or her learning in relation to expected learning outcomes' (BC Ministry of Education, 1997: 6).

Methodology

A case study approach was undertaken in both studies (Guba & Lincoln, 1989; Stake, 1995). Such an approach enables readers to learn about the case, develop understandings and see, in part, how those who participated in the study constructed their understanding. Questionnaires were distributed to all parents of students in the IF program during the first year of participation in both studies. Parent interviews were conducted in both studies, and focus group meetings with students and parents were conducted in the earlier study. EAL parent responses were highlighted in both studies.

In both studies, perspectives on why students and parents chose to participate in the program were gathered during their first year of IF. In the earlier study, two groups were polled (119 students in 4 schools in 2004 and 136 students in 5 schools in 2005), and in the more recent study, two groups were polled during one year (54 students in 2 schools in 2012), as shown in Table 2.1.

To analyze the data from questionnaires, focus group meetings and interviews, direct interpretation and categorical aggregation were used (Stake, 1995). Transcripts were open coded and emergent themes discovered through repeated occurrences. The questionnaire and follow-up interview and/or focus group were brief and open ended. The same initial three questions were asked of both parents and students in each of the two studies, but the more recent study included an additional question for parents about whether another language was spoken and/or written at home.

Table 2.1 Data collection procedures in both studies

	2005 and 2006	2012
Student-sourced data	Focus group meetings attended by 253 of 255 students (of which 85 are EAL)	Questionnaires completed by 54 of 54 students (of which 31 are EAL)
Parent questionnaires	Questionnaires completed by 120 of 253 students (EFL and EAL)	Questionnaires completed by 49 of 54 parents (of which 28 are EAL)
Parent focus groups	Focus group meetings attended by 16 parents (of which 7 are EAL)	None
Parent interviews	Interviews conducted with 2 parents (of which 1 is EAL)	Interviews conducted with 6 EAL parents

Participants

In the first study conducted in Surrey, an average of 40% of the students participating in the IF program (a higher percentage in four of the schools but only 10% in one school) spoke a home language other than English. In the second study conducted in Vancouver, about 60% of the students participating in IF were EAL learners. This difference could be attributed, in part, to the fact that one school's low percentage of EALs in the early study reduced the five-school average or the fact that the overall number of immigrants to Canada has increased from 14.2% to 17.5% during the period between the two studies (Statistics Canada, 2012a). It is worth noting, however, that the percentage of EALs in each district is very similar and has not changed significantly since the earlier study: currently, 21.7% in Surrey (B. Neveu, personal communication, 14 February 2013) and 22.5% in Vancouver (W. Wong, personal communication, 15 February 2013).

The home languages, in order of frequency, are depicted as a percentage of all languages spoken in IF schools in the two studies in Figure 2.1. The most significant difference between the new data and those in the earlier

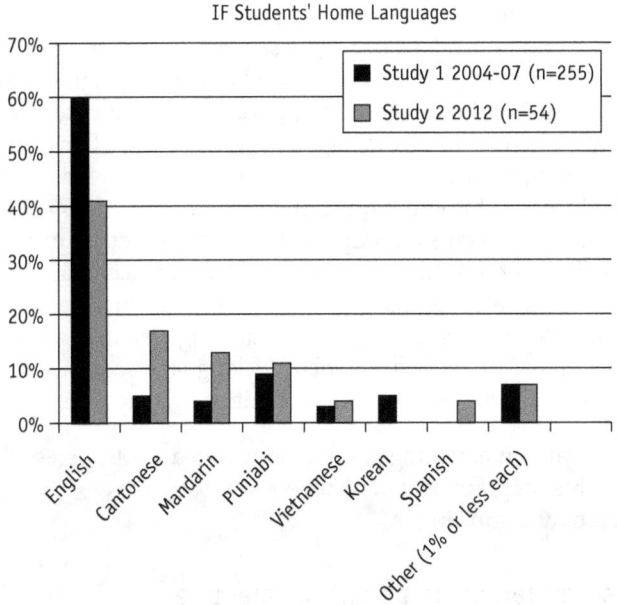

Figure 2.1 IF students' home languages

study is the more than double the number of Chinese language (Cantonese and Mandarin) speakers, a slight increase of Punjabi and Vietnamese speakers, and the presence of Spanish speakers in almost equal numbers to Korean speakers in the earlier study.

Results

The emergent themes in the recent study were very similar to those in the earlier one despite the difference in time period and context. Parents and students view the learning of French as one of Canada's official languages to be an asset worth acquiring, and some parents – both English as first language (EFL) and EAL – consider French to be an important component of a Canadian identity. In the following section, student and parent perspectives are presented according to each of these themes.

Language as an Asset

Student perspectives

Some of the reasons stated most often by students for choosing to enrol in IF related to wanting to learn a new language and seeking future advantages in high school and beyond. Many of these reasons are linked to the acquisition of future resources, such as advanced placement in high school, preparation for university and employment opportunities. Other reasons show an awareness of Canada's linguistic duality and the value of acquiring the second official language. Students expect a 'good return on [their] investment' (Norton, 2000: 10). This equation is one that Bourdieu (1977b) theorizes is inherent in all social transactions: students are, in fact, already competing for social capital in the form of knowledge and advancement opportunities. Some even see this asset as having monetary value: 'normally you have to pay [but] this is a free program'. They see learning French as a means in itself and to other ends as well. The element of language acquisition as an asset was evident as were the very real opportunities this program affords:

> I hope to gain an advantage over others who do not possess this skill.
> I joined this program so it will benefit my future.
> I want a new beginning.

English as first language parent perspectives

Parent responses indicated a consistent rationale of acquiring assets for their children, both linguistically and in terms of future advantages in high school and the job market. The academic and social benefits related to participation in the program were also noted, such as the opportunities for increased challenges and additional options in high school and beyond.

> Learning languages ignites passion for school and learning.
> It enriches the learning experience and allows her to be with other kids who are keen to learn French.
> It seems to snap kids out of their "intermediate ennui" and gets them excited about learning.

Parents articulated the advantages related to speaking an internationally recognized language and how it would increase not only their child's work and travel opportunities but also expand their understanding of the world.

> She will gain a deeper understanding of language concepts and broaden her worldview.
> This gives an expansion of her understanding of her place in the greater world.

English as additional language parent perspectives

Parents who responded to the questionnaire and indicated a home language other than English expressed many of the same perspectives as the EFL parents related to their child acquiring an asset by learning French, one of Canada's official languages.

> Participating in this program opens up all sorts of opportunities now and in the future, such as improved chances at university entrance public service work, travel, etc.
> Languages open doors. We hope she will continue to add new ones to her repertoire.
> French is one of our country's official languages. All Canadians should be able to speak both.

EAL parents raised notions of linguistic capital and plurilingualism, as was noted in the earlier study, along with statements about possible future opportunities:

> I hope [child's name] will be fluent in speaking, reading, writing and listening French so that she can have asset of knowledge of French as well as English.

> Students have opportunity to learn the language, which is really important and can take them far more towards success and bright future.
> If my child can be in this program, he will learn more languages (plus our family language, Chinese).

Themes related to economics were highlighted in several comments noting that these opportunities were available without extra cost.

> The benefits we see because we don't have to arrange any tuition fee for French class.
> I grew up speaking another language myself and I know that it is invaluable. You can't even put enough money into it. If I could go back in time, I would learn more languages myself.
> Having this opportunity for free? That's a no brainer!

Language as a Component of a Canadian Identity

Student perspectives

The acquisition of Canada's second official language was only one of many other benefits noted by students, such as enjoying languages, increasing options in high school, job possibilities, travel and so on. This is consistent with the findings in the earlier study. Only 5 out of 54 respondents mentioned that French is Canada's second language when answering the first two questions in the student questionnaire (Why were you interested in participating in this program? and What do you see as the benefits of learning French?). Two examples follow:

> I want to learn French because Canada is a bilingual country
> French and its culture are important in Canada.

The relatively small role of the official language status in student responses is different, however, from what was expressed by parents, especially EAL parents.

English as first language parent perspectives

Parent comments included references to the importance of learning French as one of Canada's official languages, as had been the case in the earlier study. The comments were often framed in the context of future jobs in government and ease of mobility within Canada and abroad. Comparisons were also made between the efficacy of an intensive versus a core program as a means of acquiring the language.

> It makes sense for students to learn both of Canada's official languages.
> This program is a more effective way to learn Canada's second language. I took French in high school but still can't speak it.

English as additional language parent perspectives

The comments gathered during interviews with EAL parents also included a strong emphasis on the importance of learning French as one of Canada's official languages.

> First of all, French is an official language of Canada and it is important to be able to use it. It's as simple as that.
> This is a second language of Canada. We hope child has opportunity to go travel, education, in politics, etc.
> If you speak a country's official language or two, you understand a lot more.
> The fact that it is an official language, that's huge. It's one of the best decisions we made.
> I'd like my son to get more from school and this second language is so important in this country. English is too.

Comments about providing one's child with opportunities or advantages that one had wanted but not necessarily achieved for oneself were also in evidence.

> I really like that my daughter is learning French because it was my dream too. Learning a new language is always beneficial. French is BC's second official language, that's why I prefer my daughter to learn French as well as English.

Discussion

As has been noted in earlier studies in FSL programs in British Columbia, the immigrant parents who participated in the two studies described in this chapter clearly associate language with capital (e.g. Berron, 1998; Carr, 2007; Dagenais, 2003; Dagenais & Berron, 2001; Dagenais & Moore, 2008). This equation was also operative for EFL parents and has been corroborated in earlier studies in French immersion in other parts of Canada (e.g. Olson &

Burns, 1983; Hart & Lapkin, 1998). For some parents, the acquisition of material and symbolic capital immediately and in the future was linked to another valued resource related to Canadian citizenship.

The bilingualism ideals set forth in federal government policy are, in fact, upheld in programs such as IF, and this is occurring in culturally and linguistically diverse sites. Both of the studies examined in this chapter took place in schools and communities where cultural and linguistic diversity is the norm. The OECD (2001) considers imperative the importance of education in ensuring future well-being in new societies and economies. This unifying purpose brought together a diverse group of parents who sought particular assets for their children.

British Columbia's draft French curriculum not only acknowledges the diversity among British Columbia students but also the multiple resources that plurilingual learners bring to language learning:

> British Columbia's students bring a rich variety of languages and cultures to the classroom. ... Many students are recent immigrants or have learned a heritage language at home. Other students have acquired language skills in one or more languages through contact in their communities or abroad. This prior linguistic knowledge is a part of who the student is. Validation of the student's ability in the language reflects the belief that all language learning is important and is a life-long endeavour. (Ministry of Education, 2011: 7)

The curriculum supports the inclusion of EAL students by stating that they already have experience learning a language or languages and noting that, in second/additional language contexts, EAL students are 'placed on an equal footing with their classmates' (Ministry of Education, 2011: 9). This inclusive view not only builds on long-established second language educational research (e.g. Cummins, 1979, 1992) but also reinforces Mady's (2007, 2010) position that EAL students play a critical role in helping Canada achieve its goals for linguistic duality, which according to the federal government (Canadian Heritage, 2003), leads to increased social cohesion.

Conclusion

Just as British Columbia's language education policy (BC Ministry of Education, 1997) has broadened the notion of linguistic duality to include knowing and learning other languages to prepare for economic prosperity, the rationale for learning French as a second or additional language encompasses benefits over and above developing linguistic proficiency. The parents of students in British Columbia's IF program sought opportunities for their children, such as academic challenges, enhanced high school options, and the acquisition of one of Canada's official languages, but they also wanted access to future benefits related to economic possibilities and increased mobility. For some parents, including those whose home language is neither French nor English, learning French as an element of Canadian citizenship was also seen as valuable. For these parents in particular, the stated link between learning French and enhancing one's Canadian identity builds on earlier research on allophone participation in French second language education and the general pursuit of assets accruing to language acquisition.

Bourdieu's (1977) conceptualization of social structures and the competition for position and capital was useful in understanding some of the dynamics in parent and student choices. In addition, the notion of common purpose around factors relating to human and social capital put forth by the OECD (2001) and others served as a lens to consider why parents and students of diverse origins came together in this program. The findings of this recent study reinforce those of an earlier one in a nearby British Columbia school district and show that common priorities related to Canada's official languages do, in fact, exert a cohesive effect on diverse groups of students and their parents.

Notes

(1) While it is unlikely that this goal will be met, it is worth noting that between 2006 and 2011, the number of people who reported being able to conduct a conversation in both of Canada's official languages increased by nearly 350,000 to 5.8 million. The bilingualism rate of the Canadian population increased slightly from 17.4% in 2006 to 17.5% in 2011 (Statistics Canada, 2012a).
(2) The number of census respondents reporting Cantonese or Mandarin as their mother tongue is underestimated because of the large number of people who report simply 'Chinese' without further specifying whether they speak Mandarin, Cantonese or another Chinese language (Statistics Canada, 2011).

References

BC Ministry of Education (1997) *Language Education in BC Schools: Policy and Guidelines*. Victoria, BC: Author.
BC Ministry of Education (2011) *Draft Curriculum – September 2011: French Elementary Secondary*, accessed October 11 2011. http://www.bced.gov.bc.ca/irp/drafts/french.pdf
Berron, C. (1998) 'When there is an opportunity, take it!' ou les raisons pour lesquelles trois parents d'origine indo-pakistanaise ont inscrit leurs enfants en immersion française. PhD thesis, Simon Fraser University.
Bilingualism and Biculturalism Commission (1969) *Book IV: The cultural contribution of other ethnic groups*, accessed June 22, 2006. http://epe.lacbac.gc.ca/100/200/301/pco-bcp/commissions-ef/dunton1967-1970-ef/dunton1967-70eng.htm

Bourdieu, P. (1977) *Outline of a Theory of Practice* (R. Nice, trans.). New York: Cambridge University Press.
Bourdieu, P. and Passeron, J. (1990) *Reproduction in Education, Society and Culture*. Beverly Hills, CA: Sage.
Bourdieu, P. and Wacquant, L. (1992) *An Invitation to Reflexive Sociology*. Chicago, IL: University of Chicago Press.
Canadian Heritage (1997) *Social Cohesion Research Workplan*, accessed December 10 2012. http://www.socialsciences.uottawa.ca/governance/eng/documents/social_cohesion_research_workplan.pdf
Canadian Heritage (2003) *Official Languages—2003–2004 Annual Report*, accessed Nov 15 2005. http://epe.lacbac.gc.ca/100/201/301/official_languages_cdn_heritage/20032004v1.pdf
Canadian Heritage (2004) *Plan Twenty Thirteen: Strategies for a National Approach in Second Language Education*. Ottawa, ON: Author.
Canadian Parents for French (2005) *The State of French Second Language Education in Canada 2005*. Ottawa, ON: Author.
Carr, W. (2007) Canada's bilingualism ideal: A case study of Intensive French in British Columbia. EdD thesis, Simon Fraser University.
Carr, W. (2009) Intensive French in British Columbia: Student and parent perspectives and English as additional language (EAL) student performance. *The Canadian Modern Language Review* 65 (5), 787–815.
Cummins, J. (1979) Linguistic interdependence and the educational development of bilingual children. *Review of Educational Research* 49, 222–251.
Cummins, J. (1992) Heritage language teaching in Canadian schools. *Journal of Curriculum Studies* 24, 281–286.
Dagenais, D. (2003) Accessing imagined communities through multilingualism and immersion education. *Journal of Language, Identity and Education* 2 (4), 269–283.
Dagenais, D. and Berron, C. (2001) Promoting multilingualism through French immersion and language maintenance in three immigrant families. *Language, Culture and Curriculum* 14 (2), 142–155.
Dagenais, D., Beynon, J. and Mathis, N. (2008) Intersections of social cohesion, education, and identity in teachers, discourses, and practices. *Pedagogies: An International Journal* 3, 85–108.
Dagenais, D. and Moore, D. (2008) Représentations des littératies plurilingues de l'immersion en français et des dynamique identitaires chez des parents chinois. *The Canadian Modern Language Review* 65 (1), 11–31.
Duff, P. (2007) Multilingualism in Canadian schools: Myths, realities, and possibilities. *Canadian Journal of Applied Linguistics* 10 (2), 149–163.
Government of Canada (2003) *The next act: New momentum for Canada's linguistic duality*. http://www.cpfnb.com/articles/ActionPlan_e.pdf
Hart, D. and Lapkin, S. (1998) Issues of social-class bias in access to French immersion education. In S. Lapkin (ed.) *French Second Language Education in Canada: Empirical Studies* (pp. 324–350). Toronto, ON: University of Toronto Press.
Heller, M. (2001) Globalization and the commodification of bilingualism in Canada. In D. Block and D. Cameron (eds) *Globalization and Language Teaching* (pp. 47–67). London: Routledge.
Jedwab, J. (2003) Social confusion: The decline of "cohesionism" in Canada and its lessons for the study of citizenship. *Canadian Diversity* 2 (1), 144–151. http://canada.metropolis.net/publications/Diversity/Diversity.Spring2003.pdf

Mady, C. (2007a) The suitability of core French for recently arrived adolescent immigrants to Canada. *Canadian Journal of Applied Linguistics* 10 (2), 177–196.

Mady, C. (2007b) Allophone students in French second-official-language programs: A literature review. *The Canadian Modern Language Review* 63 (5), 727–760.

Mady, C. (2010) Motivation to study core French: Comparing recent immigrants and Canadian-born secondary school students. *Canadian Journal of Education* 33 (3), 564–587.

Mady, C. (2012a) Official language bilingualism to the exclusion of multilingualism: Immigrant student perspectives on French as a second official language in "English dominant" Canada. *Language and Intercultural Communication* 12 (1), 74–89.

Mady, C. (2012b) Voices of immigrant adults: Perspectives and experiences with French as a second official language in "English-dominant" Canada. *Intercultural Promenades: Journal of Modern Languages and Intercultural Studies* 1 (1), 35–51.

Mady, C. and Carr, W. (2011) Immigrant perspectives on French-language learning in English-dominant Canadian communities. In C. Varcasia (ed.) *Becoming Multilingual: Language Learning and Language Policy Between Attitudes and Identities* (pp. 195–216). Bern: Peter Lang.

Netten, J. and Germain, C. (2004a) Introduction: Intensive French. *The Canadian Modern Language Review* 60 (3), 263–273.

Netten, J. and Germain, C. (2004b) Theoretical and research foundations of Intensive French. *The Canadian Modern Language Review* 60 (3), 275–294.

Norton, B. (2000) *Identity and Language Learning: Gender, Ethnicity and Educational Change*. Harlow: Pearson.

Organization of Economic Cooperation and Development (OECD) (2001) *The well-being of nations: The role of human and social capital*. http://www.oecd.org/site/worldforum/33703702.pdf

Olson, P. and Burns, G. (1983) Politics, class, and happenstance: French immersion in a Canadian context. *Interchange on Educational Policy* 14 (1), 1–16.

Stake, R. (1995) *The Art of Case Study Research*. Thousand Oaks, CA: Sage.

Statistics Canada (2011a) *Focus on Geography Series, 2011 Census – Census subdivision of Surrey, CY – British Columbia*, accessed December 4 2012. http://www12.statcan.gc.ca/census-recensement/2011/as-sa/fogs-spg/Facts-csd-eng.cfm?LANG=Eng&GK=CSD&GC=5915004

Statistics Canada (2011b) *Focus on Geography Series, 2011 Census – Census subdivision of Vancouver, CY – British Columbia*. http://www12.statcan.gc.ca/census-recensement/2011/as-sa/fogs-spg/Facts-csd-eng.cfm?LANG=Eng&GK=CSD&GC=5915022

Statistics Canada (2011c) *Immigrant languages in Canada*, accessed December 4 2012. http://www12.statcan.gc.ca/census-recensement/2011/as-sa/98-314-x/98-314-x2011003_2-eng.pdf

Statistics Canada (2012a) *Data products: October 24, 2012 – Language*, accessed December 4 2012. http://www12.statcan.gc.ca/census-recensement/index-eng.cfm

Statistics Canada (2012b) *Linguistic characteristics of Canadians*, accessed December 3 2012. http://www12.statcan.gc.ca/census-recensement/2011/as-sa/98-314-x/98-314-x2011001-eng.cfm

3 French is Hard: An English Language Learner's Experience in Core French

Jordana F. Garbati

Many Canadian schools have experienced an increase in the enrolment of English language learners (ELLs[1]) in the last several decades. Once ELLs enter the public school system, it is the school and the school board's responsibility to provide them with an equitable and inclusive education. In the province of Ontario, where English is the majority language, the Ministry of Education (2007: 7) expects that ELLs 'learn the language of instruction in English language schools at the same time as they are working towards meeting the curriculum expectations'. Instruction in French as a second language (FSL) is part of Ontario's education system and all students receive FSL instruction from Grade 4 up to at least the end of Grade 9.[2] In recent years, because of the increase in the linguistic diversity of Ontario's student population, researchers have begun exploring issues surrounding ELLs learning FSL. At the elementary level, for example, Carr (2009) has shown that ELLs in an Intensive French program outperformed their non-ELL core French (CF) peers and concluded that ELLs studying French as a third language (L3) also enhance their English (as a second language [L2]) skills.[3] At the secondary school level, Mady (2003, 2006) has shown that ELLs are more motivated than their Canadian-born peers to take FSL and that ELLs can achieve success in FSL. The qualitative case study reported here adds to the foregoing research by including a student perspective with the goal to understand the experiences of an ELL learning FSL in an Ontario elementary class.

Literature Review

Context

In addition to the approximately 250,000 permanent residents that Canada receives each year, the nation welcomes groups of temporary residents (e.g. foreign workers, foreign students and visitors). In 2011, over 1 million people were identified as temporary residents and about one-third of these people (301,842) were identified as foreign students. In other words, 29.6% of all temporary residents were foreign students. Temporary residents settle across the country, but almost half (42.1%) of all foreign students reside in the province of Ontario. The top source country for foreign students between 2009 and 2011 was China, a country where neither English nor French is spoken. While foreign students enter Canada to study at all levels, one-fifth (20.0%) of foreign students in 2011 were at the elementary or secondary school level (Citizenship and Immigration Canada, 2012).

With these statistics in mind, education in the dominant language of society (e.g. English in Ontario) is of primary importance and school boards provide support for students with no or limited English language ability in the form of English as a second language (ESL) programs. As French is an official language of Canada, the Ontario Ministry of Education mandates that all students complete an FSL program. The majority of all students in elementary and secondary schools in the province are enrolled in a CF program (Canadian Parents for French, 2012). In this program, FSL is taught as a subject and usually involves 20–45 minutes of FSL instruction per day. The aim of the Ontario CF program is to help students develop a usable command of fundamental communication skills (Ministry of Education, 1999). In addition, Ontario's equity and inclusive education strategy calls for equitable education for all students, meaning, 'a condition or state of fair, inclusive, and respectful treatment of all people' (Ministry of Education, 2009: 4). While the federal and provincial governments promote inclusive and equitable education for all, there has been some indication that ELLs experience barriers to accessing FSL (see Dagenais & Berron, 2001; Taylor, 2006, 2009; Mady & Turnbull, 2010). Research indicates that immigrants have expressed a desire to learn languages other than their own (Mady, 2003) and a reported 87% of immigrant parents in Canada believe that it is important for their children to learn a language other than English (Parkin & Turcotte, 2004). Research has also confirmed the benefits of ESL and FSL study for immigrants. In a study of three trilingual students in an early French immersion program in British Columbia, Dagenais and Day (1998) found that the teachers of these students described trilingualism as a resource that students can draw upon. Taylor (1992) questioned how ELLs adapt to and succeed in early French immersion programs, both linguistically and overall, in her case study of Victor, as he progressed from senior Kindergarten to Grade 3. She found that Victor succeeded linguistically and academically, and adapted socio-psychologically in his early French immersion program.

As far as CF is concerned, Mady's (2003) research compared the motivation of Grade 9 Canadian-born students and ELLs to learn French and found that ELLs were more motivated to learn FSL than their Canadian-born peers. She subsequently found that ELLs do in fact achieve success in CF and can often outperform their Canadian-born peers (Mady, 2007).

While the research reviewed here is relevant and provides valuable insight into the FSL education for ELLs, there has yet to be a strong focus in the research on ELLs at the elementary level in the CF program. More specifically, the question of FSL education for students who are in Canada on a temporary basis has yet to be raised. This study addresses this gap in the field as, through the use of a single case study approach, it shares an ELL's experiences in learning CF.

Theoretical Premises

L2 acquisition theorists have presented various ideas about the conditions required in order to achieve success. The literature in the field of L2 acquisition has stressed the social aspect of language learning. Edwards (1998) and Fillmore and Valadez (1986: 668) have insisted that language learning occurs in 'social settings that allow learners to come into contact with people who speak the target language well enough to help in its learning'. In this regard, communicative and social classroom activities are seen to be beneficial for the language development of L2 learners.

Theorists have also noted that children who already have literacy proficiency in one language are able to benefit from a transfer of skills when they begin reading in an L2. Edwards (1998) reported that a good foundation in the first language (L1) aids children in learning to read and write second and subsequent languages. Further, Cummins (1989, 1996) has researched the potential for knowledge and skill transfer across languages. As a result of his many years of research in the area, he believes that cross-linguistic awareness, translation between languages and the creation of bilingual texts and other resources drawing on students' L1 knowledge are underutilized. In terms of L3 acquisition, Cenoz et al. (2001) suggest that L3 learners present advantages over L2 learners because of their highly developed learning strategies, metalinguistic awareness and communicative sensitivity. Clyne (1997) and Dewaele (1998) have indicated that L3 learners use their knowledge of their L2 to help them communicate in their L3.

In terms of appropriate pedagogy for ELLs, it has been argued that an approach that promotes language awareness can help students to know those aspects of language that can be borrowed and adapted to other languages so as to improve their linguistic resources (Cenoz et al., 2001). Further,

Goldenberg (1996) suggests that ELLs are generally best served in programs that build academic knowledge in students' home languages while helping to build their proficiency in English.

In light of the theories mentioned here, I explore what a student learning an L3 (i.e. French) simultaneously with an L2 (i.e. English) experiences in CF. Additionally, what opportunities do ELLs have for social interaction or communicative language activities with their peers and to what extent are ELLs' first languages incorporated into the CF class?

Methodology

This research took a qualitative case study approach, which entails an intense, holistic description, and an analysis of a bounded phenomenon (Merriam, 1998). This approach allowed for a focus on an individual, which is one main advantage of case study research (Mackey & Gass, 2005).

Participants

The core participant in this study was Jack,[4] a Grade 8 ELL boy from Korea who was enrolled in a CF program in a public elementary school.[5] Jack had recently arrived in Canada and was in the country temporarily as part of an exchange-like program.[6] Jack's L1 was Korean, his L2 was English and his L3 was French. In order to develop an in-depth understanding of Jack's experiences in CF, additional participants were invited to participate in this study: his CF teacher, his homeroom teacher, his principal and his guardian. Jack was one of two ELLs in his class.

Data collection and analysis

Over a period of six weeks, three semi-structured interviews were conducted with Jack to glean information about his FSL development, his attitude toward learning FSL and his FSL motivation. Each of the other participants was interviewed once, also following a semi-structured protocol. In addition to the interviews, I conducted three classroom observations of the CF class within the data collection period. The first observation period was 20 minutes long and the remaining two observation periods were 40 minutes long (i.e. the duration of the French class). The Grade 8 class in this school had a 40-minute CF class on a daily basis. During these observational periods, I took detailed field notes. Other data were collected in the form of curriculum documents, school brochures and observations of French use in the school.

Interview transcripts and observational field notes were coded using an open coding technique. The codes were then organized into themes. Information from curriculum documents and the school literature was used to support the findings that emerged from the coding process.

Findings

The main findings of this study encompass the relationships between Jack and (a) the institution, (b) his host family and (c) his friends.

Institution

The institution includes the teachers, administrators, school board officials and the Ministry of Education that directly and indirectly affect Jack's experience in CF. Four main themes which affected his relationship with the institution arose in the data analysis: (a) adaptations to the FSL program, (b) FSL teacher support to Jack, (c) school or board support to the FSL teacher and (d) promotion of French in the school.

In terms of the FSL program, I observed that English was frequently used in the CF class to instruct, provide feedback and discipline the students. English was also used in spoken interactions between the students on a regular basis. Jack estimated that the FSL teacher spoke French 60% of the time and English 40% of the time.[7] Jack commented on how, when the FSL teacher spoke English, it helped him: 'The French teacher speaks French and sometimes when I can't understand French, she speaks English for me'. Commenting on the use of English in the CF class, the FSL teacher said, 'I want [the students] to know exactly what I'm expecting of them so I'll say it in French and then I repeat it in English. That way, I'll know I'm guaranteeing they know exactly what to do and how to do it'. The homeroom teacher commented, 'And certainly there's enough English spoken during French class that the [ELL] is not out of the loop. I'm in the class fairly often and I don't see it as an exclusive environment'. The use of English affected Jack's experience in the CF class but the extent to which the use of English improved his French proficiency remains unclear. For Jack, English was his L2 so he used it in order to understand his L3. During this study, it was never apparent that he used his L1 (Korean) to help him progress in French.

There was evidence that accommodations were made for Jack on a regular basis; in the province of Ontario, accommodations are understood to be changes that a teacher makes to how he/she presents information or how a student displays his/her understanding in order to be mindful of learner needs.[8] He said, 'the French teacher wrote French sentences and English sentences so I could do it... She gave us sentences and she helped us a lot'. In reference to accommodations that were made for his FSL test, Jack said, 'Everybody was doing different harder tests and I was doing easy test. ... There was one sheet and on one page there was 20 words and on the back, other questions. I didn't have to do the other questions'. Although Jack's FSL program was adapted, no one seemed to take responsibility for FSL programming for ELLs at the school. The FSL teacher took it upon herself to accommodate Jack to help him succeed, as there was no guidance or support on how to make appropriate program accommodations. Regarding the FSL program for ELLs, the French teacher said:

> To tell you the truth, no one has come to me and said really what to do. Just from experience, I've put together a package of really basic stuff. And once [the ELLs] do that, they've gone through the alphabet and numbers, I'll give them another duotang [booklet] that's a little more advanced. So I've kind of put that together myself but I haven't had anyone come and tell me what to do or how to do it.

In addition to the program accommodations, the assistance given to the ELL by the FSL teacher impacted Jack's FSL experience. During the classroom observation periods, there was some evidence of the FSL teacher trying to set Jack up for success in his learning of French. When assigned a written and oral project on the topic of careers, for example, Jack was able to work with the other ELL in the class, whereas other students were expected to complete the project independently. The FSL teacher used a variety of teaching strategies to help support Jack, including cross-curricular connections with art, group work, written tests and individual attention. By incorporating a variety of teaching methods into her program, the FSL teacher may have helped Jack achieve success. When asked what he liked about FSL, Jack replied, 'When we have French projects. We make group with friends and work together'. The FSL teacher gave Jack opportunities to work with others and it was clear that this strategy increased his enjoyment of the CF class.

While there were positive aspects of the relationship between Jack and his FSL teacher, there seemed to be a disconnect between what each of them thought was appropriate in terms of assistance. Dictionary use, for example, proved to be one area where there was some confusion. While the FSL teacher thought the dictionary was a valuable tool for Jack, he felt challenged by it. The teacher said, 'I always make sure he has a dictionary. A good one'. Whereas Jack said, 'It takes a long time to find words. [I use it] not very much'. Although the FSL teacher thought Jack was making proper use of the French-English dictionary that she provided, he found it too time consuming and difficult to use. Some teaching strategies, therefore, may not have been suitable for the ELL and a critical examination of appropriate accommodations is warranted.

While the focus of this study was on an ELL's experiences in FSL, it became apparent that one factor that influenced Jack, perhaps more indirectly than directly, was the support given to the FSL teacher. The availability, or lack thereof, of resources was an issue. The FSL teacher in this study was responsible for choosing the resources. She received no guidance about what resources could be used in her class to assist ELLs. The principal, on the other hand, felt that support was offered to the FSL teacher. When questioned about the availability of resources and teacher support, the principal said, 'I try and give [the FSL teachers] as much money for basically as many resources as they want. We give things, books, dictionaries'. When asked about the availability of FSL resources at the school, the teacher replied, 'There are French books here in the library which is helpful and there are also French games on the computer'. When probed further with regard to if and how students made use of the French library books, the FSL teacher said, 'I don't know. You'd have to talk to the librarian'. Of the computer games, she said, 'I don't know. Because I don't have computer time with them. ... I've never had computer time [at this school]'. It seemed that the FSL teacher was rather unaware of the resources available in the school that could possibly assist her in her teaching and the students in their learning. On one of my visits to the school library, there were approximately 50 French books, mainly picture books, on a shelf in a corner, tucked behind a table and a few chairs. When I asked Jack if there were French books and computer games in the library, he said that he did not know. Although FSL resources did exist at the school, their use was minimal and they did not appear to be incorporated in the FSL class. The availability of resources, as well as their effective use, is of interest in this study.

The promotion of FSL at the school was an additional theme revealed by the data. In addition to the library resources, I observed one chart paper on a hallway wall with a list of students' birthdays written in French. During observation visits, there were no announcements in French, no teachers speaking French, or any other evidence that showed that FSL was taught at the school. The French teacher did not have a classroom of her own; she travelled with a cart full of teaching materials to each of her classes. In Jack's Grade 8 classroom (where the CF class met), there was one poster in French that read *Bon Voyage*.

From the individual interviews with the FSL teacher, the homeroom teacher and the principal, it was clear that there were different perceptions of the promotion of FSL within the school. The FSL teacher commented,

'Once in a while [the teachers] will say something in French. Like a little sentence'. She also said that she made an effort to promote FSL on her own. She said, 'After kids are done their projects, I often put them up in the hall and everyone can look at them'. The homeroom teacher did not seem to think that FSL was promoted beyond the CF class. He said, 'I think the French teacher brings enthusiasm. Outside the French teacher, I don't see other people marketing it'. While the FSL teacher did not mention school-wide French events, class trips or French spoken at various times throughout the school day, the principal felt strongly that FSL was being promoted in the school. She stated, 'One of the French teachers runs a French club and kids join. They do cafés with the Grade 8s, a chocolate fondue and *tourtière* and those cultural things. And every other year the Grade 7s and 8s alternate and go to Quebec City for two nights and three days'.

Family

A second major theme that surfaced during the data analysis was with regard to the relationship between Jack and his host family. Interview data revealed that the host family had positive and negative influences on Jack's attitudes toward learning FSL because of the family's view of French as well as the use of languages in the home.

Jack's guardian did not see any advantages to Jack learning FSL, as he believed it was too difficult. The guardian said, 'I just think [learning French is] just a waste of [Jack's] time'. The guardian suggested that the focus for ELLs in the school board's exchange program is to learn English and so FSL should be a choice for them. He [the guardian] felt that the ELLs should first focus on the development of their English skills and then devote time to learning FSL.

The use of language in the home environment may have had a direct influence on Jack's skills in and attitudes toward FSL. The guardian, who speaks English, Greek and Spanish fluently, saw French as his fourth language but he admitted that he was not fluent in French. The guardian's own child was in Grade 6 at Jack's school and did not appear to be interested in learning FSL. Interviews with Jack and his guardian revealed that, while the host family was concerned about Jack's academic and social progress, French was rarely a topic of discussion at home and FSL homework never appeared in the home environment. In addition, family members rarely provided Jack with assistance in FSL because no one at home had adequate French knowledge to offer help. The guardian said he encouraged Jack to learn and practice his English, as that was the primary objective for his study in Canada.

Friends

The interview and classroom observation data also show that Jack had positive experiences in FSL that were directly related to his friendships. Working with another ELL, group work and the assistance of non-ELL friends all resulted in positive experiences for Jack. In his Grade 8 class, there was one other ELL. When speaking of his interaction with this student, Jack revealed that the other ELL helped him learn FSL; he appreciated the time that he got to work with the other ELL because he thought that this student was more proficient in FSL and could offer him some assistance. The FSL teacher had also observed that the two ELLs in the class liked to work together and, as such, she allowed them to do so for a variety of tasks. Further, on several occasions, Jack said that he found class enjoyable when he interacted with his friends. On our very first meeting, he explained that during CF class, he liked, 'When we have French projects. We make groups with friends and work together'.

Jack appeared to have positive experiences with his non-ELL friends because of the assistance they provided. He said, 'friends help me understand French' and that he called on them for help in class. When asked why he asks his friends for help rather than the FSL teacher, Jack said it was because 'friends are more comfortable to speak with'. The FSL teacher was aware of the assistance Jack received from his peers. She noticed 'certain kids, especially the ones that sit around him, trying to help him ... or he'll often go to [Student A] and ask him "what's this" or "how do you say that". They're wonderful'.

There was also evidence that Jack's peers had a negative influence on his FSL experiences. In comparing his ability and progress in FSL to that of his peers, he believed that he lacked proficiency in French. Jack admitted that, 'French was hard' several times and, in terms of homework assignments, he said that he and his friends did not do homework.

Discussion

Findings from this study both confirm and contradict ideas presented in previous research within the field. Jack's experiences in CF are in many ways parallel to what has been shown about the experiences of other immigrants to Canada who speak neither English nor French. The findings in this single case study about an ELL's experiences in CF relate to the influences, both positive and negative, that the institution (including teaching strategies, program adaptations, support from and for the teacher and the use of L1 and L2 in the L3 classroom), his family and his peers had on the ELL.

The implementation of thoughtful and engaging teaching strategies has an impact on the learning outcomes of ELLs (Coelho, 2004). Krashen (1985) stressed the importance of making input in the target language comprehensible and that, to acquire a new language, messages must be clearly understood. In order to ease the process of second (or additional) language acquisition, visual aids, reading and listening activities, building vocabulary and being concerned about whether messages are understood by students, all have important implications for comprehensible input in classroom practice (Krashen & Terell, 1983). The FSL teacher in this study often spoke French and then followed up with English. In doing so, one can question the extent to which an ELL would make an effort to understand French (his L3) when the same information would also be presented in English (his L2). In this context, Jack did not have an opportunity to use his L1 (Korean) to help him understand FSL while the non-ELLs in the class were able to use their L1 (English). Jack's temporary residency in Canada may have also influenced his motivation, or lack thereof, to participate more fully in learning French.

The FSL teacher plays a critical role in designing appropriate and motivating FSL lessons. She/he is responsible for using strategies that will support ELLs. The Ontario Ministry of Education (2005: 19) insists that ELLs 'are more likely to participate orally in class and take a positive approach to language acquisition when they are supported by teachers and peers who are sensitive to their needs and bolster their self-confidence'. In this study, the FSL teacher did attempt to create a welcoming environment for her ELLs by organizing group activities and by acknowledging their existing language skills. Additional teaching strategies that could support ELLs in every classroom, but may not have been fully implemented by the FSL teacher in this study, include completing dual-language assignments, working with same-language partners who discuss a problem and clarify information in the first language before switching to English, and creating multilingual displays or signs (Ministry of Education, 2005). Although some of these strategies were observed, the FSL teacher in this study could have incorporated additional strategies on a more regular basis to aid the ELL in his learning of FSL (e.g. appropriate personal dictionary, word lists, oral discussions and visual supports). Additionally, there were several times when Jack was rarely acknowledged in a 40-minute French class, and it was also observed that Jack used time in French class to complete independent assignments in other subject areas. These observations may indicate that a stronger relationship between teacher and student would prove advantageous.

In terms of program adaptations, a slight discrepancy was found between what the teachers believe are appropriate accommodations for ELLs and what the ELL in this study believed. In this study, there was a lack of communication between Jack and the FSL teacher and, as such, some accommodations were not successful in setting Jack up for success. More ongoing and open communication between teacher and student along with setting realistic learning goals could help structure more appropriate accommodations for ELLs in mainstream elementary CF. In this study, it was clear that there was a lack of support in place to assist the FSL teacher in her programming. Professional development opportunities for the FSL teacher were rare at both the school and school board levels. The FSL teacher in this study might have benefitted from receiving more pertinent information about how ELLs learn and about appropriate resources and strategies to assist her in her teaching.

Clyne (1997) and Dewaele (1998) suggest that L3 learners use knowledge of their L2 to help them communicate in their L3. Researchers have reported that L3 learners present advantages over L2 learners because of their high metalinguistic awareness and communicative sensitivity (see Cenoz et al., 2001; Clyne, 1997; Dewaele, 1998). On some occasions observed in this study, Jack used his knowledge of English (his L2) to assist him in understanding French (his L3). Although Jack repeatedly said, 'French is hard', he generally felt positive about understanding French by using his knowledge of English. On occasion, he spoke of making comparisons between English and French. In terms of his L1, he said, 'Korean is not similar to French so it's hard'. Jack admitted that he did not use his L1 (Korean) to help him understand his L3 (French). The exact reasons for Jack's lack of use of Korean in French class are not entirely known. It could be because of Jack's confidence in using his L1, the classroom environment, the school population or the teachers' language teaching strategies. Very probably, however, the distance between Korean and French explains why Jack was not able to draw on his L1 to understand his L3.

Jack's host family and peers had both positive and negative influences on his motivation and attitude toward learning French. We have known for a long time that motivation is a key factor in learning a second language (Gardner, 1985; Skehan, 1989). Jack's guardian did not seem interested in supporting his efforts in learning French and did not view French class as a beneficial use of Jack's time (especially due to Jack's temporary status in Canada). Jack wanted to focus on learning English and his motivation to learn English may have deterred him from becoming more involved with his French studies. Likewise, Jack's peer group did not seem keen on learning French and he seemed to have adopted a similar attitude. Krashen and Terrell (1983: 179) suggest 'peer evaluation is probably the single most important factor in the behaviour of an adolescent. For this reason it takes a very talented instructor to create an atmosphere favourable for acquisition among a group of young teenagers'. Learning that few of his friends were enthusiastic about learning French, I suggest that this could have had an effect on Jack's personal motivation for learning French and for actively participating in French activities.

Conclusion

Though a case study based on only one learner, there is valuable information for teachers, administrators and policy makers regarding CF programming for ELLs, curriculum adaptations and factors that affect the success of ELLs in CF. Jack's temporary resident status in Canada offers a new perspective on the inclusion of ELLs in elementary CF. Areas for further inquiry may include a longitudinal case study involving more than one ELL in various locations across Ontario. Additionally, researchers and and teachers could work together to investigate the importance of including temporary foreign students in CF. I suggest we also examine the curriculum guidelines for ELLs in CF and improve these documents by including program adaptation possibilities, for example, to reflect the abilities and needs of all ELLs and to assist FSL teachers who have a linguistically diverse student population. Finally, while I do not attempt to make generalizable claims from this single case study, I do note that in order for the CF program to provide ELLs with 'a valuable educational experience and the opportunity to develop a basic usable command of the French language' (Ministry of Education, 2001: 2), changes are needed.

Notes

(1) While several terms have been used in the literature (e.g. language-minority learner, allophone and non-native English speaker), for the purpose of this chapter I have adopted the term English language learner (ELL) to refer to those students in the Ontario school system who have been designated as having a mother tongue other than English. (See Ministry of Education [2005, 2007] for additional descriptions about terminology and identification.)
(2) Students in Ontario are required to successfully complete at least one FSL credit at the secondary school level (generally this is Grade 9 CF) in order to obtain a secondary school diploma.
(3) Intensive French is an FSL program option that exists is some parts of Canada (e.g. British Columbia – see Carr [2007]).
(4) Pseudonym.
(5) Kindergarten to Grade 8 represents the elementary school division in Ontario.
(6) The school board organized the exchange program. Foreign students from countries such as Korea, Japan and Mexico pay tuition to the board to be a student enrolled in a school within the board's jurisdiction. Students are placed with a host family for the period of time that they are in a school. The host parents act as their legal guardians. The duration of stay can be anywhere from a few months to a year and the students have the option of extending their stay.

(7) While length of time of French and English use by the French teacher was not calculated during the observation periods, it is estimated that English was used much more than French during the three observation periods.
(8) The Ontario Ministry of Education uses the terms 'modifications' and 'accommodations' to refer to program adaptations. Modifications mean that some or all of the course expectations have been altered. If the expectations have been altered, this is noted on the ELL's report card. Accommodations mean that additional supports have been given to the ELL in order to support his/her learning. Accommodations may include providing a student with additional time to complete assignments, extensive use of visual cues or graphic organizers, use of the student's first language or use of alternative forms of assessment (Ministry of Education, 2007). In this study, no modifications to the CF curriculum expectations were made; however, various accommodations were implemented.

References

Canadian Parents for French (2012) FSL education in Ontario 2012. Tab 3: Enrolment in FSL by grade, type and language, accessed May 20 2013. http://on.cpf.ca/wp-content/blogs.dir/1/files/Tab-3-Enrolment-in-FSL-by-grade.-type-school-language-2010-11.pdf
Carr, W. (2007) Intensive French...A BC perspective, accessed May 20 2013. http://bctf.ca/publications/NewsmagArticle.aspx?id=12418
Carr, W. (2009) Intensive French in British Columbia: Costs, benefits and connections to Canada's bilingualism ideal. *Canadian Modern Language Review* 65 (5), 787–815.
Cenoz, J., Hufelsen, B. and Jessner, U. (2001) Towards trilingual education. *International Journal of Bilingual Education and Bilingualism* 4 (1), 1–10.
Citizenship and Immigration Canada (2012) *Canada Facts and Figures. Immigration Overview: Permanent and Temporary Residents*. Ottawa, ON: Minister of Public Works and Government Services Canada.
Clyne, M. (1997) Some of the things trilinguals do. *International Journal of Bilingualism* 1, 95–116.
Coelho, E. (2004) *Adding English*. Don Mills, ON: Pippen.
Cummins, J. (1989) *Empowering Minority Students*. Sacramento, CA: Association for Bilingual Education.
Cummins, J. (1996) *Negotiating Identities: Education for Empowerment in a Diverse Society*. Sacramento, CA: Association for Bilingual Education.
Dagenais, D. and Berron, C. (2001) Promoting multilingualism through French immersion and language maintenance in three immigrant families. *Language, Culture and Curriculum* 14 (2), 142–155.
Dagenais, D. and Day, E. (1998) Classroom language experiences of trilingual children in French immersion. *The Canadian Modern Language Review* 54 (3), 376–393.
Dewaele, J.M. (1998) Lexical interventions: French interlanguage as L2 versus L3. *Applied Linguistics* 19, 471–490.
Edwards. V. (1998) *The Power of Babel: Teaching and Learning in Multilingual Classrooms*. Stoke-on-Trent: Trentham Books.
Fillmore, L.W. and Valadez, C. (1986) Teaching bilingual learners. In M.C. Wittrock (ed.) *Handbook of Research on Teaching* (3rd edn) (pp. 648–685). New York: Macmillan.
Gardner, R.C. (1985) *Social Psychology and Second Language Learning: The Role of Attitudes and Motivation*. London: Arnold.

Goldenberg, C. (1996) The education of language-minority students: Where are we, and where do we need to go? *The Elementary School Journal* 96, 353–361.
Krashen, S.D. (1985) *Inquiries and Insights. Second Language Teaching. Immersion & Bilingual Education. Literacy. Selected Essays.* Hayward, CA: Alemany Press.
Krashen, S.D. and Terrell, T.D. (1983) *The Natural Approach: Language Acquisition in the Classroom.* Hayward, CA: Alemany Press.
Mackey, A. and Gass, S.M. (2005) *Second Language Research: Methodology and Design.* Mahwah, NJ: Lawrence Erlbaum.
Mady, C.J. (2003) Motivation to study and investment in studying core French in secondary school: Comparing English as a second language students and Canadian-born students. Unpublished master's thesis, Ontario Institute for Studies in Education, University of Toronto.
Mady, C.J. (2006) The suitability of core French for recently arrived English as a second language adolescent immigrants. Unpublished doctoral dissertation, Ontario Institute for Studies in Education, University of Toronto.
Mady, C. (2007) The suitability of core French for recently arrived adolescent immigrants to Canada. *Canadian Journal of Applied Linguistics* 10 (2), 177–196.
Mady, C. and Turnbull, M. (2010) Learning French as a second official language: Reserved for Anglophones? *Canadian Journal of Educational Administration and Policy* 99, 1–23.
Merriam, S.B. (1998) *Qualitative Research and Case Study Applications in Education.* San Francisco, CA: Jossey-Bass.
Ministry of Education (1999) *The Ontario Curriculum. Grades 9 and 10. French as a Second Language-Core, Extended and Immersion French.* Toronto, ON: Queen's Printer for Ontario.
Ministry of Education (2001) *French as a Second Language: Extended French. Grades 4–8. French Immersion. Grades 1–8.* Toronto, ON: Queen's Printer for Ontario.
Ministry of Education (2005) *Many Roots Many Voices: Supporting English Language Learners in Every Classroom. A Practical Guide for Ontario Educators.* Toronto, ON: Queen's Printer for Ontario.
Ministry of Education (2007) *English Language Learners: ESL and ELD Programs and Services. Policies and Procedures for Ontario Elementary and Secondary Schools, Kindergarten to Grade 12.* Toronto, ON: Queen's Printer for Ontario.
Ministry of Education (2009) *Realizing the Promise of Diversity: Ontario's Equity and Inclusive Education Strategy.* Toronto, ON: Queen's Printer for Ontario.
Parkin, A. and Turcotte, A. (2004) *Bilingualism: Part of Our Past or Part of Our Future?* Montreal, QC: Centre for Research and Information on Canada (CRIC).
Skehan, P. (1989) *Individual Differences in Second Language Learning.* London: Edward Arnold.
Taylor, S.K. (1992) Victor: A case study of a Cantonese child in early French immersion. *Canadian Modern Language Review* 48 (4), 736–759.
Taylor, S.K. (2006, June) ESL in bilingual education with a *twist*: Immigrant children in Canadian French immersion. *Bilingual Basics* 8, 1, accessed May 20 2013. http://www.tesol.org/read-and-publish/newsletters-other-publications/interest-section-newsletters/bilingual-basics/2011/11/03/bilingual-basics-news-volume-8-1-(june-2006)
Taylor, S.K. (2009) The caste system approach to multilingualism in Canada: Linguistic and cultural minority children in French immersion. In T. Skutnabb-Kangas, R. Phillipson, A.K. Mohanty and M. Panda (eds) *Social Justice Through Multilingual Education* (pp. 177–198). Bristol: Multilingual Matters.

Part 2

Heritage Language and Culture Maintenance for Immigrants and Their Families

4 Fostering Heritage Languages and Diasporic Identities: The Role of Grassroots Initiatives in Alberta and British Columbia

Martin Guardado and Ava Becker

To find an ethnic community without grassroots groups would not be an easy task. Indeed, so pervasive are such groups among immigrant populations that it is somewhat surprising that their role in heritage language development (HLD) has received far less attention than the role of the communities in which they operate (Fishman, 1991; Zentella, 1997). Grassroots groups exist to address the needs that community members have identified as important to their existence in the host country, such as housing and spiritual leanings, and frequently operate under the direction of volunteers with limited temporal, material and financial resources. Whether language and culture maintenance is part of a group's explicit agenda, the primary language of interaction in these self-formed groups is almost invariably the heritage language (HL), at least among the older generations. In turn, this linguistic practice fosters a particular cultural environment in which their bilingual children are also actors. To our knowledge, the second-generation's responses to the cultural and linguistic environment in grassroots groups have only recently begun to be documented (Blackledge & Creese, 2010; Guardado, 2008a).

The few studies that have examined the effects of grassroots group participation on HLD have highlighted their ability to create sites of cultural and linguistic validation (e.g. Guardado, 2008a). Drawing on Mary Louise Pratt's concept of *safe houses* (Pratt, 1991),[1] Guardado interpreted such spaces as places where newcomer parents can unwind in their own language, and raise their children alongside parents with shared cultural values. And because children learn language and culture through interaction (Schieffelin & Ochs, 1986), grassroots groups provide them with a rare opportunity to expand their quotidian circle of interaction and become more proficient HL speakers while growing up in the diaspora.

Ethnolinguistic minorities do not form a homogeneous group, however, and must not be treated as such (Zentella, 1996). The first large waves of immigration from Latin America to Canada were comprised of primarily leftist political refugees from Chile in the 1970s, followed by Salvadoreans in the 1980s and 1990s (del Pozo, 2006). Yet, refugees in general enjoy little representation in the language maintenance literature, making it relatively unclear in what ways the HL and identity experience of this type of migrant differ from or parallel that of those coming for more volitional reasons (e.g. family reunification and economic). Therefore, in this chapter, we will examine data from three studies in Western Canada: one in Metro Vancouver, involving families with school-aged children who had arrived as landed immigrants, and two in Edmonton, involving families with (now) adult children who had arrived, officially or unofficially, as political exiles from Chile in the 1970s. The following analysis will shed light on how refugee and non-refugee family participation in grassroots groups supported Spanish language development by responding to disruptions to family networks, and providing fertile ground for cultural reconstruction and the emergence of resilient diasporic ethnic identities.

Forging Heritage Cultures and Identities

Because the ability to maintain the HL in a dominant language context enables ethnic minorities to develop a strong identity and sense of self, having a strong ethnic identity has been identified as an important factor conducive to language maintenance (e.g. Guardado, 2006). However, much about the relationship between ethnic identity development and HLD remains enigmatic. Studies examining this link rarely problematize or account for the inevitable reconstruction of culture that takes place in the diaspora, effectively excluding a potentially rich – if not central – avenue of HLD analysis (for exceptions, see Baquedano-Lopez, 2000; Zentella, 1997).

Illustrations of the complex dynamics of ethnic identity and HLD can be found in a variety of studies. The participants in Schecter and Bayley's (1997) study, for instance, understood first language (L1) loss as cultural identity loss; however, despite parents' best efforts to socialize their children into Mexican identities and the Spanish language, they were not always successful. It is possible that, growing up outside of Mexico, the children – at least within the time frame of the study – simply did not feel a connection to the Mexican cultural heritage that their parents presented to them, which included speaking Spanish. Indeed, the extent to which one identifies with his/her L1 culture in HL contexts may be shaped by where he/she feels such culture is situated. In Kouritzin's (1999) study of language loss in Canada, one participant, Helena, talked about Hungarian culture in Hungary as 'theirs' and Hungarian culture in Canada as 'ours', clearly demonstrating a locally cultivated ethnic identity. Along similar lines, a 17-year-old male participant in King and Ganuza's (2005: 186) study in Sweden described his ethnic identity as Chilean, 'but from Stockholm'. These reflections speak to the particular cultural environment that is created in the diaspora, and beg further examination for their implications for language maintenance.

Diasporic Familism

Immigrants often seek out surrogate family relationships (Guardado, 2008a) in response to the familial void created by migration. But, in cultures where *familism* is a salient feature, the void is even more pronounced. Familism is defined as a set of central values that embrace loyalty to and solidarity with the family unit, which includes both the nuclear family as well as the extended family, and a strong reliance on members of this unit for support (Sabogal et al., 1987). According to a well-established research tradition in cultural psychology, Hispanics exhibit higher levels of familism than other groups (Mindel, 1980; Sabogal et al, 1987), sometimes viewing fellow Hispanic immigrants as their extended family (Suárez-Orozco, 1993) – a phenomenon that Guardado (2008a, 2008b) has termed *diasporic familism*.

Guardado's (2008a, 2008b) ethnography with Hispanic families in Vancouver found that most participants defined themselves in relation to their membership in large families. The grassroots groups in which many of the study participants were involved became 'surrogate extended families' (Guardado, 2008a) to many of them. This diasporic familism also incorporates elements that are crucial to the continuation of their cultures and languages. Surrogate extended families, then, become important sources of input and support for the home language and culture and one of the aims of families' HL socialization efforts.

Grassroots Groups as Safe Houses

The lack of recognition of the social, cultural and linguistic capital of immigrant minorities has been frequently decried (e.g. Li, 1999; Rodríguez, 1982; Schecter & Bayley, 1997, 2002; Valdés, 1996). It has been posited that families' efforts to foster their home languages in their children are a crucial step in the process of empowering and validating themselves (Zhou & Trueba, 1998), and giving them voice to affirm their own culture (Pennycook, 2001). A common immigrant strategy to achieve self-validation in the host society is through the formation of grassroots groups – clusters of community networks created by individuals seeking to achieve common goals. These groups are often characterized by relationships based on shared cultural affinities (Milroy, 1980), such as the Saturday HL schools present in most linguistic minority communities. They have been called *safe houses* (Guardado, 2008a), in the sense that they serve to mitigate the tensions that arise from unequal relations of power and potentially disparate cultural value orientations and languages between those found in their homes and those of the host culture.

In the face of potential conflicts emerging from such asymmetrical relations and clashing interactions, or contact zones, Pratt (1991: 36) argues that 'people need places for healing and mutual recognition, safe houses in which to construct shared understandings, knowledges, claims on the world that they then bring into the contact zone'. Some immigrants in multicultural societies, regardless of their immigration status or level of fluency in their additional languages, may feel unable to attain a genuine sense of belonging in their new environments; participation in grassroots groups offers them an extra-domestic place to socialize their children around people who grew up in a cultural context somewhat similar to where they were raised. It offers them a place where they can speak their language freely, and be themselves in a society where part of them feels perpetually foreign (Guardado, 2008a). In order to further explore the role that these self-organizing spaces play for Hispanics living in two Canadian provinces, this chapter examines the following central question: How does participation in ethnic grassroots groups impact HL use and cultural identity development?

The Three Studies

The data samples used in this chapter came from three separate qualitative investigations of HLD in Hispanic grassroots groups in Edmonton, Alberta and Metro Vancouver, British Columbia (see Table 4.1). While the studies differed in terms of the data collection period, location, and specific recruitment criteria, they all sought to uncover factors that contributed to HLD in these communities. The chapter will not fully report on each of these projects; rather, it will draw on overlapping themes identified in each individual study in order to demonstrate the interconnectedness between the findings of all three.

Table 4.1 Overview of studies

Study/fieldwork period	Grassroots group	No. of families	National origin	Length of residence in Canada (years)	Study location
Study 1 (2008)	The Co-Op	2	Chile	30+	Edmonton, Alberta
Study 2 (2011–2012)	REPARA	2	Chile	30+	Edmonton, Alberta
Study 3 (2005–2006)	La Casa Amistad	8	Chile, Argentina, Mexico, Canada	2–20+	Vancouver, British Columbia

The two Alberta projects involved Chilean political exile families. The first was a pilot study that sought to uncover factors that contributed to HL maintenance in the second generation of two families in the community. The participants interviewed had both resided in a Chilean housing cooperative (The Co-Op) that was created initially to meet settlement needs. Parents from both families reported having lived there with their families for approximately two decades before moving. Each participant was interviewed once using a list of guiding questions rooted in the language maintenance literature.

The second Edmonton study, conducted three years later, interviewed two more Chilean families from the same community. The interview questions probed the relationship between Spanish language maintenance and the political nature of this community that the pilot study helped to uncover. The families were selected based on the involvement of at least one of their now adult children in REPARA (Recordar Para Actuar/Remembrance for Action),[2] a local grassroots group formed to preserve the memory of the progressive political culture that their community had brought from Chile in the 1970s. Two semi-structured interviews were conducted with each participant following the completion of a background questionnaire that included a self-report language assessment and political orientation items.

The Vancouver study was an ethnography focusing on the socialization of language ideologies and practices related to HLD. The 34 participating families in the larger study came from several Spanish-speaking countries and many were involved in grassroots organizations. In this chapter, we highlight one such group, La Casa Amistad (Friendship House), a group consisting of eight middle-class families who met weekly with the goal to transmit the Spanish language and associated cultures to their children through arts and crafts-based activities. Data collection strategies included demographic questionnaires, multiple interviews with parents and children, and weekly participant observations over 18 months.

The present cross-case analysis mainly draws on data samples from interviews with the study participants. All three sets of interview data were analyzed and categorized according to standard qualitative data analysis procedures, such as Bogdan and Biklen's (1998) guidelines and Ryan and Bernard's (2003) recommended steps. These procedures served in the development of coding categories and the identification of emergent themes. These themes were then analyzed across the three grassroots groups and commonalities were developed into new categories that collectively formed the coherent argument advanced in this chapter.

Data Analysis and Discussion

In total, three main themes emerged in response to the guiding question: (1) grassroots groups as sites of validation and identity formation; (2) grassroots groups as promoters of diasporic familism; and (3) claiming diasporic identities. Each theme represents an aspect of the response and collectively they become building blocks for the central argument put forward in the chapter.

Grassroots groups as sites of validation and identity formation

La Casa Amistad

Although Canada's official policy of multiculturalism has been the object of much criticism (e.g. Bissoondath, 1994), some of the parents in La Casa Amistad felt that it validated their grassroots group, which became a local, extra-domestic space where their language was a legitimate means of communication in Canadian society for at least two hours a week. One parent felt that the time the family spent in the group complemented home efforts and allowed for:

> A moment in which, again, the importance of the language is emphasized. So they see that I'm not the only lunatic (loca) in space and that Orlando [Mr. Ramírez] and I emphasize Spanish. (Mrs Aguirre)

Another parent, Mrs Cooper, commented that the group provided:

> A natural environment [where] everyone [...] speaks Spanish. [...] It's a powerful environment; it's not like just one parent speaking [Spanish] at home.

Part of the group's power was in motivating and contextualizing Spanish use by fostering cultural pride and creating and/or strengthening cultural identity (Guardado, 2009). According to Ms Juárez, her daughter, Sandra, used to have 'zero interest' in her heritage, but once they started attending La Casa Amistad, her daughter began to identify herself more with her Latin roots, especially her Chilean roots, and developed an interest in learning the language:

> What I have noticed is that Sandra is more interested now in the language than she was before. She's trying to read on her own. A *spark* has been lit that she didn't have before. So in that sense, I'm very grateful to the group because I can see in her that she makes more of an effort and she tries to speak, read and listen to more Latin American music and she tries to follow along. And so in that sense I think it's fostering *cultural identity*. That she feels proud.

The Co-Op

Perhaps in part because the parents in The Co-Op were having a (forced) out-of-country and out-of-language experience (Rushdie, 1991),³ those interviewed expressed that The Co-Op provided them with a welcome sense of place and belonging:

> It was like a little Chile in the middle of a sector of Edmonton. (Ernesto)

The Co-Op was a place where families could use their language freely and socialize their children according to their cultural values without concerning themselves with things like childcare:

> [Living in The Co-Op] was really rewarding because for once you could talk, use your language, and get together and share food, share ideas and you know, have friends that sort of, have basically the same basic ideas. [...] [It] helped us a lot, in a sense that you know, there was no worries right? [...] [And we] help[ed] each other to raise the children, because when both of you have to work I mean somehow *somebody* have to look after, you know, after your kids right? (Pablo)

The children also benefitted from the cultural and linguistic validation that the group provided, albeit differently:

> It was funny, like *once* we left The Co-Op and we're outside and we speak Spanish, you know? But usually in there, you know when we were

playing and stuff like that we usually kept it to English. [...] We are really proud you know, to call ourselves Chilean and we weren't ashamed of it that we spoke Spanish, and I think that we almost kinda flaunted it you know, that we were different, because Canada does embrace that and we were able to do that. (Rafael)

Growing up in The Co-Op's mixed language environment appears to have laid the foundation for some to use Spanish proudly outside of the group, in childhood and into adulthood. Indeed, Rafael's sister, Gabriela, went on to become a teacher in a local Spanish bilingual school. Seeing their home language used in a communal setting offered them a wealth of early input, which Au (2008) has found to be useful for revitalization years later.

The Co-Op was a permanent, physical space where cultural socialization efforts typically relegated to the home domain could take place naturally, in front yards, over fences, and in Spanish. Gabriela recalled teachers and friends 'always being interested to learn more' about her unique living situation, and being happy to tell them about it. For the youth, their experience in The Co-Op became inextricable from their ethnic sense of self as they grew older:

I lived the first eighteen years of my life [in The Co-Op]. So that was a huge part of my identity. [...] That helped, you know, me grow up in that whole kind of environment, to retain my language. (Rafael)

Some participants, however, shared memories of life before The Co-Op. Diego recalled being unaware of his ethnic heritage until his family moved to The Co-Op:

[It wasn't until I moved to] The Co-Op [that] I realized that I was actually Chilean and I learned more about my culture that way [...]. The only thing I knew was just I spoke Spanish when I got home, right?

An essential step in the cultural and linguistic validation that took place in these grassroots groups was that of ethnocultural discovery (Guardado, 2008b). Indeed, it has been argued that childhood can be a time of ethnic unawareness (Tse, 1999), which for Diego was interrupted by his grassroots group participation. Furthermore, until he was introduced to The Co-Op environment where he could see Spanish spoken by others in a broader sociocultural context, his HL had limited social and linguistic opportunities to develop (Fishman, 1991; Thomas & Cao, 1999).

Grassroots groups as promoters of diasporic familism

La Casa Amistad

Most parents and children commented spontaneously on the importance of family to them. They often expressed this in relation to their home countries, where almost all of the group families had their networks of relatives. During a home observation, six-year-old Florencia, one of the Aguirre-Ramírez daughters, proudly and candidly offered that her preference for Mexico was simply because she had family members there:

Florencia: Can I tell you why I like Mexico better?
Martín: why?
Florencia: than here?
Martín: yes
Florencia: because
Perla: there
Florencia: I have my cousins there

It is unsurprising, then, that feelings about family seemed unavoidable when talking about La Casa Amistad. For instance, Mrs Aguirre remarked that:

> The parents' idea was for the children to practice Spanish. But if you analyze each parent's personal reasons, it was not only for the children to speak Spanish. It was also to connect with other families at a more intimate level.

Although most of the families in the group frequently traveled to their heritage countries, because of their grassroots group involvement in Vancouver, the language became something that was relevant for future trips to Latin America, for home communication and as a passport to central membership and participation in La Casa Amistad. The group members interviewed stated that they had established close relationships with other members and both the parents and the children in the group saw themselves as family. As Mrs Aguirre noted, forming surrogate family ties was part of the necessary process of recreating oneself in the diaspora:

> That aspect that is very important; family support. We start to grow our own roots here among us, right? You can make it more your own, right? It's a country that is more your own.

The Co-Op

In The Co-Op, surrogate family relationships were explicitly named through the use of *tía* and *tío* (aunt and uncle):

> I always call Spanish people, like adults, *tío* and *tías*, because those were the *tío* and *tías* I had right? [...] Because to my parents, we were all one community, right? We were all one family, so everybody was *tío* and *tía*. And I never knew the difference, but then when I got to Chile [as an adult] they were like, "Well, how come you say *tío* and *tía* to everybody?" (Diego)

Indeed, the surrogate family relationships that some Chilean youth forged with their *tíos* and *tías* in the diaspora – Chilean or other Latin American, as indicated by Diego's 'Spanish people' comment – were stronger than those they had with their biological family members in Chile, because, as Gabriela put it:

> My aunts and uncles here were closer to me 'cause most of them had known me since I was a baby, since I was born, so *those* are my aunts and uncles. (Gabriela)

Without the economic and political freedom to travel and foster biological family bonds face-to-face, the surrogate families described in The Co-Op appeared to be somewhat more intense than in La Casa Amistad. By the time The Co-Op youth traveled to Chile, often as young adults, the diasporic families had already replaced their biological family ties in many ways:

> [...] when I came back to Edmonton [from visiting Chile], **this** was home. This was where all my friends were. This was where people that mean the most to me live. Right? Not saying that I don't love my *grandparents* [in Chile], but I didn't really get to know 'em. (Diego)

Claiming diasporic identities

The focal participants from REPARA, Adriana and Victor, did not grow up in an ethnic housing co-operative or have Spanish-only policies at home, and their families were not active in Chilean community groups to the extent that the other participants were.[4] However, immersion in a particular 'refugee culture' (Victor) while growing up may be seen as a form of group participation. At different ages, they became aware of their parents' leftist political ideologies, and of the reasons that they had sought refuge in Canada in the 1970s. As they grew older, these 'refugee culture' narratives became the pulse of their diaspora identities, which their involvement in groups such as REPARA would further nurture. Their ethnic self-identification was enmeshed in the Chilean socialist movement whose symbolic death in the 1973 coup d'état found continuity in their community's exile (Power, 2009). As a result, their 'ethnic' identities were firmly rooted in their local community, as we will see in the following sections.

Adriana

Our interviews showed that Adriana was proud to identify culturally as Chilean, but 'in a different context than *Chilenos* in *Chile* are'. She spoke confidently and passionately about the political context out of which her community had sprung, and her sense of belonging to it:

> My context is really special because it was, it's a context that really preserved the amazing years of 1970, or 1971–1973, because it's that context and the community that I come out of, the Chilean-Canadian community, that was founded and framed by the supporters of *Salvador Allende*, and like, these were the founders of the community, so the culture of this Canadian-Chilean community is different then than what happened in Chile because it grew in a different context. [...] For me it's something really special I think.

Adriana identified with her Chilean-Canadian community, yet her Chilean identity differed from the nationally hyphenated identities that often emerge in the literature (Schecter & Bayley, 1997). Instead, the ethnic identity that she described was defined by the specific diasporic context in which she grew up (King & Ganuza, 2005; Kouritzin, 1999). At the time of the interviews, Adriana felt very little connection to Chile (the country) at all:

> I am not a Chilean citizen and when I go to *Chile* I go as a tourist. I don't claim any status in *Chile*.

On the other hand, within her Chilean-Canadian community she had formed a powerful circle of interaction in which she was happy to use Spanish in order to learn more about her special context:

> Spanish was a key tool in so many parts of my life. For me, yeah and connecting with senior members of the community has been one of the most beautiful things, right?

Victor

A highly proficient heritage speaker who, in addition to having taken some Spanish classes in university and travelling extensively in Latin America, Victor continued to use the language on a regular basis with a range of Spanish speakers at different community events. Perhaps somewhat surprisingly, he did not worry that the community's 'youth are losing *castellano*'[5] for a variety of reasons, the most relevant to the present discussion being that subsequent generations should not

> Get caught up in "oh, I just need to learn the language," because I mean, the language will come. The ideas are what's more important.

Indeed, after he began acquiring English in day care, his Spanish fell increasingly into disuse until a family trip to Mexico prompted him to revitalize his dormant L1 at age 17. For Victor, the language *did* come once he came to identify with the 'ideas' (the political and ideological history of his community), and he subsequently found relevance for Spanish in his adult life in Edmonton. By age 18, he had become active in the city's Latin American community, regularly attending meetings where his English-influenced Spanish did not go unnoticed. But because of his strong identification with deep elements of local Latin American/refugee culture (Hall, 1976) and his agenda to incorporate their activist past into continuing community-building efforts in the diaspora, he was able to overcome the community elders' negative reactions to his non-native Spanish:

> [...] Spanish was spoken at those meetings all the time, so it became—and of course you know, you go through that stage where you're speaking Spanish with an accent, to a certain degree. You're trying your best to put on your best Chilean accent but all of a sudden like these *gringuísmos*[6] come out, right? And you're like—and you know like people laugh at it and it's like ha, ha, ha. And you got a choice at that point. You can either feel ashamed and shut up, or be like I don't care I'm gonna keep talking here.

Victor's comment reminds us that having some proficiency in the HL does not necessarily lead to acceptance as an authentic member of the ethnic community (e.g. Dagenais & Day, 1999), and that the heritage speaker has the potential to be silenced based on the nature or variety of their Spanish. It also takes the emphasis away from travel to the country of origin as the primary provider of a community of native speakers, and brings our attention to the role of native speakers and their attitudes about group membership in the diaspora.

Conclusion

The preceding cross-case analysis discussed data samples from three different studies in two provinces. The discussion centered on the experiences and perspectives of members and former members of three grassroots organizations. Both La Casa Amistad and The Co-Op acted as sites of cultural and linguistic discovery and validation for their members while providing children with a natural context for language practice. For the members of both groups, these became their Spanish-speaking community and settings where a special type of familism thrived in the diaspora.

REPARA, a group formed by second-generation young adults, provides a glimpse into the potential effects that grassroots group participation – and the accompanying diasporic familism – may have on members as they get older. Grassroots groups often disband after they have served their settlement-related purposes, but REPARA is an example of the kind of cultural revitalization effort that can emerge after childhood when minoritized youth develop a strong connection to their local ethnic community. Adriana and Victor's reported experiences and perspectives may challenge contemporary notions that essentialize the link between ethnicity and cultural identity. There is, for instance, an abundance of often conflicting positions on the presence, experiences and seeming affiliations of ethnolinguistic minorities in Canada. Some of these perspectives highlight the individual and societal values of maintaining languages and distinct ethnic identities (e.g. Taylor, 1994) and others claim that the opposite is true. Critics of multiculturalism, such as Bissoondath (1994), argue that an emphasis on ethnic identities leads to the creation of ghettos, fragments society and endangers national unity. However, the data analyzed in this chapter suggest that these claims may often be irrelevant and instead point to the agentive and highly transformative experiences of group participants, which ultimately lead to a sense of rootedness and *not* of separateness in Canada. Moreover, as several participants remarked, home is where their family is, and thus the surrogate family ties that flourished in these groups helped to establish Canada as their home. By extension, then, conversing in Spanish with their grassroots families also served to validate their home language in the diaspora.

The foregoing analysis suggests that grassroots group participation offers more than just contexts for language practice. It may also have lasting effects on the language use and identity development of future generations. A contribution to theory in HLD contexts, then, lies in the role that grassroots groups play in the validation, construction and recreation of cultures and identities. Where nationally hyphenated identities often represent the (willing or reluctant) compromise that heritage speakers make when none of their (perhaps assigned) national allegiances alone adequately captures their lived experience, diasporic identities affirm the legitimacy of their unique cultural and linguistic practices unapologetically. Given that this analysis revealed the existence of synergistic and creatively self-constituted identities, future research might examine how grassroots groups contribute to the process of reimagining locally situated cultures and their role in the ways that diasporic identities are chosen and enacted across the lifespan.

Educational leaders, policymakers and practitioners might consider the present findings insightful as they endeavor to gain access to phenomenological examinations of diverse groups in alternative informal and non-formal learning contexts. The findings emerging from this interpretive study can potentially become important building blocks upon which educators can construct increasingly nuanced understandings of the cultural and social lives of highly diverse student populations. This updated awareness may further inform the conceptualization of pedagogical experiences that are more consonant with families' lives outside school, an arguably necessary factor in the provision of a sound education.

In closing, group participation not only provided an opportunity for the children to see other families speaking Spanish, but it also showed them that there were other families in similar circumstances who did not have their extended families near and, for the Vancouver children, who made plans to visit them abroad during holidays. It normalized their attitude about such experiences, and motivated some of the children to explore their cultural and linguistic heritage further. While a shift away from the HL in childhood is often understood to be an indicator of loss (Chumak-Horbatsch, 1999), Adriana and Victor's stories corroborate findings that revitalization is possible with changes in identity and motivation (Tse, 1997) and remind us that fluctuations in language proficiency are a natural part of being bilingual (Grosjean, 2010; Valdés, 2005). Their grassroots group participation continued to fortify and validate their chosen diasporic identities and gave continued purpose to Spanish use, which may bode well for its transmission to another generation of bilingual or multilingual Latin Americans in the Canadian diaspora.

Notes

(1) Ironically, Pratt was inspired by a 1200-page letter written by the Quechua Andean Gauman Poma to the King of Spain in 1631 to denounce the injustices committed by the Spaniard empire in Peru.

(2) All group and participant names are pseudonyms.
(3) This refers to the parents' experiences outside the home, but in the case of mixed-language families, at times the out-of-language experience was partially true also at home.
(4) It is relevant to note that Adriana's family was fairly involved in their Latin American community church, but Adriana stopped attending around the time her participation in REPARA and other activist organizations began.
(5) Spanish.
(6) Anglicisms.

References

Au, T.K-F. (2008) Salvaging heritage languages. In D. Brinton, O. Kagan and S. Bauckus (eds) *Heritage Language Education: A New Field Emerging* (pp. 337–351). New York: Routledge.

Baquedano-Lopez, P. (2000) Narrating community in doctrina classes. *Narrative Inquiry* 10 (2), 429–452.

Bissoondath, N. (1994) *Selling Illusions: The Cult of Multiculturalism in Canada*. Toronto, ON: Penguin.

Blackledge, A. and Creese, A. (2010) *Multilingualism: A Critical Perspective*. London: Continuum.

Bogdan, R. and Biklen, S.K. (1998) *Qualitative Research for Education: An Introduction to Theory and Methods*. Boston, MA: Allyn and Bacon.

Chumak-Horbatsch, R. (1999) Language change in the Ukrainian home: From transmission to maintenance to the beginnings of loss. *Canadian Ethnic Studies* 31 (2), 61–75.

Dagenais, D. and Day, E. (1999) Home language practices of trilingual children in French immersion. *Canadian Modern Language Review* 56 (1), 99–123.

del Pozo, J. (2006) Las organizaciones comunitarias de chilenos en la provincia de Québec, Canadá. In J. del Pozo (ed.) *Exiliados, Emigrados y Retornados: Chilenos en América y Europa, 1973–2004* (pp. 127–147). Santiago de Chile: RIL Editores.

Fishman, J.A. (1991) *Reversing Language Shift: Theoretical and Empirical Foundations of Assistance to Threatened Languages*. Clevedon: Multilingual Matters.

Grosjean, F. (2010) *Bilingual: Life and Reality*. Cambridge, MA: Harvard University Press.

Guardado, M. (2006) Engaging language and cultural spaces: Latin American parents' reflections on language loss and maintenance in Vancouver. *Canadian Journal of Applied Linguistics* 9 (1), 51–72.

Guardado, M. (2008a) Language socialization in Canadian Hispanic communities: Ideologies and practices. PhD thesis, University of British Columbia.

Guardado, M. (2008b) Language, identity and cultural awareness in Spanish-speaking families. *Canadian Ethnic Studies* 40 (3), 171–181.

Guardado, M. (2009) Speaking Spanish like a boy scout: Language socialization, resistance and reproduction in a heritage language Scout troop. *Canadian Modern Language Review* 66 (1), 101–129.

Hall, E.T. (1976) *Beyond Culture*. Garden City, NY: Anchor Press.

King, K. and Ganuza, N. (2005) Language, identity, education, and transmigration: Chilean adolescents in Sweden. *Journal of Language, Identity, and Education* 4 (3), 179–199.

Kouritzin, S.G. (1999) *Face[t]s of First Language Loss*. Mahwah, NJ: Lawrence Erlbaum.

Li, X. (1999) How can language minority parents help their children become bilingual in familial context? A case study of a language minority mother and her daughter. *Bilingual Research Journal* 23 (2 and 3), 211–223.

Milroy, L. (1980) *Language and Social Networks*. Baltimore, MD: University Parks Press.

Mindel, H. (1980) Extended familism among urban Mexican Americans, Anglos and Blacks. *Hispanic Journal of Behavioral Sciences* 2 (1), 21–34.

Pennycook, A. (2001) *Critical Applied Linguistics: A Critical Introduction*. Mahwah, NJ: Lawrence Erlbaum Associates.

Power, M. (2009) The U.S. movement in solidarity with Chile in the 1970s. *Latin American Perspectives* 36 (6), 46–66.

Pratt, M.L. (1991) Arts of the contact zone. *Profession* 91, 33–40.

Rodríguez, R. (1982) *Hunger of Memory: The Education of Richard Rodríguez*. Boston, MA: Bantam Books.

Rushdie, S. (1991) *Imaginary Homelands: Essays and Criticism, 1981–1991*. London: Granta.

Ryan, G.W. and Bernard, H.R. (2003) Techniques to identify themes. *Field Methods* 15 (1), 85–109.

Sabogal, F., Marin, G., Otero-Sabogal, R., Marin, B.V. and Perez-Stable, E.J. (1987) Hispanic familism and acculturation: What changes and what doesn't? *Hispanic Journal of Behavioral Sciences* 9, 397–412.

Schecter, S.R. and Bayley, R. (1997) Language socialization practices and cultural identity: Case studies of Mexican-descent families in California and Texas. *TESOL Quarterly* 31 (3), 513–541.

Schecter, S.R. and Bayley, R. (2002) *Language as Cultural Practice: Mexicanos en El Norte*. Mahwah, NJ: Lawrence Erlbaum Associates.

Schieffelin, B.B. and Ochs, E. (1986) Language socialization. *Annual Review of Anthropology* 15, 163–191.

Suárez-Orozco, C.E. (1993) Generational discontinuities: A cross-culture study of familism and achievement motivation in Mexican, Mexican immigrant, Mexican American, and white non-Hispanic adolescents. PhD thesis, California School of Professional Psychology.

Taylor, C. (1994) The politics of recognition. In A. Gutmann (ed.) *Multiculturalism: Examining the Politics of Recognition* (pp. 25–74). Princeton, NJ: Princeton University Press.

Thomas, L. and Cao, L. (1999) Language use in family and in society. *English Journal* 89, 107–113.

Tse, L. (1997) Ethnic identity development and the role of the heritage language. PhD thesis, University of Southern California.

Tse, L. (1999) Finding a place to be: Ethnic identity exploration of Asian Americans. *Adolescence* 34 (133), 121–138.

Valdés, G. (1996) *Con Respeto: Bridging the Distances between Culturally Diverse Families and Schools*. New York: Teachers College Press.

Valdés, G. (2005) Bilingualism, heritage language learners, and SLA research: Opportunities lost or seized? *The Modern Language Journal* 89 (3), 410–426.

Zentella, A.C. (1996) The 'chiquitafication' of U.S. Latinos and their language, or why we need a politically applied Applied Linguistics. Paper presented at the Plenary address to the American Association for Applied Linguistics Annual Meeting, Chicago, IL.

Zentella, A.C. (1997) *Growing up Bilingual: Puerto Rican Children in New York*. Oxford: Blackwell.

Zhou, Y. and Trueba, H.T. (eds) (1998) *Ethnic Identity and Power: Cultural Contexts of Political Action in School and Society*. New York: SUNY Press.

5 Self, Identity and Motivation in the Development and Maintenance of German as a Heritage Language

Kimberly A. Noels

The development and maintenance of the linguistic and cultural competencies of members of minority ethnolinguistic groups is a topic of interest for scholars across many disciplines, including linguistics, sociology, education and psychology. This chapter takes a social psychological perspective to review some research on heritage language learners' (HLLs) and non-heritage language learners' (non-HLLs) motivation for learning German, primarily in the context of post-secondary language courses. More specifically, it draws from Self-Determination Theory (SDT) (Deci & Ryan, 1985; Ryan & Deci, 2002) to argue that the more learners feel that the target language is important to their sense of self, the more motivated they will be to learn the language. German HLLs, because of their unique experience with the German community, are particularly likely to feel that German is integral to their sense of identity, although the strength of this identity may depend on the situational context.

German in Canada

Contemporary German HLLs in Canada are largely descendants of immigrants who arrived during one of several waves of migration of German speakers that began in the latter half of the 1700s and continued until the 1960s. In the 1971 census, German was reported to be the most widely spoken non-official mother tongue in Canada. Since that time 'German's share of the allophone population has been steadily shrinking, from 19% in 1971 to 7% in 2006' (Statistics Canada, 2012), with the exception of a slight rise in 2006 (possibly due to increases in the Hutterite and Mennonite communities [M. Prokop, personal communication, January 2013]). English, French, Punjabi, Chinese, Spanish and Italian speakers now outnumber German speakers; German is currently Canada's fifth most commonly spoken non-official mother tongue (Statistics Canada, 2013). Not only is German declining, but also its speakers are aging: 65.4% are 45 years or older and only 18% are 24 years or younger (Statistics Canada, 2013). The 2011 census indicates that there are around 430,000 people who claim German as their mother tongue, of which 29% claim to use German most often and 27% claim to use it regularly at home. Although German speakers comprise a rather small percentage of the total Canadian population (approximately 1.2%), almost 10% of the population claims some German ancestry (Statistics Canada, 2008). One possible implication of these numbers is that many Canadians with a German-speaking background do not consider themselves speakers of the language, even though German may have been used by family members.

Although the German-Canadian population is declining, German language education remains available across Canada at most age levels.[1] In earlier years, options include community language classes, bilingual programming and German language courses in public schools. At the post-secondary level, German courses are available in all provinces; approximately 57% of Canadian universities offer at least basic German language courses, and of these, 66% offer undergraduate major or minor programs and 21% offer graduate studies programs. Many students are interested in learning German because they see it as an important international language that is useful for scientific, commercial and aesthetic reasons. Additionally, a not insignificant number of students desire to learn German to communicate with family members in Canada and overseas, to learn more about their cultural heritage and to pass the language on to their offspring.

Motivation and Learning German

Early research on students' reasons for learning German was influenced by Gardner and Lambert's seminal work on language learning motivation (1972; see Gardner, 2010 for a review). In their framework, reasons for language learning were termed 'orientations', and these, along with positive attitudes and a desire to learn the language, could predict effortful engagement in learning, which in turn could predict linguistic and non-linguistic outcomes. Gardner and Lambert (1972) claimed that a learner may have several orientations for learning a language, including instrumental orientations that reflect pragmatic benefits for learning the language (e.g. getting course credit or a well-paying job), a desire to travel or a desire to control the target language community. The most intensively studied orientation was the integrative orientation, which refers to a desire to learn the language in order to have contact and possibly identify with people from other ethnolinguistic communities. Although many orientations could foster motivated engagement in learning, Gardner (2010) maintains that, because of its link with positive attitudes, the integrative orientation is a relatively consistent predictor of motivational intensity and, indirectly, proficiency.

With regard to learning German in the Canadian context, Bausenhart (1984) found that English-speaking and French-speaking university students in German classes reported integrative reasons for learning the language. Prokop (1975) found that if university students had positive attitudes toward German speakers, they were more likely to achieve higher grades in German than those who expressed instrumental reasons. Focusing more directly on HL students, Prokop (1974) compared monolingual English students and bilingual German-English students with a German background, and found that the groups endorsed both the integrative and the instrumental orientations; however, for both groups, greater endorsement of an integrative orientation was linked with better grades. In his examination of children in German language schools, Bausenhart (1971) found that pupils were more instrumentally than integratively oriented. He suggested that these children might not be integratively oriented because there was little opportunity for them to engage with German community members, who were widely dispersed across the urban area where these children lived.

Richard Clément and I (1989) examined the motivational orientations of university-level German learners following an approach taken by Clément and Kruidenier (1983). Clément and Kruidenier found that although four orientations were common to learners of French and English across a wide variety of Canadian contexts, the integrative orientation was only evident in specific contexts. The four orientations included a desire to travel to regions where the language was spoken, to develop friendships with speakers of the language, to increase their knowledge about the language and the culture, along with utilitarian reasons for learning the language (i.e. the instrumental orientation). In our study, we also found evidence that both HLLs and non-HLLs were learning German for travel, friendship, knowledge and instrumental reasons (Noels & Clément, 1989). An additional orientation, however, differentiated HLLs from non-HLLs. Termed an identity-influence orientation, it highlighted HLLs' desire to identify with and make friends with German-speaking Canadians, gain influence over the German-speaking community and understand the problems of German-speaking people in a predominantly English community. These reasons correlated with the belief that knowing German would contribute to their success and better pay in business. Thus, this orientation was about HLLs' participation in and contribution to the German community. It seems reasonable that such a desire for a meaningful impact could be realized through a career in which German figured prominently.

The theme of identity evident in Noels and Clément's (1989) study also emerges in other theoretical formulations. Several scholars have argued that its notion of integrativeness, with its emphasis on contact and identification with a specific target group, might be recast into a somewhat broader framework in which the self serves as the central organizing concept (e.g. Edmondson, 2004). For instance, Norton (2000) argued that learners invest in developing their second language (L2) skills to the extent that their sense of self and their membership in desirable 'imagined communities'. Elsewhere, Dörnyei's (2005) L2 Self-System Model maintains that a person's vision of themselves in the future as a masterful user of the target language is an important predictor of motivated engagement and learning outcomes. Consistent with this focus on the self and identity, I suggest that the focus on intergroup relations highlighted in 'integrativeness' might be well complemented by a framework that underscores the importance of internalizing the target language as a central aspect of one's self-concept (Noels, 2001, 2009). A useful framework in this regard is SDT (Deci & Ryan, 1985; Ryan & Deci, 2002).

SDT (Deci & Ryan, 1985) maintains that people who engage in an activity such as learning German because they feel it is consistent with their other values and integral to their sense of self tend to be more engaged in that activity and experience more positive outcomes. However, his or her sense of self. Instead, they may recognize that learning German is relevant to their personal goals, although it is not integral to their identity (e.g. 'Learning German will help me when I visit with my relatives in Germany'; 'German is widely used in physics, and so knowing it will help me in my physics career'). Alternatively, some learners might feel that they ought to learn German as a result of the internalized norms of its importance (e.g. 'losing my German skills would be a waste'; 'I feel guilty not being able to speak with my grandmother') still others may face situational circumstances that reward or punish their engagement in language learning (e.g. program requirements and impending exams). These motivational orientations can be situated along a continuum describing the extent to which the decision to engage in the activity is regulated by self-determined reasons (termed 'integrated' and 'identified' regulations) or by the demands of internalized pressures or external circumstances (termed 'introjected' and 'external' regulations, respectively). Importantly, any one person can have multiple reasons for learning a language, some of which might be more salient at different times.

The degree to which an activity is internalized into and regulated by the self is distinct from the notion of intrinsic motivation. Intrinsic motivation refers to engagement in the activity because it resonates with an inherent tendency to explore novel situations and challenge one's capacities. A learner who describes aspects of learning German as invigorating and satisfying would be expressing the sentiment associated with intrinsic motivation. Intrinsic motivation is similar to the more internalized forms of extrinsic motivation described earlier, in terms of the degree of self-determination and positive outcomes.

Using the SDT framework, a survey of university-level learners of German found that both HLLs and non-HLLs strongly endorsed the position that they were learning German because they found it intrinsically interesting and enjoyable and because they identified personally important reasons for learning the language (see Figure 5.1; Noels, 2005; note: integrated regulation was not assessed in this study). Consistent with these quantitative findings, their responses to an open-ended question about why they were studying German often included themes relating to strong feelings of appreciation for the language and enjoyment the language, as well as reasons indicating a personal connection and investment in the language, as illustrated in the following quote:

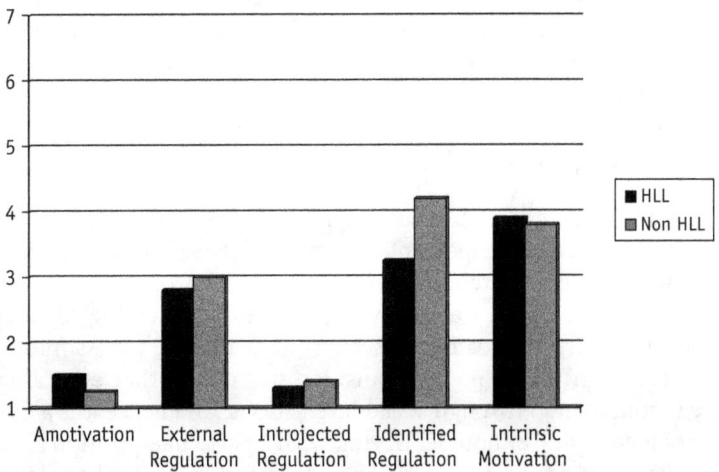

Figure 5.1 Mean orientation endorsement as a function of learner group (Adapted from Noels, 2005)

I needed one more elective credit so I thought I'd take something I enjoy and am good at. It will boost my grades a little. Also, my background (relatives) is German and I've been to Germany and loved it. I love the sound of the language. It's important not to be confined by not knowing more than one language. (HLL)

Not all reasons were so strongly positive. As indicated in the quotation, there were also practical constraints to be met (i.e. 'It will boost my grades a little'). Thus, the students also endorsed and expressed reasons for language learning that reflected external pressures to learn the language, such as completing a program requirement. Finally, there was very little endorsement of items and few written expressions of reasons reflecting a self-inflicted pressure that one 'ought to' learn the language, or explicit indications of amotivation.

The HLL and non-HLL groups differed only in the extent to which they were learning the language because it was personally meaningful, such that the HLLs more strongly endorsed this orientation. The significance of the language to their sense of self is corroborated by the findings that HLLs indicated a stronger German identification (but no difference in English identification) and a stronger integrative orientation toward the German community. Perhaps more importantly from an educator's perspective, the more strongly learners expressed self-determination reasons for learning German, the more likely they were to report that they engaged actively in learning German, they intended to study German after the current course was completed and they considered themselves as having strong German language skills.

Identifying as a HLL

Given the evidence that the internalization of a language into the learner's self-concept is important for motivated engagement in language learning and linguistic outcomes, a further question concerns how identity should be defined. There are many approaches to studying identity and a myriad of aspects that can be assessed (for a review, see Ashmore *et al.*, 2004). A common theme in L2 acquisition research is that ethnolinguistic identity is constructed through social interactions, and hence it is a dynamic 'process of identifying or not identifying with a particular position in life and continually negotiating and modifying this position and attitudes toward it' (Val & Vinogradova, 2010). Consistent with this sociocultural position, I define ethnolinguistic identity as a feeling of belonging to one or more ethnolinguistic reference groups that is contextually variable, reflecting power differentials between groups in contact and the situational dynamics of face-to-face interactions (Clément & Noels, 1992; see also Noels *et al.*, 2004).

Using a quantitative approach forwarded by Clément and Noels (1992), we can re-examine the data reported in the Noels (2005) study to understand situational variations in German learners' ethnolinguistic identity. In that study, German learners separate scales ranging from 1 to 5 to rate their identification with German and with English speakers across six situational domains (with family, with friends, at school, during leisure activities, at work and in the general public). When the identity indices were averaged across domains, both HLLs and non-HLLs indicated stronger English than German identity, although HLLs expressed greater German identity than did the non-HLLs.

An analysis of situational variations in identity reveals that patterns of identity are much more nuanced than this general index would suggest. As can be seen in Figure 5.2(a), for non-HLLs, English identity is much stronger than German identity, and it varies little across situations. By contrast, ratings of German identity, although relatively low across all domains, show some evidence of situational variability. Non-HLLs report stronger German

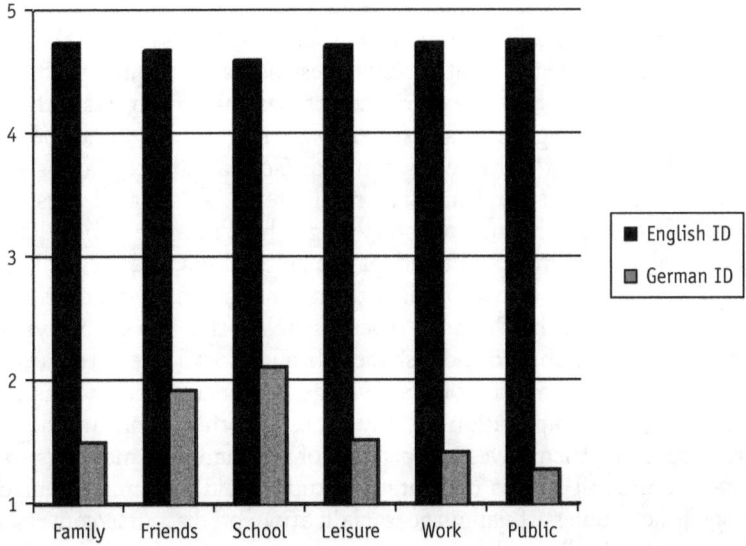

Figure 5.2 (a) Mean identity as a function of reference group and situation for non-heritage learners of German. (b) Mean identity as a function of reference group and situation for heritage learners of German

identity when in school (where German is taught) and among friends (some of whom might be students from school) than the community, work, leisure and family domains. Thus, even among these relatively novice learners of German, we can see that their ethnolinguistic identity shifts toward that of their interlocutors' in situations where intercultural contact is more likely to take place.

This profile of situational variation in the identities of non-HLLs can be contrasted with that of HLLs. In their case, English identity was also stronger than German identity across all domains, but we can see a clear variation in this general pattern. German is strongest in the family domain, followed by the school domain and the friendship domain, and weakest in the leisure, work and community domains. In a complementary manner, English identity is weakest in the family domain (although this difference is only statistically significant in comparison with the work and community domains). Thus, when one interacts with at least some family members of German descent, we see that German identity is relatively strong, and approaches equivalence with English identity. Although weaker than in the family domain, German identity is relatively strong in other contexts where there is more opportunity for interactions with German speakers (i.e. with friends and at school). Although this is a small sample, these identity profiles are consistent with those of larger-scale studies of minority groups (e.g. Noels et al., 2004, 2009).

These results suggest that global assessments of identity potentially misrepresent the identity experience of language learners. Had we only considered the general assessment, we might have concluded that German HLLs have a rather weak sense of German identity and seem to have assimilated into the Canadian mainstream. A situated perspective indicates that although this possibility might hold in more public domains (where it might be functional to adopt the cultural practices of the broader society), it is less descriptive of identity in more intimate domains. These findings corroborate the claims of several scholars that the self is dynamic, contextualized, and shaped and reshaped through social interaction (e.g. He, 2004, 2010). This snapshot of the average tendencies within this group encourages greater exploration of how HLLs and the people around them create a sense of themselves as speakers of German and members of the German community. This quantitative study could be complemented by ethnographic studies of language socialization or discourse/conversation analyses that delve more deeply into the process by which people negotiate identities across different social interactions.

Significant others, identity and motivation

If the maintenance and development of German as a HL is valued in Canada, is imperative to explore how a sense that German is personally meaningful can be fostered in German HLLs. There are many accounts of the circumstances under which one might invest in learning a language and claim ownership of that language as a key aspect of the self. One important consideration is the extent to which the student feels that she/he has a sense of agency in the learning process (Norton, 2000; Benson, 2011). This theme of agency is taken up in SDT, which posits that there are three 'psychological needs' that must be filled to facilitate self-regulation (Ryan & Deci, 2002). Autonomy, or the sense that one has voluntarily chosen to engage in an activity because it is personally relevant, is regarded as the key to motivated learning and general well-being. A second need is competence, which refers to a feeling of confidence that one is 'effective in one's ongoing interactions with the social environment and experiencing opportunities to exercise and express one's capacities' (Ryan & Deci, 2002: 7). The need for competence is associated with seeking out 'optimal challenges' that can help a person to enhance their capabilities. Relatedness refers to the sense that one has an emotional connection or 'secure communion' with significant others, who return the feeling. These people might include the teacher and classmates in the language classroom, members of one's family, members of the target language community or any other individual or group who is relevant to the learner. Although these needs can be differentiated theoretically, practically they work in concert to promote well-being, personal growth and motivated engagement.

Some support for this claim in the context of learning German indicates that these three perceptions are associated with a more active engagement in language learning, the intention to continue German studies and a more intrinsic orientation (Noels, 2005). Moreover, HLLs were more likely to endorse these perceptions, and also have greater interaction with the German community, stronger self-evaluation of German competence and stronger German identification. These findings have been followed up with a larger questionnaire survey of German students enrolled in German courses across Canada that considered how family members, German teachers and members of the German community might affect students' self-determination (Noels & Saumure, 2013; see also Noels *et al.*, 2007). The results for non-HLLs indicated that all three fundamental needs were associated with a more self-determined motivational orientation, although autonomy was the strongest of these predictors. Although the teacher was perceived as the most important supporter of all three needs, family members and members of the German community also fostered non-HLLs motivation by providing constructive feedback on their German and a sense of connectedness. The results for HLLs showed that a more self-determined orientation was associated with a sense of autonomy and, particularly, a strong feeling of connectedness with others. This support came primarily from the German community and the family; in comparison, the German teacher played virtually no role in supporting the motivation.

These results underscore the important differences in the learning contexts for non-HLLs and HLLs. For the foreign language student, it would seem evident that the language teacher would have the greatest influence. The teacher has considerable control over the learning process, from the design of the curriculum, to the choice of course materials and to the manner of evaluation; he/she is the most important provider of feedback to develop the learner's sense of competence; and he/she is likely the most important person with whom the student can establish a sense of connectedness with the German community and culture. By contrast, for HLLs, family and other members of the German community may figure more prominently in their social ecology. Especially in a university-level course with a duration of only a few months, the teacher's impact on student motivation may be modest in comparison. These results suggest that community-based curricula might offer a particularly effective teaching approach for HLLs (e.g. Carriera & Kagan, 2011), along with other opportunities to participate in German culture and communities, such as study abroad programs in German-speaking regions. Within the classroom, instructors might consider teaching conversational strategies, developing pragmatic skills and providing background information essential for initiating and sustaining interaction with German speakers, including family members and others who habitually address the student in English rather than German.

Issues for Future Consideration

This review of the motivational aspects of German HLLs highlights a recurrent theme in much recent research on L2 learning, that of the central role of self and identity in language development. For both HLLs and non-HLLs, the more German was internalized into the learners' sense of self, the more engaged, persistent and confident the learners. HLLs have an advantage in that they have a distinctively strong connection to the language and culture, and it would seem reasonable to think that they would be particularly successful learners. Some limitations to the studies discussed here, as well as developments in the HLL area more generally, raise several issues that should be addressed in future research.

One limitation of this research is that it is solely focused on learners who are enrolled in formal language classes. Thus, most of the HLLs investigated are those who already have a sufficiently strong and positive connection with the German language and culture that they would invest their time, energy and money in the rather difficult process of language learning. To better understand how one's sense of self is relevant to learning and maintaining a HL and culture, it would be important to explore the issues raised here with those members of the German community who do not feel the need, desire or compunction to enroll in a language class.

Comparisons with L2 learners usefully reveal the distinct motivational and identity profile of HLLs, but comparisons with other HL groups would also be valuable. It is probably safe to say that the majority of research on HL is focused on Asian and Latino Americans, groups that have a strong and increasing vitality in the regions where they study. Given their different opportunities for interaction in public spheres, their potential influence in educational and political realms and their importance to the commerce in their region, the experience of these larger minority language groups might be expected to be substantially different from those of smaller groups. Indeed, scholarly definitions that emphasize the linguistic expertise of the HLL might focus concern on larger minority groups and divert attention from smaller minority groups that are equally deserving of consideration. Particularly in the Canadian context, where multiculturalism and HL maintenance are supported through governmental policies, it is important to use a broad scope to understand the diversity of HLL experiences, including minority groups with less widely spoken languages.

Comparisons across HL groups also provide insight into motivational dynamics that are culturally specific. For instance, Comanaru and Noels (2009) found that Chinese HLLs were similar to the German HLLs studied by Noels (2005) in their endorsement of self-determined reasons for learning the HL, but the two groups differed in that the German group reported levels of introjected regulation similar to those of non-HLLs, whereas the Chinese learners reported much. It is not altogether clear why Chinese speakers report a greater obligation to learn their HL. Perhaps because the Chinese community is large and growing relative to the German community, Chinese HL learners experience more interpersonal interactions in which it is expected that they will communicate effectively in their HL. There may be greater cohesiveness among members, along with a greater sense of commitment to the community. Alternatively, there may be cultural differences in motivational dynamics: a growing body of research indicates that European Americans tend to regard conformity to the wishes of others as undermining their autonomy, but Asian Americans students do not have such strong negative sentiments about obliging the expectations of close others (Iyengar & Lepper, 1999). Thus, comparisons of motivational and identity processes in culturally distinct groups could provide a much needed analysis of the role of cultural values in academic learning.

Further unpacking of the definition of a 'German HLL' would also be helpful. German-Canadians are not a homogeneous group; they originate from not only Germany, Austria and Switzerland, but also Russia, the former Austro-Hungarian empire, other parts of Eastern Europe and other parts of the world. In the face of this diversity, some maintain that developing a cohesive German-Canadian community and articulating a common German-Canadian identity is problematic (e.g. Hoerder, 1998 as cited by Prokop, 2007). Bassler (1998) argues that such difficulties are not insurmountable, since German-Canadians are not bound to identities framed in terms of their countries of origin, but can articulate identities that fit their Canadian experience, including recognition of the fact that German-Canadian identity is subject to regional variations and is changeable over time. His conceptualization of identity, with its emphasis on spatial and temporal dimensions, complements the situated conception of identity presented here. The importance of a temporal dimension is further underscored by Eubel's (2008) finding that advanced students express greater intrinsic motivation to learn German than lower-level students.

In addition to articulating what it means to be affiliated with an ethnolinguistic group, we need to further consider how language and identity figure into the definition of a 'heritage' learner. For some, a narrow definition focused on the linguistic proficiency and patterns of usage is sufficient, especially for linguistic analyses (e.g. Valdès, 2000; Polinsky & Kagan, 2007). For others, a broader definition is preferred, including anyone who claims an ancestral connection to the language, whether the language is used in the home or not (e.g. Fishman, 2001; Kondo-Brown, 2005). Identification as a HLL is not isomorphic with HL exposure, use and proficiency, or ancestral background. For instance, in the research described earlier, I found that although the classification of German students as HLLs according to whether one or both of their parents had a 'German-speaking background' showed good correspondence with the response to the question 'Would you consider yourself a heritage language learner (that is, is German a part of your cultural background)?', it was not perfect: 13.8% of those whose parents had a German background did not consider themselves to be a HLL. As observed by Dressler (2010), not all people who could be designated as a German HLL on the basis of their ethnolinguistic background assume this identity whole-heartedly. There is a variety of reasons for their reluctance, including a lack of exposure in the home, a perceived lack of ability, dialect differences between the school and home and, for some, concerns of stigmatization (Prokop, 2007).

In a complementary manner, we need to consider the experience of people who do not claim a German ancestral background, but who nonetheless have considerable familiarity with German. For example, Dressler (2010) points out that Canadian bilingual programs include children who do not claim German ancestry, but who are linguistically proficient due to an extended stay abroad. Likewise, adult learners may have lived in German-speaking countries and/or have romantic partners or spouses who speak German. For instance, in one of our studies a participant checked a box to indicate that she did not have a HL background, but penciled in 'not mine, but my husband is German'. She elaborated more fully when asked to describe her reasons for learning German:

> I study German because my husband is German. It is part of my children's heritage – my husband's parents immigrated to Canada – many relatives are still in Germany. I want to better understand their culture and also the language so we can converse. Also my son attends German Saturday school and we can learn together this way.

These learners' familiarity with German ways of being and sense of German as a part of themselves is unlike that of many other L2 learners. However, Dressler notes that although some might feel some affiliation with the German culture and/or community, they may not be perceived to have the linguistic expertise or the proper 'inheritance' that would confer on them the status of HLL by members of the German community. As arguments for the creation of HL-focused classes are mounted, one might wonder how such learners might also be accommodated in a way that recognizes not only their linguistic capacities but also their ownership of the language and their distinctive experience with the culture and the community.

Conclusion

Over the last decade, L2 acquisition research has increasingly emphasized the important role of the self and identity in the development of linguistic and cultural competencies. This chapter further underscores the importance of this theme by articulating how SDT can usefully frame the issues of internalization, agency and motivation in German HL learning. Additionally, it offers a situated approach to understanding the dynamics of HL identity. It is hoped that this perspective, along with other discussions of identity, can help elucidate what He (2010) terms 'the heart of heritage', thereby complementing the contributions of other disciplines to the understanding of the unique linguistic, pedagogical, social and psychological dynamics of HL learning.

Acknowledgements

The author would like to thank Shadi Mehrabi for her research assistance, Manfred Prokop for his informative and enjoyable discussions about the German Canadian community, the Social Science and Humanities Research Council of Canada for their financial support, and Callie Mady and Katy Arnett for their helpful comments on earlier versions of this chapter.

Notes

(1) Although precise numbers are difficult to determine, options in earlier years include community language classes, bilingual programming and German language courses in public schools.

References

Ashmore, R.D., Deaux, K. and McLaughlin-Volpe, T. (2004) An organizing framework for collective identity: Articulation and significance of multidimensionality. *Psychological Bulletin* 130 (1), 80–114.

Bassler, G.P. (1998) German-Canadian identity in historical perspective. In A.E. Sauer and M. Zimmer (eds) *A Chorus of Different Voices: German-Canadian Identities* (pp. 95–98). New York: Peter Lang.

Bausenhart, W.A. (1971) The attitudes and motivation of German language school children in Canada. *Word* 27, 342–358.

Bausenhart, W.A. (1984) Attitudes and motivation of Anglophone and Francophone university students of German. *Canadian Modern Language Review* 40 (2), 208–217.

Benson, P. (2011) *Teaching and Researching Autonomy in Language Learning*. Harlow: Pearson Education.

Carreira, M. and Kagan, O. (2011) The results of the national heritage language survey: Implications for teaching, curriculum design, and professional development. *Foreign Language Annals* 44 (1), 40–64.

Clément, R. and Kruidenier, B.G. (1983) Orientations in second language acquisition: I. The effects of ethnicity, milieu, and target language on their emergence. *Language Learning* 33, 273–291.

Clément, R. and Noels, K.A. (1992) Towards a situated approach to ethnolinguistic identity: The effects of status on individuals and groups. *Journal of Language and Social Psychology* 11 (4), 203–232.

Comanaru, R. and Noels, K.A. (2009) Self-determination, motivation, and the learning of Chinese as a heritage language. *Canadian Modern Language Review* 66 (1), 131–158.

Deci, E.L. and Ryan, R.M. (1985) *Intrinsic Motivation and Self-Determination in Human Behavior.* New York: Plenum Press.
Dornyei, Z. (2005) *The Psychology of the Language Learner: Individual Differences in Second Language Acquisition.* Mahwah, NJ: Lawrence Erlbaum.
Dressler, R. (2010) 'There no space for being German': Portraits of willing and reluctant heritage language learners of German. *Heritage Language Journal* 7 (2), 1–21.
Edmondson, A.C. (2004) Individual motivational profiles: The interaction between external and internal factors. *Zeitschrift für Interkulturellen Fremdsprachenunterricht* 9 (2) http://zif.spz.tu-darmstadt.de/jg-09-2/beitrag/edmondson2.htm
Eubel, S. (2008) Why study German? A survey among students studying German. In *Preparing for the Graduate of 2015. Proceedings of the 17th Annual Teaching Learning Forum*, 30–31 January 2008. Perth: Curtin University of Technology. http://otl.curtin.edu.au/tlf/tlf2008/refereed/eubel.html
Fishman, J.A. (2001) 300-plus years of heritage language education in the United States. In J.K. Peyton, D.A. Ranard and S. McGinnis (eds) *Heritage Languages in America: Preserving a National Resource* (pp. 81–90). Washington, DC: Delta Systems; and McHenry, IL: Center for Applied Linguistics.
Gardner, R.C. (2010) *Motivation and Second Language Acquisition: The Socio-Educational Model.* New York: Peter Lang.
Gardner, R.C. and Lambert, W.E. (1972) *Attitudes and Motivation in Second Language Learning.* Rowley, MA: Newbury House.
He, A.W. (2004) Identity construction in Chinese heritage languages classes. *Pragmatics* 14 (2/3), 199–216.
He, A.W. (2010) The heart of heritage: Sociocultural dimensions of heritage language learning. *Annual Review of Applied Linguistics* 30, 66–82.
Iyengar, S.S. and Lepper, M.R. (1999) Rethinking the value of choice: A cultural perspective on intrinsic motivation. *Journal of Personality and Social Psychology* 76 (3), 349–366.
Kondo-Brown, K. (2005) Differences in language skills: Heritage language learner subgroups and foreign language learners. *The Modern Language Journal* 89 (4), 563–581.
Noels, K.A. (2001) New orientations in language learning motivation: Towards a model of intrinsic, extrinsic and integrative orientations. In Z. Dörnyei and R. Schmidt (eds) *Motivation and Second Language Acquisition* (pp. 43–68). Honolulu, HI: University of Hawai'i Second Language Teaching and Curriculum Centre.
Noels, K.A. (2005) Orientations to learning German: Heritage background and motivational processes. *Canadian Modern Language Review* 62, 285–312.
Noels, K.A. (2009) The internalization of language learning into the self and social identity. In Z. Dörnyei and E. Ushioda (eds) *Motivation, Language Identity and the L2 Self* (pp. 295–313). Bristol: Multilingual Matters.
Noels, K.A. and Clément, R. (1989) Orientations to learning German: The effects of language heritage on second language acquisition. *Canadian Modern Language Review* 45, 245–257.
Noels, K.A., Clément, R. and Gaudet, S. (2004) Language and the situated nature of ethnic identity. In S.H. Ng, C.N. Candlin and C.Y. Chiu (eds) *Language Matters: Communication, Culture, and Identity* (pp. 245–266). Hong Kong: City University of Hong Kong Press.
Noels, K.A., Leavitt, P.A. and Clément, R. (2010) 'To see ourselves as others see us': On the implications of reflected appraisals for ethnic identity and discrimination. *Journal of Social Issues* 66 (4), 740–758.

Noels, K.A. and Saumure, K.D. (2013) Motivation for learning German as a heritage vs. foreign language: A self-determination perspective on the role of the social context in supporting learner motivation. Unpublished manuscript, University of Alberta.

Noels, K.A., Stephan, S. and Saumure, K.D. (2007) Supporting the motivation of heritage and nonheritage learners of German. In C.L. Rieger, J.L. Plews and C. Lorey (eds) *Intercultural Literacies and German in the Classroom: Festschrift for Manfred Prokop* (pp. 29–48). Germany: Gunter Narr Verlag.

Norton, B. (2000) *Identity and Language Learning: Gender, Ethnicity and Educational Change.* Harlow: Pearson Education.

Polinsky, M. and Kagan, O. (2007) Heritage languages: In the 'wild' and in the classroom. *Language and Linguistics Compass* 1 (5), 368–395.

Prokop, M. (1974) Differences between attitudes of French-American and German-Canadian speakers toward the foreign culture. ERIC Document Reproduction Service No. 094578.

Prokop, M. (1975) The stability of student attitudes toward German language and culture over an academic year. Paper presented at Meeting of the Canadian Association of Second Language Teachers, Edmonton, Alberta, Canada. (Eric Document Reproduction Service No. ED113968.)

Prokop, M. (2007) *A History of Alberta's German-speaking Communities; Volume 1: From the 1880s to the Present.* Okotoks, AB: Manfred Prokop.

Ryan, R.M. and Deci, E.L. (2002) Overview of Self-Determination Theory: An organismic-dialectical perspective. In E.L. Deci and R.M. Ryan (eds) *Handbook of Self-Determination Research* (pp. 3–33). Rochester, NY: University of Rochester Press.

Statistics Canada (2008) *Canada's Ethnocultural Mosaic, 2006 Census.* Ottawa, ON: Ministry of Industry. http://www12.statcan.ca/census-recensement/2006/as-sa/97-562/pdf/97-562-XIE2006001.pdf

Statistics Canada (2012) *Canada Yearbook 2011: Languages* (11-402-X). http://www.statcan.gc.ca/pub/11-402-x/2010000/chap/lang/lang-eng.htm

Statistics Canada (2013) 2011 Census of Population, Statistics Canada Catalogue no. 98-314-XCB2011016. http://www12.statcan.ca/census-recensement/2011/dp-pd/tbt-tt/Rp-eng.cfm?LANG=E&APATH=3&DETAIL=0&DIM=0&FL=A&FREE=0&GC=0&GID=0&GK=0&GRP=1&PID=103251&PRID=0&PTYPE=101955&S=0&SHOWALL=0&SUB=0&Temporal=2011&THEME=90&VID=0&VNAMEE=&VNAMEF=

Val, A. and Vinogradova, P. (2010) What is the identity of a heritage language speaker? Heritage Briefs. McHenry, IL: Center for Applied Linguistics. http://www.cal.org/heritage/pdfs/briefs/what-is-the-identity-of-a-heritage-language-speaker.pdf

Valdés, G. (2001) Heritage language students: Profiles and possibilities. In J.K. Peyton, D.A. Ranard and S. McGinnis (eds) *Heritage Languages in America: Preserving a National Resource* (pp. 37–77). Washington, DC: Delta Systems; and McHenry, IL: Center for Applied Linguistics.

6 Learning Chinese as a Heritage Language

Patricia A. Duff and Duanduan Li

Heritage language (HL) learning, teaching and research have been important areas of applied linguistics in Canada since 1971, when a national multicultural policy was implemented (Jedwab, 2000; Pendakur, 1990). Canadian HL education research soon began to examine the experiences of children from a variety of HL backgrounds learning their HLs through educational programs and not simply at home (see reviews in Ashworth, 1988; Benyon & Toohey, 1991; Cummins, 1983, 1991, 1992, 1993; Cummins & Danesi, 1990; Danesi et al., 1993; Duff, 2008).[1] These studies also examined teachers' and parents' satisfaction with bilingual (HL) programs, HL students' participation, attitudes, levels of HL and English proficiency, academic achievement and feelings of self-esteem, cultural identity and intra-family communication. The research also benefited from earlier Canadian scholarship on ethnolinguistic identity and vitality in relation to language learning, retention and attitudes (see Duff, 2012a).

Since the beginning of the 21st century, there has been considerable interest in Canada and internationally in processes, outcomes and educational structures supporting HL learners both in and out of school and over their lifespan (e.g. Brinton et al., 2008; Hornberger, 2005; Wiley & Valdés, 2000). The research agenda has also expanded from studies based on social and cognitive psychology, to more sociocultural, post-structural and critical approaches to language learning (see Swain & Deters, 2007), as well as linguistic analyses of intriguing differences between HL and non-HL learners' grammars (e.g. Montrul, 2010). Studies have also examined HL or first language (L1) loss to a greater extent and not just the challenges and rewards of (re)learning a HL (e.g. Kouritzen, 1999). Currently, a prominent theme in HL research worldwide is connected with identity and language learning, retention (or resilience) and language loss (Blackledge & Creese, 2008; He, 2008, 2010; Hornberger & Wang, 2008; Leung et al., 1997; Liu & Lo Bianco, 2007; Norton & Toohey, 2011).

In this chapter, we focus on issues connected with students from Chinese backgrounds in Chinese HL education contexts, recognizing that other immigrant groups and domestic Francophone and (larger) Aboriginal communities in Canada may face similar challenges (Duff & D. Li, 2008). The relative status and vitality of their ancestral languages at home, in public, private or community schools and in society more generally, is an important shared factor, as is the desire on the part of elders to pass on to their children cherished aspects of their linguistic and cultural heritage and to nurture intergenerational bonds and lines of communication that support the well-being of families, groups, traditions and languages themselves.

Changing Contexts for Research on Chinese as a Heritage Language

Research on Chinese populations and the development and use of their HLs has received increased attention and visibility in the past decade (e.g. He & Xiao, 2008; Lo Bianco, 2007; Tao, 2006; Tsung & Cruickshank, 2011). This trend in Chinese language education stems from a number of interrelated demographic, sociopolitical and economic factors. First is the dramatically changing status and visibility of Chinese language(s) internationally, particularly Mandarin, in Chinese diaspora and non-diaspora contexts (Duff *et al.*, 2013; McDonald, 2011; Tsung & Cruickshank, 2011). Coinciding with this visibility are the demographics of recent waves of immigrants to North America from 'Greater China' – principally from Hong Kong, the People's Republic of China and Taiwan – who often have higher levels of education, bilingualism in Chinese and English and socioeconomic status, and thus, different social, cultural and economic capital and clout at their disposal, than their predecessors in the 19th- and 20th-century diaspora (P. Li, 1998). These newer immigrants are often very proactive in establishing language schools and community centers while actively maintaining their transnational ties and travel to Chinese-speaking regions.[2]

The cumulative effect of Chinese immigration and language retention in North America has been that 'Chinese' (i.e. the languages/dialects included under that label) has for a number of years been the primary home language census category for a large proportion of the Canadian population, ranking third after English and French (Statistics Canada, 2011). The growing number of 'families with children from China' (international adoptions) has also stimulated interest in Chinese heritage language (CHL) programs, even in families with non-Chinese-background parents (Duff, submitted).

Kindergarten to Grade 12 (K-12) Chinese educational programs either established within the public education sector or, more commonly, run privately through community schools have long been an option for Chinese-background learners in major cosmopolitan areas around the world (Chen, 2006; Jiang, 2010). However, now, in addition, HL students have more opportunities to enroll in Chinese courses in public post-secondary institutions, reflecting a number of demographic and educational changes (D. Li & Duff, 2008; Liu & Lo Bianco, 2007). In the United States, the development of the College Board's SAT II Chinese Test with Listening and the Chinese Advanced Placement examination, according to McGinnis (2008), has been a powerful impetus for CHL students to exert themselves to learn and retain their knowledge of Chinese, typically through community or private CHL instruction that leads to advanced university coursework.

In Canada, national assessment tools and funding have not played the same role in fostering language retention by CHL speakers since educational curriculum, policies and assessment are, for the most part, governed and funded provincially. However, the advent of provincial Ministry-approved Mandarin-language (challenge) examinations in British Columbia (the province we are most familiar with) has encouraged students to develop and maintain their proficiency in Chinese up through the high school years. For those wishing to subsequently continue their (Mandarin) Chinese studies formally, university placement screening procedures direct them to appropriate courses for CHL students with reasonably advanced proficiency, where more academic language and literacy skills and metalinguistic awareness can be developed further using textbooks specifically designed for CHL students (D. Li & Duff, 2008; D. Li *et al*., 2003).

The foregoing contextual factors attest to the tremendous commitment, in general, on the part of many who identify as Chinese and to the wider educational community now, to the preservation, use, value and teaching of standard modern Chinese (i.e. Mandarin) (X. Wang, 1996). However, the label *Chinese* in the term *Chinese Heritage Language* points to many additional issues, connected to the geopolitical and linguistic complexities and sensibilities associated with the different dialects of Chinese that are spoken, learned, taught and used in public media in Canada and elsewhere, the different writing (script) systems, the sheer size of the population, the perceptions of the economic significance and (soft) power of Greater China, the active engagement of the Mainland Chinese and Taiwanese governments in promoting Chinese language education by supplying teachers and textbooks for CHL teaching and providing other instructional opportunities, and the growing number of Chinese-background language learners at the post-secondary level (Duff *et al.*, 2013; D. Li & Duff, 2008). Many of these ideological, contextual and practical matters are being investigated in research on 21st-century Chinese language education (e.g. Duff *et al.*, 2013; Duff & Lester, 2008).

CHL Education and Research in Canada vs. the United States: Examining National Discourses

The challenges facing CHL populations and educators in Canada are similar in many ways to their counterparts in other English-dominant countries. However, Canada's social, political, cultural and educational context and history are also distinct, particularly given our federal policies and laws connected with official bilingualism and multiculturalism. The unique colonial linguistic *duality* of Canada (settlement by Anglophones and Francophones) has detracted from the importance and role of other minority languages (immigrant and Indigenous alike). Therefore, when news media broach the subject of increasing instruction in Asian languages such as Mandarin Chinese in English-dominant provinces like British Columbia, there is often a public outcry in defense of French language education, citing its crucial role in maintaining national unity and mutual understanding, thereby according French a somewhat privileged default status in the Canadian Anglophone school curriculum (with some exceptions). For decades, the desire among particular ethnic communities to have publicly funded opportunities to pursue HL education has been contentious in Canada, related to highly politicized questions about the HL community members' Canadianness, loyalty, social integration and good citizenship, official language mastery, appropriate uses and purposes of taxpayer-funded language education and Anglo-Franco unity, among other recurring themes (e.g. Ashworth, 1988; Duff, 2008).

One solution to some of these sensitivities has been to reframe *heritage* languages as *international* languages, the latter term being perceived to have a less culturally conservative connotation and seen as important for the strategic interests of the nation as a whole in the context of globalization, and not just ethnic interest groups (see Tavares, 2000). Yet, despite newspaper and magazine headlines proclaiming the 'Asia-Pacific Century' and the 'rise of China' or about (Western) Canada being part of the 'Asia-Pacific Gateway' (Duff *et al.*, 2013), Chinese language education and Chinese applied linguistics research are underdeveloped in Canada both for CHL and non-Chinese-background students. In terms of the provision of language education programs for Canadian HL learners through public education (e.g. bilingual, immersion and second-language programs in schools), the Canadian record has been somewhat checkered in recent years. Canada is naturally well known internationally for its ever-popular and widely subscribed French immersion programs and has supported bilingual programs for certain other languages as well (e.g. Hebrew, Ukrainian and Chinese). However, US-type dual-immersion or two-way bilingual programs that serve, reciprocally, the bilingual and academic goals of both HL (minority) learners (e.g. Korean, Spanish and Mandarin) and Anglophones within the same programs are much less widespread in Canada than in the United States (Genesee & Lindholm-Leary, 2008).

On a more positive note, Canada has not needed to invoke discourses and federal agencies connected with 'homeland security' or national defense to argue for the value of HL education in the way that the United States has (i.e. for protectionist reasons, positioning certain 'critical' languages and their speakers as potentially dangerous to national interests). Yet, interestingly, the post-2001 US politics around language, global terrorism and fear has helped leverage and mobilize major federal funding for HL education and research at all (K-16) program levels (see, e.g. Everson & Xiao, 2009; McGinnis, 2005, 2008). Applied linguists have carefully navigated these new waters, attempting to reposition the debates somewhat away from a defensive international stance to a recognition of the benefits of cultivating the national resources that languages and cultures represent (Brecht & Ingold, 1998; Peyton *et al.*, 2001), and making a case for funding on that basis (but see Ricento [2005] for a critique of the language-as-resource argument).

Themes in Canadian and international research in CHL

(1) Language and literacy socialization through children's home and school interactions and textbooks

A growing body of ethnographic research has examined CHL children's socialization or enculturation into and through Chinese oral and literate practices at home and at school (e.g. Duff, 2010, 2012b, submitted; He, 2012; Jia, 2006). Curdt-Christiansen (2006, 2008, 2012; Maguire & Curdt-Christiansen, 2007) demonstrated the very rich resources and creative, multilingual and often syncretic (hybrid) practices that CHL children in Montreal engaged in, through socialization practices with parents, grandparents, peers and siblings. Children's appropriation of Chinese, English, French and various other semiotic resources (e.g. cartoons) in their multilingual environments, their literacy activities, interactions and language play at home and at school reflected not just their literacy learning and academic achievement, but other social, cultural and intellectual values that were embodied in the texts and interactions themselves.

G. Li's (2006) ethnographic CHL language socialization research in the Metro Vancouver area explored differences in the way that three young CHL elementary-school children attending an 'English-only' school were being socialized into bi/multilingual (Cantonese, Mandarin and English) and biliterate (Chinese and English) practices and identities at home versus school, and the tensions between the roles and status of English and Chinese in some cases. For example, one of the Canadian-born children whose parents had originally come from Hong Kong refused to acknowledge knowing Chinese at his public school and eventually spoke English almost exclusively at home and at school. The Mainland Chinese parents of the second child in the study had come as wealthy investment-class immigrants and did not speak (much) English; they wanted to keep their options open for the future, entertaining the possibility of returning to China some day. They therefore tried to instill in their child a solid foundation in Chinese language and literacy to ensure transnational mobility options. Yet, they valued the child's development of English proficiency and cultural knowledge in the meantime. The third study participant was from a trilingual Cantonese-English-Mandarin-speaking, investment-class family from Hong Kong who put a lot of stock in the boy's English development, since his older brother had struggled in school in Canada because of his limited English literacy. The younger brother engaged freely with English pop culture literacy activities (e.g. video games, comic books and cartoons) and read English books for leisure but had some difficulties producing English writing. The parents' expectations regarding the young boy's Chinese language and literacy attainment were therefore relatively low and, despite attending Chinese language school for several hours a week, he apparently made little progress. Thus, various circulating ideologies or discourses that children and their families encounter, combined with their familial migration histories and trajectories, influence decisions and choices about which languages to cultivate in their children, and how and why to do so.

Unfortunately, apart from the previous studies, little if any research has explored classroom discourse, instruction and ideologies involving K-16 CHL learners in Canada. On the other hand, recent Canadian research has looked closely and critically at how textbooks and curricula mediate children's language and literacy development and socialize learners into certain identities and ideologies, some of which may be problematic. For example, Curdt-Christiansen (2008) and Chiu (2011) examined CHL textbooks produced by either Mainland China or Taiwan and distributed freely for CHL programs in Canada and the United States. They noted certain recurrent themes across the two widely used series: an emphasis on perseverance, diligence, seniority (respect for elders, conformity), modesty, education, knowledge of classic texts and proficiency in Chinese, visits to iconic monuments and geographical landmarks, and in the Taiwanese texts primarily, what Chiu called 'family values'. These themes were presented to children as obligatory aspirations and goals for learning Chinese and being authentic Chinese. Both authors emphasized that while some of the themes may represent important aspects of Chinese historical and cultural knowledge, others conflict with those that the children encounter in mainstream educational and social contexts or experience in their everyday lives as Chinese-Canadians. Chiu's textbook study was informed not just by literacy-as-social-practice perspectives but also by her personal experience as a CHL researcher, teacher and immigrant from Taiwan whose younger sister had dropped out of Chinese language school in Alberta at an early age, abandoning Chinese. Chiu argued that the very dull, pedantic, authoritarian nature of these CHL textbooks socialized students into 'closed discourses' and identities, offering no alternatives, no critique, no discussion and no contextualization or possibility of third spaces or cultural hybridity for generation 1.5 immigrant Canadians. To make matters worse, these messages are often delivered through very traditional teaching methods by well-meaning but untrained, foreign-educated volunteer teachers (or parents), driving many children and youth away from CHL education and language retention.

Jiang (2010) also examined from a sociohistorical perspective how CHL textbooks and instruction from the establishment of the earliest Chinese schools in British Columbia have always been highly politicized and conservative, reflecting trends in political movements in China, especially throughout the tumultuous 20th century. However, just as these traditional means of CHL enculturation may discourage and disengage contemporary language learners, so too can current textbooks, materials, teaching methods, and curricula at the post-secondary level that assume not that CHL learners are displaced citizens of regions in Greater China, but that they are monolingual, monocultural Anglophones with no prior Chinese cultural knowledge or experience in learning Chinese as a 'foreign' language (D. Li & Duff, 2008). This has necessitated the development of special tracks and materials for students from CHL backgrounds (D. Li *et al.*, 2003).

(2) Motivation and identity among young adult CHL learners

Closely connected with issues of early home and school-based socialization and curricular and textbook issues are key questions about motivation and identity in CHL learning. Much of the relevant research involves CHL learners at North American universities who persist with

Chinese studies beyond the first semester. Studies from Western Canadian university settings include those by D. Li (2005; see also D. Li & Duff, 2008, forthcoming) and Comanaru and Noels (2009).

D. Li's survey of HL learners of Chinese at a Western Canadian university (D. Li, 2005; D. Li & Duff, 2008) revealed that although CHL learners are by no means homogeneous in terms of their language and literacy profiles, they generally require advanced-level conversational skills (and lexico-grammatical features to support them), more sophisticated pragmatic competence, oral academic discourse, literacy and a more in-depth exploration of Chinese culture. Her findings revealed that most participants studied Mandarin for both integrative and instrumental reasons: to learn more about themselves and their ethnic cultures and to increase their future career opportunities related to the burgeoning Chinese economy. However, unlike their university CHL experiences, which they described using positive terms, such as *enjoyable, fun, rewarding, satisfying, important, helpful, interesting* and *fascinating*, their childhood HL learning experiences were described in negative terms: *difficult, annoying, bothersome, unwilling, painful, isolated, lonely, uncomfortable, scared, intimidating, embarrassed, not free, stuck* and *a burden*. Li also examined their values and hence preferences for the simplified versus traditional script and the reasons for their preferences, stemming primarily from their countries of origin. Finally, she analyzed students' attitudes toward different dialects of Mandarin (e.g. Beijing and Taiwanese) and their reasons for affiliating with one or another variety (and sometimes shifts), and the connection between these varieties and their evolving identities.

Our subsequent research (Duff & D. Li, 2008, forthcoming) examined more closely the diverse multilingual identities and repertoires of a subset of five CHL students who had completed questionnaires and then volunteered to take part in further interviews. The five CHL learners (born in Hong Kong, Taiwan, China, Indonesia and Canada) revealed their complicated linguistic histories and investments. Collectively, they had had prior experience with several dialects of Chinese, but they had also learned English and other languages to reasonably high levels (French, Indonesian, Danish, German and Japanese). We also tracked the students over a number of years as they moved from Canada to other countries to pursue work or further studies; only one participant, the woman originally from Beijing, remained in Canada at the end of our study. This unforeseen development reinforced for us the transnationalism and different forms of cultural (linguistic) capital the participants had at their disposal. It not only affected their language choices and use, but also their dialect and script preferences and the other languages in which they were competent and also invested to some degree (e.g. French for the Beijing native). The study thus demonstrated the value of longitudinal research with CHL learners spanning different geopolitical regions, time, space and languages.

A concurrent, multiple case study of five long-term *non*-Chinese learners of Chinese in British Columbia (Duff *et al.*, 2013) pointed to interesting similarities and differences across the two sets of participants. In both studies, the learners' displayed diverse trajectories, goals, achievements and even misgivings at times regarding their learning and use of Chinese and about how they were sometimes positioned in terms of their Chinese competence or Sinophone identities. For the non-HL learners, confusion surrounding oral dialects and orthographic systems, the need to negotiate access to communities of (Mandarin) Chinese speakers, their desire for more engaging Chinese leisure reading materials and their yearning for identities as legitimate, (multi)literate, cosmopolitan, transnational speakers of Chinese and other languages were more pronounced than they were for the HL students and also underscored some of the shared challenges for learners of Chinese in Canada.

Comanaru and Noels' (2009) research at a university in Alberta also explored social-psychological aspects of CHL. The study involved 145 CHL and non-CHL Mandarin learners. Their analysis was primarily quantitative but included some open-ended/extended responses to questions about the students' motivations to study Chinese. The authors reported that 'the more learners felt they were learning Chinese because it was personally meaningful and fun, the more they engaged in the learning process. This orientation was promoted to the extent that learners felt a connection with the Chinese community and, particularly for heritage learners, a sense of personal control over the learning process' (Comanaru & Noels, 2009: 131). The CHL learners were, they found, more driven than the non-HL students in the study based on identity or 'self-concept' issues as well as familial obligation. However, they found no meaningful differences in this regard whether those HL learners were Mandarin-dominant or English-dominant.

(3) Additional areas of research, scholarship and professional development in CHL

Professional development enabling teachers to accommodate the needs of diverse Chinese learners has surfaced as a priority in several English-dominant countries (Duff *et al.*, 2013; Duff & Lester, 2008; Everson & Xiao, 2009; Xiao, 2009). Other areas of research that offer many possibilities but have not been addressed sufficiently in Canada are the following: corpus development to examine differences between CHL and native Chinese oral and written forms among university learners (e.g. Tao, 2008); the development of morphological awareness and literacy in school-aged CHL learners (e.g. studies in He & Xiao, 2008); morphological and grammatical development in CHL (e.g. aspect marking; Jia & Bayley, 2009); CHL learners' language and identity development, and their dispositions toward and use of Chinese, English and other languages from early childhood through adulthood, and cross-generationally (He, 2008; W. Li, 1994); and curriculum and placement decisions for CHL learners, since many programs do not differentiate well between heritage and non-heritage learners and assume that learners are either monolingual and monocultural Anglophones or are homogeneous CHL groups (Kelleher, 2008; Wong & Xiao, 2010).

Conclusion

As policies and population demographics change within Canada, and globalization shrinks the world and expands opportunities to learn and use Chinese, CHL education and research beg more attention. More in-depth case studies and larger-scale studies are needed of learners at various points across their lifespan at home, in school and in extracurricular, community and virtual settings, generating new understandings of the (sometimes conflicted) desires, pressures, positionings, struggles and rewards of learning and using Chinese in Canada and abroad.

However, beyond capturing learners' acquisition and use of their HL and literacy skills and their personal and familial attitudes toward HL maintenance, many progressive educators now incorporate students' languages, narratives and literacy traditions into the mainstream English or French school curriculum. This is done to raise (all) students' metalinguistic awareness, to strengthen children's literacy skills across languages and to support their diverse linguistic identities and abilities, and relationships with relatives who can serve as resources (e.g. Cummins, 2005; Cummins & Early, 2011). Canadian scholars have demonstrated convincingly that students who are able to retain their HLs and literacy skills perform well – indeed, often better than their English L1 peers – in both English-medium and French immersion or core French program contexts (e.g. Swain & Lapkin, 1991, 2005). It is now incumbent on (language) educators to seize opportunities to expand the vision of what is possible, innovative, engaging and effective in Chinese education and to create opportunities for new generations to develop their multilingual competencies.

Acknowledgment

The authors gratefully acknowledge funding from the Social Sciences and Humanities Research Council of Canada, which has supported the preparation of this chapter.

Notes

(1) In the Canadian context, heritage languages (HLs) are generally synonymous with immigrant languages, distinct from either official languages (English and French) or Indigenous languages (Duff, 2008; Duff & D. Li, 2009).
(2) In British Columbia alone, there are more than 200 CHL language schools. Students can opt to take Mandarin in public secondary schools that offer it, although the courses were designed for *second* rather than *heritage* language learners. The reality is that many of the students in the highest grade levels are CHL learners, however (P. Hao, personal communication, November 2012).

References

Ashworth, M. (1988) *Blessed with Bilingual Brains: Education of Immigrant Children with English as a Second Language*. Vancouver: Pacific Educational Press.
Benyon, J. and Toohey, K. (1991) Heritage language education in British Columbia: Policy and programs. *Canadian Modern Language Review* 47, 606–616.
Blackledge, A. and Creese, A. (2008) Contesting 'language' as 'heritage': Negotiation of identities in late modernity. *Applied Linguistics* 29 (4), 533–554.
Brecht, R.D. and Ingold, C.W. (1998) Tapping a national resource: Heritage languages in the United States. *ERIC Digest*. Washington, DC: ERIC Clearinghouse on Language and Linguistics.
Brinton, D., Kagan, O. and Bauckus, S. (eds) (2008) *Heritage Language Education: A New Field Emerging*. Mahwah, NJ: Lawrence Erlbaum.
Chen, Y.J. (2006) Balancing goals and emotional responses to learning Chinese as a heritage language. Unpublished PhD dissertation, University of Texas.
Chiu, L. (2011) The construction of the 'ideal Chinese child': A critical analysis of textbooks for Chinese heritage language learners. Unpublished MA thesis, University of British Columbia.
Comanaru, R. and Noels, K. (2009) Self-determination, motivation, and the learning of Chinese as a heritage language. *Canadian Modern Language Review* 66 (1), 131–158.
Cummins, J. (ed.) (1983) *Heritage Language Education: Issues and Directions*. Ottawa: Minister of Supply and Services Canada.
Cummins, J. (ed.) (1991) Heritage languages [Special issue]. *Canadian Modern Language Review* 47 (4), 601-832.
Cummins, J. (1992) Heritage language teaching in Canadian schools. *Journal of Curriculum Studies* 24, 287–296.
Cummins, J. (1993) The research basis for heritage language promotion. In M. Danesi, K. McLeod and S. Morris (eds) *Heritage Language and Education: The Canadian Experience* (pp. 1–21). Oakville: Mosaic Press.
Cummins, J. (2005) Proposal for action: Strategies for recognizing heritage language competence as a learning resource within the mainstream classroom. *The Modern Language Journal* 89, 585–592.
Cummins, J. and Danesi, M. (1990) *Heritage Languages: The Development and Denial of Canada's Linguistic Resources*. Montreal: Our Schools/Our Selves Education Foundation.
Cummins, J. and Early, M. (eds) (2011) *Identity Texts: The Collaborative Creation of Power in Multilingual Schools*. Stoke-on-Trent: Trentham Books.

Curdt-Christiansen, X.L. (2006) Teaching and learning Chinese: Heritage language classroom discourse in Montreal. *Language, Culture and Curriculum* 19 (2), 189–207.
Curdt-Christiansen, X.L. (2008) Reading the world through words: Cultural themes in heritage Chinese language textbooks. *Language and Education* 22 (2), 95–113.
Curdt-Christiansen, X.L. (2012) Implicit learning and imperceptible influence: Syncretic literacy of multilingual Chinese children. *Journal of Early Childhood Literacy*, doi:10.1177/1468798412455819.
Danesi, M., McLeod, K. and Morris, S. (eds) (1993) *Heritage Languages and Education: The Canadian Experience*. Oakville: Mosaic Press.
Duff, P. (2008) Heritage language education in Canada. In D. Brinton, O. Kagan and S. Bauckus (eds) *Heritage Language Education: A New Field Emerging* (pp. 71–90). New York: Routledge/Taylor & Francis.
Duff, P. (2010) Language socialization. In N.H. Hornberger and S. McKay (eds) *Sociolinguistics and Language Education* (pp. 427–455). Bristol: Multilingual Matters.
Duff, P. (2012a) Identity, agency, and SLA. In A. Mackey and S. Gass (eds) *Handbook of Second Language Acquisition* (pp. 410–426). London: Routledge.
Duff, P. (2012b) Second language socialization. In A. Duranti, E. Ochs and B. Schieffelin (eds) *Handbook of Language Socialization* (pp. 564–586). Malden, MA: Wiley-Blackwell.
Duff, P. (submitted) Language socialization into Chinese language and 'Chineseness' in diaspora communities. In X. L. Curdt-Christiansen and A. Hancock (eds) *Learning Chinese in Diasporic Communities: Many Pathways to Becoming Chinese*. Amsterdam: John Benjamins.
Duff, P., Anderson, T., Ilnyckyj, R., Lester, P., Wang, R. and Yates, E. (2013) *Learning Chinese: Linguistic, Sociocultural, and Narrative Perspectives*. Berlin/Boston, MA: De Gruyter.
Duff, P. and Lester, P. (eds) (2008) *Issues in Chinese Language Education and Teacher Development*. Vancouver: University of British Columbia Centre for Research in Chinese Language and Literacy Education.
Duff, P. and Li, D. (2008, August) Negotiating language, literacy and identity: Chinese heritage learners' language socialization. World Congress of Applied Linguistics, Essen, Germany.
Duff, P. and Li, D. (eds) (2009) Indigenous, minority, and heritage language education in Canada [Special issue]. *Canadian Modern Language Review* 66 (1).
Duff, P. and Li, D. (forthcoming) Learning Chinese as an additional, transnational language: Negotiating identity, community, and legitimacy. In M. Primsloo and C. Stroud (eds) *Educating for Language and Literacy Diversity*. London: Palgrave Macmillan.
Everson, M. and Xiao, Y. (eds) (2009) *Teaching Chinese as a Foreign Language*. Boston, MA: Cheng & Tsui.
Genesee, F. and Lindholm-Leary, K. (2008). Dual language education in Canada and the USA. In S. May and N.H. Hornberger (eds) *Encyclopedia of Language and Education, Vol. 5, Bilingual Education* (pp. 253–263). New York: Springer.
He, A.W. (2008) An identity-based model for the development of Chinese as a heritage language. In A. He and Y. Xiao (eds) *Chinese as a Heritage Language: Fostering Rooted World Citizenry* (pp. 109–124). Honolulu, HI: National Foreign Language Resource Center, University of Hawaii.
He, A.W. (2010) The heart of heritage: Sociocultural dimensions of heritage language acquisition. *Annual Review of Applied Linguistics* 30, 66–82.

He, A.W. (2012) Heritage language socialization. In A. Duranti, E. Ochs and B. Schieffelin (eds) *The Handbook of Language Socialization* (pp. 587–609). Malden, MA: Wiley-Blackwell.
He, A.W. and Xiao, Y. (eds) (2008) *Chinese as a Heritage Language: Fostering Rooted World Citizenry.* Honolulu, HI: National Foreign Language Resource Center.
Hornberger, N.H. (ed.) (2005) Heritage/community language education: US and Australian perspectives. *International Journal of Bilingual Education and Bilingualism* 8 (2&3) [special issue].
Hornberger, N.H. and Wang, S. (2008) Who are our heritage language learners? Identity and biliteracy in heritage language education in the United States. In D. Brinton, O. Kagan and S. Bauckus (eds) *Heritage Language Education: A New Field Emerging* (pp. 3–35). New York: Routledge.
Jedwab, J. (2000) *Ethnic Identification and Heritage Languages in Canada.* Montreal: Université de Montréal and Les Éditions Images.
Jia, L. (2006) The invisible and the visible: Language socialization at the Chinese heritage language school. Unpublished PhD Dissertation, University of Texas at San Antonio.
Jia, L. and Bayley, R. (2009) The (re)acquisition of perfective aspect marking by Chinese heritage language learners. In A. He and Y. Xiao (eds) *Chinese as a Heritage Language: Fostering Rooted World Citizenry* (pp. 205–222). Honolulu, HI: National Foreign Language Resource Center.
Jiang, H. (2010) A socio-historical analysis of Chinese heritage language education in British Columbia. Unpublished MA thesis, University of British Columbia.
Kelleher, A. (2008) Placements and re-positionings: Tensions around CHL learning in a university Mandarin program. In A.W. He and Y. Xiao (eds) *Chinese as a Heritage Language: Fostering Rooted World Citizenry* (pp. 239–258). Honolulu, HI: National Foreign Language Resource Center, University of Hawai'i at Manoa.
Kouritzen, S.G. (1999) *Face[t]s of First Language Loss.* Mahwah, NJ: Lawrence Erlbaum.
Leung, C., Harris, R. and Rampton, B. (1997) The idealized native speaker, reified ethnicities, and classroom realities. *TESOL Quarterly* 31, 543–560.
Li, D. (2005) Attitudes, motivations and identities in learning Chinese as a heritage language. Paper presented at the 14th World Congress of Applied Linguistics, Madison, Wisconsin, August.
Li, D. (2008) Issues in Chinese language curriculum and materials development. In P. Duff and P. Lester (eds) *Issues in Chinese Language Education and Teacher Development* (pp. 49–69). Vancouver: University of British Columbia Centre for Research in Chinese Language and Literacy Education.
Li, D. and Duff, P. (2008) Issues in Chinese heritage language education and research at the postsecondary level. In A.W. He and Y. Xiao (eds) *Chinese as a Heritage Language: Fostering Rooted World Citizenry* (pp. 13–33). Honolulu, HI: National Foreign Language Resource Center, University of Hawai'i at Manoa.
Li, D., Liu, I., Liu, L., Wang, H., Wang, Z. and Xie, Y. (2003) *A Primer for Advanced Beginners of Chinese.* New York: Columbia University Press.
Li, G. (2006) Biliteracy and trilingual practices in the home context: Case studies of Chinese Canadian children. *Journal of Early Childhood Literacy* 6 (3), 359–385.
Li, P.S. (1998) *The Chinese in Canada.* Toronto: Oxford University Press.
Li, W. (1994) *Three Generations, Two Languages, One Family: Language Choice and Language Shift in a Chinese Community in Britain.* Clevedon: Multilingual Matters.
Liu, G-Q. and Lo Bianco, J. (2007) Teaching Chinese, teaching in Chinese, and teaching the Chinese. *Language Policy* 6, 95–117.

Lo Bianco, J. (ed.) (2007) The emergence of Chinese. [Special issue]. *Language Policy* 6 (1).
Maguire, M. and Curdt-Christiansen, X.L. (2007) Multiple schools, languages, experiences and affiliations: Ideological becomings and positionings. *Heritage Language Journal* 5 (1), 50–78.
McDonald, E. (2011) *Learning Chinese, Turning Chinese: Challenges to Becoming Sinophone in a Globalised World.* New York: Routledge.
McGinnis, S. (2005) More than a silver bullet: The role of Chinese as a heritage language in the United States. *Modern Language Journal* 89, 592–594.
McGinnis, S. (2008) From mirror to compass: The Chinese heritage language sector in the United States. In D. Brinton, O. Kagan and S. Bauckus (eds) *Heritage Language Education: A New Field Emerging* (pp. 229–242). Mahwah, NJ: Lawrence Erlbaum.
Montrul, S. (2010) Current issues in heritage language acquisition. *Annual Review of Applied Linguistics* 30, 3–23.
Norton, B. and Toohey, K. (2011) Identity, language learning, and social change. *Language Teaching* 44 (4), 412–446.
Pendakur, R. (1990) *Speaking in Tongues: Heritage Language Maintenance and Transfer in Canada.* Ottawa: Multiculturalism and Citizenship Canada.
Peyton, J., Ranard, D. and McGinnis, S. (eds) (2001) *Heritage Languages in America: Preserving a National Resource.* McHenry, IL: Delta Systems.
Ricento, T. (2005) Problems with the 'language-as-resource' discourse in the promotion of heritage languages in the U.S.A. *Journal of Sociolinguistics* 9 (3), 348–368.
Statistics Canada (2011) Census in brief: Immigrant languages in Canada. Language, census of population, 2011. http://www12.statcan.gc.ca/census-recensement/2011/as-sa/98-314-x/98-314-x2011003_2-eng.pdf
Swain, M. and Deters, P. (2007) 'New' mainstream SLA theory: Expanded and enriched. *The Modern Language Journal* 91 (5), 820–836.
Swain, M. and Lapkin, S. (1991) Heritage language children in an English-French bilingual program. *Canadian Modern Language Review* 47, 635–641.
Swain, M. and Lapkin, S. (2005) The evolving sociopolitical context of immersion education in Canada: Some implications for program development. *International Journal of Applied Linguistics* 15, 169–186.
Tao, H. (ed.) (2006) Chinese as a heritage language. [Special Issue]. *Heritage Language Journal* 4 (1).
Tavares, A. (2000) From heritage to international languages: Globalism and Western Canadian trends in heritage language education. *Canadian Ethnic Studies* 32 (1), 156–172.
Tsung, L. and Cruickshank, K. (eds) (2011) *Learning and Teaching Chinese in Global Contexts: Multimodality and Literacy in the New Media Age.* London: Continuum.
Wang, X. (ed.) (1996) *A View from Within: A Case Study of Chinese Heritage Community Language Schools in the United States.* Washington, DC: National Foreign Language Center.
Wiley, T. and Valdés, G. (2000) Heritage language instruction in the United States: A time for renewal, Editors' introduction. *Bilingual Research Journal* 24 (4), iii–vii.
Wong, K.F. and Xiao, Y. (2010) Diversity and difference: Identity issues of Chinese heritage language learners from dialect backgrounds. *Heritage Language Journal* 7 (2), 153–187.
Xiao, Y. (2009) Teaching Chinese as a heritage language: Keys to success. In M. Everson and Y. Xiao (eds) *Teaching Chinese as a Foreign Language: Theories and Applications* (pp. 175–191). Boston, MA: Cheng & Tsui.

Part 3
Individuals with Disabilities and Second Language Study

7 The Genesis and Perpetuation of Exemptions and Transfers from French Second Language Programs for Students with Diverse Learning Needs: A Preliminary Examination and Their Link to Inclusion

Katy Arnett

The issue of whether/how/when students with diverse learning needs[1] should pursue French second language (FSL) study in Canada has taken on renewed attention in the new millennium, as schools are expected to facilitate and promote more inclusive[2] learning environments than ever before (Hutchinson & Martin, 2012). In its last two annual reports, Canadian Parents for French (2010, 2012) has emphasized the need to develop and promote policies that make FSL study accessible (from both admission and pedagogical standpoints) to students who have diverse needs, including students who are gifted, have a special need or are Allophones.[3] The research community has also started to consider this issue: studies have shown that students with disabilities and other needs are able to develop competencies in FSL programs (e.g. Arnett, 2008; Mady, 2007; Rousseau, 1999). Nonetheless, questions persist about the appropriateness of this language learning context for certain minority student populations (e.g. Fortune & Menke, 2010; Mannavaryan, 2002). Six provinces/ territories currently allow for students with disabilities and other diverse learning needs to be exempted, transferred or otherwise excused from FSL programs or FSL requirements on the basis of a disability, giving FSL a unique status in Canada as the only school subject from which students with disabilities can be excluded (Arnett, 2013a).

While there is evidence of inclusion in some FSL classrooms (e.g. Arnett, 2003, 2010), the goal of this chapter is to explore some of the reasons why FSL programming continues to be plagued by questions about its appropriateness for students with diverse needs and why some jurisdictions have protocols that seem to promote exclusion. In this chronicle, there are three particular strands that deserve attention: the construct of the 'ideal' in language education, the construct of disability/diverse learning needs and the construct of 'inclusion'. The chapter will demonstrate how the genesis of exclusion from FSL was a result of a confluence of events within FSL education and special education, but that its perpetuation may be linked to other factors, including issues of leadership and parents.

FSL Programming and Requirements in Canada

In Canada, only the Anglophone provinces of Ontario and eastward (New Brunswick, Newfoundland & Labrador, Nova Scotia and Prince Edward Island) require students to study FSL for any number of years. British Columbia and Yukon require all students to study a second language, but French is one of many options. Alberta, Saskatchewan, and Manitoba, along with the territories of Northwest Territories, and Nunavut do not have official FSL study requirements. Exemptions from FSL requirements based on a disability are permitted in British Columbia, Ontario, New Brunswick, Newfoundland & Labrador, Prince Edward Island and Yukon. Three of the four FSL program models will be mentioned throughout this chapter: core French, Intensive French (IF) and French immersion. The inter-relationship among these programs also has implications for the question of inclusion within FSL.

Core French is the most popular model for FSL study and has existed since the 1800s (Canadian Parents for French, 2010; Carr, 2007). In a core French program, French is studied as another subject in the student's day, just like music, math or history. Core French can begin as early as Grade 1, though most programs begin in Grade 4 as a result of the recommendations of the National Core French Study (NCFS) (LeBlanc, 1990). Classes meet for 20 to 90 minutes, three to five times a week (Carr, 2007).

In some parts of Canada, core French programs are being replaced by IF, which begins in Grade 5 or 6. For half of the year (usually at the start of the year), the students exclusively focus on French, following a literacy-based approach that emphasizes the development of strong speaking and listening skills (Netten & Germain, 2004). In subsequent years, students complete the 'Post-Intensive' program that resembles the timetable of core French, but still draws on the principles of literacy-based instruction (Netten & Germain, 2004).

French immersion programs are available across Canada, though entry points for the programs vary from one province/territory to the next. Though the FSL requirements can be fulfilled through French immersion, the program is generally regarded as an 'enrichment option' for FSL study (Mady & Arnett, 2009). According to the most recent and available data, French immersion enrolments are on the increase in Canada, largely at the expense of declining enrolments in core French (Canadian Parents for French, 2010).

Most of the research on the issue of inclusion in FSL programming has focused on the immersion context above all others (see Mannavaryan, 2002, for a review). The notion of 'transfers' out of immersion and subsequently, 'exemptions' from requisite FSL study for students with atypical needs can be traced to studies in the mid-1970s, which suggested that students with language-based learning difficulties in French immersion may benefit more from moving to the English program (Trites, 1976; Trites & Price, 1976, 1977). The documented practice of transferring students out of French immersion when a student has been identified with a learning difficulty (e.g. Mady & Arnett, 2009) has a direct influence on the other FSL programs in the school, particularly in jurisdictions where FSL study remains a requirement. In some circumstances, there is a disproportionate number of students with atypical needs in non-immersion classrooms (Rushowy, 2009). For example, in the core French class featured in the case study of Arnett (2003), 17 of the 27 students had some special education need, behavioral challenge or a language-related challenge. Thus, across the FSL program portfolio, there can be great unevenness in the numbers of students with atypical needs.

The construct of the 'ideal' in relation to language education and development

At various points throughout the development of an understanding of language competency, of second language education and of learner needs, the notion of an 'ideal' is found repeatedly. It is argued that several of these moments have coalesced to create and, to some degree, perpetuate exclusion, while one of the moments may mark the recognition of the role of FSL instruction in inclusion.

According to Chin and Wigglesworth (2007), the first noted definition of a bilingual individual appeared in the 1930s, when Bloomfield (1933: 55) described someone who had 'native-like control of two languages'. Though alternate definitions appeared in the 1950s, Mackey's (1962: 52) suggestion that an individual was bilingual when he/she could 'use more than one language' created the dichotomous view of what constitutes bilingual proficiency that is still debated today (Chin & Wigglesworth, 2007). At their core, the conceptions of bilingualism that prevailed in the era when French immersion was developed were not just concerned with 'how much' language one needed to know, but 'how well' it needed to be known (Chin & Wigglesworth, 2007). An individual was believed to be an 'ideal bilingual' when he/she was able to perfectly use two languages within a variety of contexts. This ideal became attached to the goals of French immersion (Lambert & Tucker, 1972).

Within the same decade as the expansion of 'bilingualism', scholars in first language linguistics were confronting the implications of Bernstein's (1964) assertion that deficient language skills in the children of working-class parents were responsible for their lack of success in school and Labov's (1969) response disproving it. The Deficit Hypothesis was congruent with other discussions that were happening in the era, in that there was again an emphasis on the idea of an 'ideal' way of speaking English and those who did not speak it were somehow inferior. This may have helped to reinforce views of what it meant to be an 'ideal bilingual'.

When French immersion was launched in 1965 with the St Lambert experiment, the notions of an 'ideal' were not a part of the student profile (Lambert & Tucker, 1972). The notion of an 'ideal' arrived in 1976, when Trites published the results of a study of struggling students in French immersion. Trites (1976) suggested that students be screened for challenges with auditory processing prior to entry into immersion, and promoted the transfer of struggling students out of immersion. Further, the study revealed that teachers 'were not willing to deal with the wide range of learning abilities within the context of the immersion program; students who were considered less bright or of low socioeconomic status were sometimes discouraged from entering the program or recommended for transfer out of the program' (Fortune & Menke, 2010: 8). This coincides with the ideas presented in the aforementioned Deficit Hypothesis from the era. More recently, Demers' (1994) publication of the characteristics of 'successful' and 'unsuccessful' immersion students seemed to promote the idea of some students being 'better suited' for immersion, as a way to help inform possible decisions about transfers out of immersion.

The notion of the 'ideal' has also been a part of the more populous program of core French; the NCFS (LeBlanc, 1990) was most concerned with the 'ideal' way to teach French in that context. Particularly inspired by the criticisms (Stern, 1976), one of the goals of the NCFS was to understand the ways in which core French was being taught. LeBlanc (1990) found that there were uneven conceptualizations of 'communicative language teaching', which led to instructional delivery models that were not really emblematic of communicative teaching. Much of the observed instruction was found to be decontextualized examinations of certain aspects of language, showing little relevance to students' lives and interests (LeBlanc, 1990). By acknowledging the role of FSL teaching methodology as the reasons for poor learning outcomes in the students – and not the students themselves – the NCFS marked an important shift in thinking about FSL study. Success in FSL was not just about the students in the classes (which was an idea from immersion), but the way in which French was being taught. This aligns well with the ideas of 'inclusive teaching'.

The construct of disability and diverse learning needs

Since for nearly as long as can be chronicled, it has been presumed that individuals with a disability have a permanent 'flaw' or 'deficit' that prevents them from being normal; much is denoted by the word 'disability' (Valle & Connor, 2011). Though supports have long existed to help the individual access aspects of life (i.e. the use of canes/crutches and eyeglasses), it has also been the case that individuals who are different have been removed from society/situations (Winzer, 1993). Thus, there is a strong historical precedent to remove/exclude individuals who do not align with the majority; the suggestion by Trites and Price (1976, 1977) to transfer struggling students out of French immersion was highly consistent with practices and beliefs about how best to respond to someone whose needs were different from the larger community. The subsequent advent of exemptions in core French at this time was also consistent with thoughts and practices on how to address diverse learning needs ('Fabrice',[4] personal communication).

In 1963, two years prior to the launch of the St Lambert experiment,[5] the term 'learning disabilities' entered the education lexicon (Lerner, 2006). At that time, the interest in streaming students based on ability led researchers to consider those students whose achievement (i.e. grades) did not align with their potential (as determined by IQ scores). To the researchers then, it did not make sense that a student with a good IQ would struggle in school. As they were defined at the time, learning disabilities were associated with a 'minimal brain dysfunction' that always had a negative influence on how a person perceived, processed and/or expressed language (Lerner, 2006). This perspective likely explains the approach of Trites and Price (1976, 1977) in their research, in that some of their data collection methods attempted to identify neurological differences in struggling students through both brain scans and IQ tests. Though criticized for their methods (e.g. Cummins, 1983), their work at the time was consonant with the presumptions about learning disabilities.

Many of those initial ideas remain in current definitions of learning disabilities, and there is still much debate about this largest category of special education need (Hutchinson, 2012). The lack of a definitive sense of 'learning disability' may explain some of the continued practices of exemptions and transfers from FSL programs in Canada. Because each province and territory in Canada sets its own policies for the identification and diagnosis of a learning disability (Kozey & Siegel, 2008), it would be reasonable to argue that those definitions could influence views on inclusion in FSL, particularly when it comes to exemptions. For example, Kozey and Siegel (2008) found that eight provinces in Canada continued to be influenced by the increasingly unpopular IQ-achievement discrepancy to define and/or diagnose a learning disability, and five of those provinces, at the time, allowed for exemptions from FSL based on a learning disability (British Columbia, New Brunswick, Newfoundland & Labrador, Nova Scotia and Ontario). Thus, it could be that the province or territory's views of learning disabilities influence ideas about exclusion from FSL, rather than understandings of second language learning. This should be explored further.

The construct of inclusion

Within Canadian education, the principle and practice of inclusion has existed in various forms since the 1980s (Arnett, 2013b). Though definitions vary across the country, inclusion is typically conceptualized to emphasize the right and need for all students to have access and acceptance in an educational environment (Hutchinson & Martin, 2012). In some cases, the notion of 'benefit' from the setting is also directly emphasized, but there are also instances in which the notion is an implied part of the definition. (Arnett, 2013b). In other words, inclusion is about making sure that students are able to gain entry into the learning environment (access), and once there, that they have a right to have their learning needs met in a way that is best for them (benefit). Inclusion is generally regarded as a contentious element of modern education, in that questions are regularly raised about its success, influence on students, funding demands, time demands for teachers and implementation (Arnett, 2013b).

For FSL, the question of access to its programs has been a concern of the advocacy group, Canadian Parents for French, for several years (e.g. Canadian Parents for French, 2010, 2012; Demers, 1994). They commissioned a recent review by Mady et al. (2010) to determine the extent to which provincial and territorial policies protect and ensure access to FSL programs for students with atypical learning needs. Mady et al. (2010) found that only 2 of the 13 provinces and territories (Manitoba and Nova Scotia) have policies that explicitly provide for support for gifted students and students with academic challenges in FSL. One province (New Brunswick) has a specific policy that permits students with academic challenges to be admitted into FSL programs, while the province of British Columbia has a policy that is actually the contrary. The absence of official policies concerning the admission of students to FSL and the provision of support – even though there may be legal protections for students with disabilities in schools – may be a reason for the continued practice of exemptions/transfers. In some cases, it is the absence of a policy that permits the continuation of a practice.

The notion of 'benefit' in relation to inclusion is best understood through the implications of the *Emily Eaton* v. *Brant County Board of Education* Supreme Court Decision of 1998. The decision maintained that there was no legal basis for presuming that inclusion was best achieved by placing the student in the general education classroom, but rather that inclusion was achieved by placing the student in the learning setting that was in his/her best interests (aka 'of benefit') (Van Nuland, 2011). In other words, access (entry) to the same classroom as other students may not be preferable for all students and could preclude them from benefiting from the classroom in a way that was consistent with their needs. It could be the case that exemptions/transfers from FSL are being viewed as compliant with the findings of the *Emily Eaton* case, in that their use acknowledges that FSL may not be the best environment for all students. However, if such logic has been applied for those policies that do exist, it is immediately flawed because exemptions/transfers do not exist in other subject areas.

Finally, the notion of 'benefit' in inclusion has also been presented in relation to two paradigms: social benefit (interpersonal skills for students) and academic benefit (what students learn) (Arnett, 2013b). For such benefits to be achieved for students with atypical needs, teachers are expected to provide supports (sometimes referred to as accommodations or adaptations) to help the student understand, express his/her understanding about the concept and/or engage in particular behaviors. Such strategies have been shown to be consistent with conceptualizations of good FSL instruction, particularly in the context of core French (Arnett, 2003).

Inclusion within FSL: Perspectives from Four FSL Stakeholders

A total of four semi-structured interviews (each lasting 45–90 minutes) were conducted as part of this inquiry to gain insight into some current and longitudinal views about exemptions and transfers. To a degree, I had worked with all four of the stakeholders in previous projects, which may explain their willingness to discuss ideas that have been previously documented as difficult to explore (e.g. Monhindra, 2001); all responded to email requests I sent to be interviewed. Pseudonyms and changes to identifying details are used to protect the anonymity of the sources.

Participant 1 is Jean, who works in Nova Scotia, the only province in the past decade that eliminated exemptions from FSL study. He has spent his over 30-year career in FSL, as both a teacher and as an administrator and was implicated in the end of the exemption policies there. Participant 2, Fabrice, has also been involved in FSL for over 30 years and currently works in a central office position supporting FSL teachers in Ontario; he was also a classroom teacher and administrator. Participants 3 and 4, Emmanuelle and Josette, are both current classroom teachers. Emmanuelle is in her ninth year of teaching and is a Grade 7 French immersion teacher in Newfoundland & Labrador. She has taught at other levels of FSL previously and is currently pursuing graduate work. Josette is in her fourth year of teaching, entering FSL teaching as a career change. She works in the Catholic system in Ontario, teaching core French at the elementary level. Both Fabrice and Josette have sons with learning disabilities who studied French.

Three of the four interviews were conducted over the telephone and two were audio recorded to facilitate transcription. The third telephone interview, at the request of the participant, was not audio recorded. During the interview, I took notes, which were then reviewed by the participant. The fourth interview occurred over Skype, which was video recorded. Transcripts were created to facilitate analysis; these were analyzed following the principles of comparative analysis (Glaser & Strauss, 1967). Several themes emerged in the analysis, including 'leadership', 'parents', 'communication', 'previous practice' and 'resources'. Though all themes are in need of additional development in the research literature on inclusion in FSL, this section will focus on ideas emerging from the themes of 'leadership' and 'parents' that point to additional reasons for the perpetuation of exemptions and transfers.

Leadership

Previous work focusing on the inclusion of students with disabilities in the general education classroom has confirmed the influence of leadership views on inclusive practice (e.g. Stanovich & Jordan, 1998). From this small case study, it appears that the same holds true when French is the subject in question. In the case of all of our participants, school leadership at various levels – Minister of Education, school principal and/or department head – played a role in questions about whether students with atypical learning needs should remain in FSL.

Jean reported that the impetus for phasing out the exemptions from the core French requirement grew from the alignment of several factors: a Minister of Education who felt it unreasonable for students to be exempt from a requirement, the advent of a new Action Plan for education in the Nova Scotia province and the adoption of IF as a program. The minister 'wanted the policy gone', and because of changes already in motion due to the new Action Plan, it was easier to implement this gradual change. Recognizing the cultural shift that the end of the exemption policy would inspire, the province included in its plan a protocol for not only adding to teachers' understanding of the new teaching model, but also about facilitating inclusive teaching within the FSL classroom. Using a 'trainer of trainers' like-model, 'key school personnel were brought on board' to help the leaders develop the expertise that they could then take back to their schools and share with colleagues. Thus, leadership at multiple levels was involved in the change.

Emmanuelle acknowledged during the interview that she was 'one of five' in a school of 'over fifty' teachers who seemed to hold the belief that students with disabilities can/should remain in French immersion; she was acutely aware of her minority view. To a degree, she believed that her minority view may be why she was 'cut off from the conversation' about whether a struggling student should remain in her class; both her department head and the school principal were in favor of the student transferring out of the French immersion class after two months of study. Emmanuelle reported that conversations between herself and her principal and department head about her interest in working to support the student, and 'doing whatever it took to help her, um, do well in French', were met with responses indicating that her efforts would be for naught. In this particular instance then, it seems that even when a teacher is interested in supporting and including a student in French immersion, leadership can stop it.

Josette reported that at her school, 'the exemption policy is not at the forefront of my school's, my principal's thoughts. In speaking with my principal about this with my AQ [additional qualification] course, my principal said that it would be a rare occurrence for a child to be exempt at the elementary school level'. When prompted further, Josette indicated that she understood the principal's position to be one that left the entire decision with the parents, noting that 'it [an exemption] would only occur if the parents insisted on it'. In this case, while there is not any evidence that the principal personally believes that students with atypical learning needs can/should be included in core French, it seems that parental views could hold more sway in some schools than in others.

In summary, the comments from these stakeholders reveal, somewhat not surprisingly, differences in the role of leaders in shaping inclusion within FSL; some insist upon its practice, others may go against it, even if the teacher is in favor of it, and others may leave the decision up to the parents. As Wise (2010) noted, these differences in views have implications for funding related to the support of included students in FSL, particularly French immersion. The recent work of the Canadian Parents for French (2012) has argued that this unevenness is problematic for ensuring equitable access to FSL and again underlines the need for official policies to be developed.

Parents

Fabrice, Emmanuelle and Josette all confirmed in their interviews that French immersion has the perception of being promoted and protected for the academic elite in a school setting; most of the literature that has critiqued the original Trites and Price (1976, 1977) research on French immersion, in general, has also touched on this theme of elitism (e.g. Wise, 2010). Emmanuelle suggested that parents may also play a role in this mindset:

> I find that parents are uh, they think, uh, because their child is, uh, because their child is in French immersion, their child is academically strong, and that they need to be in this program because they don't want them in the English stream...I don't know. It's really weird. There is this negative attitude um, as of late, like parents see that putting their child in French immersion will eliminate them from being in a class with other children who might have behavioural disorders, learning disabilities, um, what have you, so they want them to be segregated from that, so they put them in French immersion.

Emmanuelle's comments point to parents' growing interest in class paths that 'protect' their children from classroom contexts in which the teacher may be challenged by a wider range of needs – in other words, an 'inclusive classroom'. While she does not mention why parents hold this belief, it could be evidence of how the legacy of exclusions and transfers has come to shape popular thinking about FSL instruction and inclusion; here, one FSL program is being used to avoid another kind of FSL program because of parent fears of student differences.

As mentioned previously, both Fabrice and Josette had experiences as parents of children with learning difficulties pursuing FSL study. The comments they shared about their own experiences as parents confronting the exemption/transfer questions provide some additional insight into reasons why FSL has an uneven record with inclusion. First, Josette was in favor of her Grade 8 son (who has learning disabilities and ADHD) being exempted from the Grade 9 core French requirement because she was 'afraid that he's going to be in a class with someone who doesn't believe he should be there. If I knew that he would have the same kind of experience he's having this year – and I knew he would tell me that if Mme. X was teaching it next year, he'd do French – I'd do it. It's not a risk we're willing to take'. At other points in the interview, she made mention of her experiences working with others within FSL who had expressed 'strong objections to students like my son taking French. As a mother, I just found that horrible. As someone who works with them, I found it horrible. Even though there are a lot of people who want all of the kids in the class, it's not everywhere'. As was found in Mady and Arnett (2009), parents' decision to go along with an exemption is sometimes made to protect the student from individuals who do not have favorable views of inclusion within FSL; thus, exemptions are perpetuated because of fears about teachers who may still favor them.

On the other hand, Fabrice's son, who was identified as being gifted and having learning disabilities, remained in core French all the way through Grade 12 because he really wanted to study it. The progression was not always smooth though and was made particularly challenging because Fabrice was Department Head in French at the time Pierre was a student. Fabrice recounts,

> He almost dropped French from this teacher because there were no accommodations made for him, really, because she thought it was like cheating. Because he can't memorize, and things have to be in context and whatnot for him to learn, so she just didn't do it. And I couldn't get involved. It all came through the SERT [Special Education Research

Teacher], but what I did do as a result of that was realize, that as a department, we needed to work on that and make it a concerted effort to accommodate. And so we worked on it together. What did happen when Pierre was in Grade 11 was that his teacher actually had learning disabilities and understood totally and was able to accommodate for him. His marks jumped.

Fabrice's example represents a somewhat extreme case, in that the position of leadership that he/she held at the time trumped the role of a parent wanting to advocate for one's child. However, being a parent of a child with an atypical learning need, it influenced what happened from the leadership post following the experience, in regard to supporting students with special needs. While it was mentioned in the interview that Fabrice's colleagues never learned about the challenges facing his son, it does provide another illustrative example of how leadership influences the experience of students with atypical needs. The example also points to lack of teacher knowledge and the influence of teacher beliefs, themes that have been explored in other literature (e.g. Arnett, 2010).

In summary, the interview data shared in this section point to the influences of leadership and parents on the end and/or perpetuation of exemptions and transfer policies. It would be useful to pursue a larger research project that incorporates interviews with more stakeholders.

Conclusion

Within Canada, FSL education and issues implicating special education are highly sensitive in many jurisdictions, and bringing them together for research can be particularly challenging. This chapter aimed to show how certain contextual factors conspired to lead to the ideas of exemptions and transfers from FSL in the first place, and offers some preliminary reasons for why the practices continue, in order to, perhaps, more actively question their benefit to FSL. School boards and provincial/territorial bodies need to be more open to research that examines exemptions and transfers (or even students who never get to study French because of a disability) and inclusion within FSL. Researchers and other stakeholders also need to more vigorously pursue projects that chronicle and examine the experiences of students with disabilities in FSL; the other two studies in this section are an excellent start. Within FSL, many are concerned with the general public's common ascription of elitism and irrelevance to discussions of its programs. Promoting more research into this issue could help respond to this concern, enabling more focus on ways to make FSL open and valuable to all.

Notes

(1) Throughout this chapter, a variety of terms will be used to describe students whose learning needs are less common in a classroom. Though most of the 'atypical learning needs' presented in this chapter are linked to 'learning disabilities', the use of the varying terms aims to capture the various ways in which learner differences are currently being conceptualized.
(2) The construct of 'inclusion' and 'inclusive teaching' will be defined in a later part of this chapter.
(3) Allophones are students who are adding both English and French to their linguistic portfolios.
(4) 'Fabrice' is one of the participants of this study.
(5) Within Canada, the 'St Lambert experiment' was the term used to describe the research project that chronicled and assessed the potential of French immersion. The first French immersion program was held in St Lambert, Quebec (Lambert & Tucker, 1972).

References

Arnett, K. (2003) Teacher adaptations in core French: A case study of one Grade 9 class. *The Canadian Modern Language Review* 60 (2), 173–198.
Arnett, K. (2008) Exploring the use of student perspectives to inform topics in teacher education: Issues in creating an inclusive core French classroom. *Canadian Journal of Applied Linguistics* 11 (1), 63–81.
Arnett, K. (2010) Scaffolding inclusion in a Grade 8 core French classroom: An exploratory case study. *The Canadian Modern Language Review* 66 (4), 603–628.
Arnett, K. (2013a) French second language exemptions: Should students with learning disabilities be excused from French class? *Education Canada* 53 (2). http://www.cea-ace.ca/fr/education-canada/article/french-second-language-exemptions
Arnett, K. (2013b) The philosophies, politics, and practice of inclusion: Pathways for facilitating reflection and dialogue in the school community. *The CAP Journal,* 20, (4),12-17.
Bernstein, B. (1964) Elaborated and restricted codes: Their social origins and some consequences. *American Anthropologist* 66 (6), 55–69.
Bloomfield, L. (1933) *Language.* New York: Holt, Reinhart, & Wilson.
Canadian Parents for French (2010) *The State of French-Second-Language Education in Canada 2010 Executive Summary.* Ottawa: Canadian Parents for French.
Canadian Parents for French (2012) *The State of French-Second-Language Education in Canada 2012 Executive Summary: Academically Challenged Students and French Second Language Programs.* Ottawa: Canadian Parents for French.
Carr, W. (2007) *Teaching Core French in British Columbia: Teachers' perspectives.* BCATML/BCTF Research Report, accessed 12 January 2013. www.bcatml.org/CFinBC2007.pdf
Chin, N.B. and Wigglesworth, G. (2007) *Bilingualism: An Advanced Resource Book.* New York: Routledge.
Cummins, J. (1983) *Bilingualism and Special Education: Issues in Assessment and Pedagogy.* Clevedon: Multilingual Matters.
Demers, D. (1994) *Learning Disabilities and Cross-Linguistic Interference in French Immersion: When to Transfer, When Not to Transfer.* Manitoba: Learning Disabilities Association of Manitoba.

Fortune, T.W. and Menke, M.R. (2010) *Struggling Learners and Language Immersion Education: Research-Based, Practitioner-Informed Responses' to Educators' Top Questions.* Minneapolis, MI: University of Minnesota, The Center for Advanced Research on Language Acquisition.

Genesee, F. (2007) French immersion and at-risk students: A review of research evidence. *The Canadian Modern Language Review* 63 (5), 655–687.

Glaser, B.G. and Strauss, A.L. (1967) *The Discovery of Grounded Theory: Strategies for Qualitative Research.* Chicago, IL: Aldine Publishing Company.

Hutchinson, N. and Martin, A. (2012) *Inclusive Classrooms in Ontario Schools.* Toronto: Pearson Education Canada.

Kozey, M. and Siegel, L. (2008) Definitions of learning disabilities in Canadian provinces and territories. *Canadian Psychology* 49 (2), 162–171.

Labov, W. (1969) The logic of non-standard English. *Georgetown Monographs on Language and Linguistics* 22, 1–31.

Lambert, W.E. and Tucker, G.R. (1972) *Bilingual Education of Children: The St. Lambert Experiment.* Rowley, MA: Newbury House Publishers.

LeBlanc, R. (1990) *The National Core French Study: A Synthesis.* Ottawa: The Canadian Association of Second Language Teachers.

Lerner, J. (2006) *Learning Disabilities and Related Disorders: Characteristics and Teaching Strategies* (10th edn). Boston, MA: Houghton Mifflin.

Mackey, W. (1962) The description of bilingualism. *The Canadian Journal of Linguistics* 7 (5), 51–85.

Mady, C. (2007) The suitability of core French for recently arrived adolescent immigrants to Canada. *Canadian Journal of Applied Linguistics* 10 (2), 177–196.

Mady, C. and Arnett, K. (2009) Inclusion in French immersion in Canada: One parent's perspective. *Exceptionality Education International* 19 (2), 37–49.

Mady, C., Black, G. and Fulton, K. (2010) *Review of Ministry Education Policies Affecting Equitable Access to FSL Programs.* Ottawa: Canadian Parents for French.

Mannavarayan, J.M. (2002) *The French Immersion Debate: French for All or All for French?* Calgary: Detselig Enterprises.

Mohindra, A. (2001) Student exemptions from elementary core French programs in Ontario. Unpublished Master's research paper, The Ontario Institute for Studies in Education of the University of Toronto.

Netten, J. and Germain, C. (2004) Theoretical and research foundations of Intensive French. *The Canadian Modern Language Review* 60 (3), 275–294.

Rousseau, N. (1999). A French immersion disabilities program: Perspectives from students, their parents, and their teachers. *Mosaic* 6, 16–26.

Rushowy, K. (2009, March). French immersion debate: Oakville parents claim French immersion bias, accessed 13 January 2013 http://www.parentcentral.ca/parent/article/606543

Stanovich, P. and Jordan, A. (1998) Canadian teachers' and principals' beliefs about inclusive education as predictors of effective teaching in heterogeneous classrooms. *Elementary School Journal* 98, 221–238.

Stern, D. (1976) The Ottawa-Carleton French project: Issues, conclusions, and policy implications. *The Canadian Modern Language Review* 33 (2), 216–243.

Trites, R.L. (1976) Children with learning difficulties in primary French immersion. *The Canadian Modern Language Review* 33 (2), 193–207.

Trites, R.L. and Price, M.A. (1976) *Learning Disabilities Found in Association with French Immersion Programming.* Ottawa: University of Ottawa Press.

Trites, R.L. and Price, M.A. (1977) *Learning Disabilities Found in Association with French Immersion Programming: A Cross-Validation*. Ottawa: University of Ottawa Press.
Valle, J.W. and Connor, D.J. (2011) *Rethinking Disability: A Disability Studies Approach to Inclusive Practices*. New York: McGraw Hill.
Van Nuland, S. (2011) Ten Supreme Court cases that have an impact on teachers. In R.C. Flynn (ed.) *Rights and Reason: Shifting Tides in Law & Education, Proceedings of the Twenty-Second Annual Conference of the Canadian Association for the Practical Study of Law in Education* (pp. 345–378). Toronto: CAPSLE.
Winzer, M.A. (1993) *The History of Special Education: From Isolation to Integration*. Washington, DC: Galludet University Press.
Wise, N. (2010) Access to special education for exceptional students in French immersion: An equity issue. *The Canadian Journal of Applied Linguistics* 14 (1), 177–193.

8 Reading Without Borders: At-Risk Students Transitioning from L1 to L2 in French Immersion

Renée Bourgoin and Joseph Dicks

French immersion (FI) programs are an integral part of Canada's education landscape. The pedagogical underpinnings of this second language approach focus on learning the language, learning about the language and learning through the language. Students learn literacy and content areas such as mathematics, sciences and social sciences using the second language as the medium of instruction. Supported by over 40 years of research, FI is a viable and popular option for many students, including the 300,000 who are currently enrolled in the program (Canadian Parents for French, 2006). And, with this increase in popularity, many FI programs are populated by a wide range of learners, including students at risk for learning difficulties. According to Genesee (2007: 656), 'at-risk' students are those who have 'language, literacy, and academic difficulties or who are likely to experience such difficulties, whether they stem from what might be considered clinical factors (reading disability or language impairment) or from non-clinical factors (generally low levels of academic ability)'.

Studies examining the suitability of FI for academically at-risk students, although limited, have consistently shown that at-risk students are at no greater disadvantage when enrolled in FI, both with respect to their English language development and their overall academic achievement (Bruck, 1982; Cummins, 1983; Genesee, 1992, 2007; Genesee et al., 2004). Unfortunately, many young students either choose not to enter FI or they exit the program because of academic difficulty related primarily to literacy (Bournot-Trites, 2008; Keep, 1993). Reading difficulties, in particular, seem to be major contributors to the success of FI students. As they progress from one year to the other, students are expected to read increasingly complex content in French. Academic success can be jeopardized if French reading skills are inadequate.

The early identification of students who may be at risk for reading difficulties is crucial to providing remedial help as quickly as possible (Bournot-Trites, 2008). However, difficulties can arise when attempting to identify students in second language contexts. In some cases, waiting to diagnose students until they attain a certain level of proficiency in their second language leads to under-diagnosis. However, identifying students too quickly can lead to over-diagnosis (Geva, 2006; Wise & Chan, 2009). Because languages do not develop in isolation from one another, it has been recommended whenever possible 'to collect information about the children's competence in both languages' (Genesee et al., 2004: 211).

This study seeks to examine FI students' experiences with reading acquisition with regard to development in their first language and in French. In particular, it seeks to create a deeper understanding of the differences between at-risk and high-performing beginning second language readers by examining the range of strategies employed by learners at different levels of ability (Anderson, 1991; Chamot & El-Dinary, 1999; Chamot & O'Malley, 1994; Cornaire, 1991; Macaro, 2001).

Literature Review

The act of reading entails the construction and reconstruction of meaning from print, message getting and problem solving. It is a complex task requiring both automatic and conscious mental activity including the use of multiple processes and strategies (Alderson, 2000; Clay, 1991). Strategies are methods, actions, steps, operations and/or techniques organized and integrated within a learner's long-term memory (Van Grunderbeeck, 1994). They are employed by the learner to obtain, comprehend, learn, retain, retrieve and use information (Chamot, 2005; Chamot & El-Dinary, 1990; Cornaire, 1991; Grabe, 2009; Oxford, 1990; Rubin, 1987; Wenden, 1987).

Orchestration of reading strategies

Proficient readers understand the purpose of the reading task and the options available to them, and they are able to adjust to different reading purposes and to changing conditions. They understand that the effectiveness of strategies is dependent on the particular reading situation and they are able to apply strategies to a new situation and know why they are doing so (Koda, 2005; Paris et al., 1994). They effectively consolidate their understanding of the reading process because they have strategic control over the reading task (Clay, 1991). When encountering a problem, they draw upon their strategies in an integrated way and use them appropriately in combination with one another instead of over relying on isolated strategies (Pinnell & Scharer, 1987; Van Grunderbeeck, 1994).

Metacognitive strategies

Having strategic control over the reading task is referred to as metacognition (Grabe, 2009). Metacognition is responsible for such processes as self-monitoring, predicting, verifying and coordinating other cognitive processes (Saint-Laurent et al., 1995). Related *meta* concepts include metacognitive knowledge, metacognitive experience (Garner, 1994) and metalinguistic awareness (Bialystok, 2001). By using metacognition, strategic readers know why they read and continue to do so throughout the reading as they resolve difficulties, reflect, evaluate and integrate information in various ways (Grabe, 2009). Poor readers lack or have inadequate metacognitive strategies. They also have a harder time adapting their strategies to the reading task because their use of strategies is not as flexible as they are for strong, strategic readers (Geva & Clifton, 1994; Saint-Laurent et al., 1995).

Second language reading research

Reading research conducted in second language contexts has found that, similarly to first language research, being strategic plays an important role in second language reading (Koda, 2005). Strong second language readers use metacognitive strategies to plan for and monitor their comprehension of texts (Chamot & O'Malley, 1994), understand how to use appropriate strategies when difficulties arise (Anderson, 1991; Cornaire, 1991) and effectively use a combination of strategies (Macaro, 2001). This accentuates second language reading development because 'prior literacy-learning experience fosters an explicit understanding of what is to be accomplished in the task, and this, in turn, may expedite the process by allowing learners to be more reflective and strategic' (Koda, 2008: 74). The literature on linguistic transfer suggests that bilingual students who read strategically in one language also do so in their other language (August & Shanahan, 2006; Geva & Clifton, 1994). More specifically, readers who use good meaning-making strategies in one language transfer these strategies to other languages (Genesse et al., 2006). Transfer is possible in these cases because these strategies are metacognitive, and thus transfer across languages (Durgunoglu, 2002; van Gelderen et al., 2003).

Method

Context

This study took place in a FI program that begins in Grade 3. Students receive their instruction in English starting in Kindergarten until the end of Grade 2, at which point, they can choose to enroll in FI or continue in English. This unique context provided an opportunity to explore students' French reading development with the understanding that they were entering the second language program having had three years of formal English reading instruction. Two questions were central to this study: (1) what can be learned from exploring at-risk and high-performing students' first and second language reading development? and (2) what can be learned from examining at-risk and high-performing students' knowledge of and use of reading strategies in their second language?

Participants

This study involved Grade 3 FI students from two urban elementary schools who were participating in a larger research project.[1] From that larger-scale research, four typical at-risk readers and four typical high-performing readers (as noted by their scores on previous literacy assessments) were randomly selected to provide preliminary insights into differences that would be followed up with a larger sample to determine trends. All eight students selected for this study came from English first language backgrounds.

Procedures and measures

Using an ethnographic case study approach, data were collected over a two-year period. Students individually met with the researchers twice in Grade 2 while they were still in the English program and four times in Grade 3, once they had enrolled in FI. During each of these sessions, students completed a number of reading tasks. Some tasks were designed to assess students' performance on reading measures (Dynamic Indicators of Basic Early Literacy Skills [DIBELS] and Indicateurs dynamiques d'habiletés précoces en lecture [IDAPEL]) while others assessed students' knowledge of and perceived use of reading strategies (interview/think-aloud protocol).

Assessing early reading skills

In Grade 2 English, prior to enrolling in the FI program, students were administered the DIBELS (Good et al., 2004), a set a norm-referenced, standardized English reading assessments. For the purposes of this study, the sub-tests related to fluency and comprehension were used. As a timed task, students read as much of a reading passage within the one-minute allotted time and, subsequently, were asked to do an oral summary of what was read within this time frame. The task was repeated three times using different reading passages. These measures were administered twice in Grade 2: at the mid-year point and, again, at the end of the year. Similar measures using a French version of DIBELS – the IDAPEL – were administered three times (November, March and June) in Grade 3, once students started the FI program.

Reading passage and think-aloud protocol
In Grade 3, a think-aloud task was administered four times throughout the year in September, November, March and June. Each time, two French reading passages were selected to determine each child's approximate reading level (Fountas & Pinnell, 2001). Students were asked to read the stories and do an oral summary of the passages. Using this reading task as a base point, students were then asked to participate in a think-aloud protocol loosely based on the one designed by Graham *et al*. (1993). Although initially designed to assess students' knowledge of writing, the questions were redesigned to access students' knowledge of reading and their perceived use of reading strategies. Further modifications were made to account for students' age and development. Follow-up questions were used to elicit clarification, gain additional information or provide students with the opportunity to expand upon their answers. Think-aloud interviews were also audio-recorded and transcribed.

Data Analysis

The Grade 2 data obtained from the English fluency and comprehension measures, along with teacher-administered reading assessments, were used to identify high-performing readers and students who were at-risk for reading difficulties in their first language. In cases where there were inconsistencies between students' fluency scores and comprehension scores, DIBELS oral retell measures were examined further. English fluency data were analyzed by comparing them to the Grade 3 end-of-year French IDAPEL fluency measures. This analysis was useful in exploring students' reading profiles and students' reading development in both languages.

Think-aloud interviews were transcribed and analyzed. This involved the identification of 'units of analysis' representing occurrences when the student mentioned and or described strategies and their use. Once identified, 'units of analysis' were coded, categorized and sub-categorized in terms of type and number using a slightly modified version of Oxford's (1990) second language learning strategies schemata. A rubric was developed to code students' answers into one or more of the five different types of second language reading strategies: cognitive strategies, memory strategies, metacognitive strategies, compensation strategies and socio-affective strategies. A deeper analysis was conducted by further sub-categorizing these five types of strategies: cognitive (i.e. practicing, receiving and retrieving messages, analyzing and reasoning, creating structure for input and output); memory (i.e. creating mental links, applying images and sound, employing actions); metacognitive (i.e. centering, arranging and planning, evaluating); compensation (i.e. guessing intelligently, substituting); and socio-affective (i.e. social strategies, affective strategies).

Results

Fluency data from the end-of-year Grade 2 DIBELS revealed important differences among individual students. Allan, Lillian, Owain and Luke, for example, each read under 90 English words during the 1-minute timed task, placing them in the 'at-risk' category for this norm-referenced measure. At the other end of the spectrum, Marcelle, Heidi, Gwen and Jessa exceeded expectations by scoring above 125 words a minute (see Figure 8.1). These baseline data were helpful in identifying at-risk students because this oral reading fluency measure is effective in determining the reading competencies of children in the lower elementary grades (Good *et al.*, 2004). Moreover,

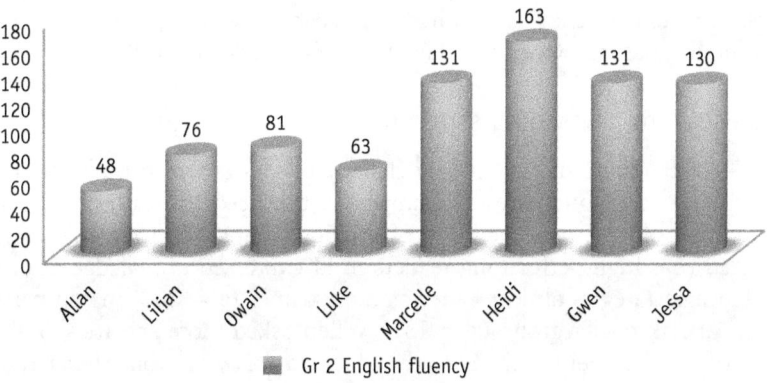

Figure 8.1 End-of-year Grade 2 English fluency scores of at-risk students and high-performing students

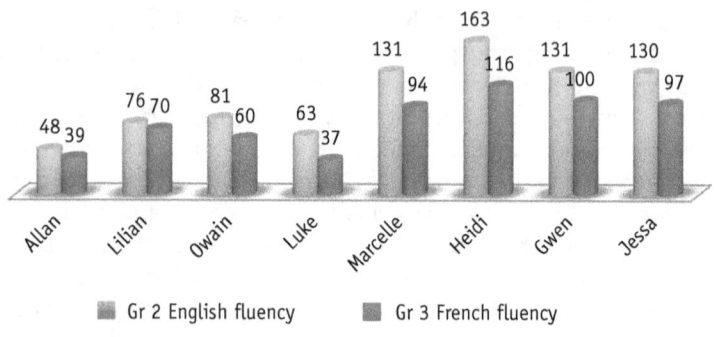

Figure 8.2 Grade 2 English and Grade 3 French fluency scores of at-risk and high-performing students

since first and second language reading skills are closely correlated (Dressler & Kamil, 2006; Skutnabb-Kangas & Toukomaa, 1976), Grade 2 English results were used to identify and track students who could be at risk for French reading difficulties in FI.

The IDAPEL was administered in Grade 3 at the end of students' first year in FI. French fluency data from this test revealed that students were following similar patterns of reading development in both languages (see Figure 8.2). In other words, students who had been identified in Grade 2 as at-risk for reading difficulties in English were again performing below their high-performing peers in terms of French reading fluency. Students had not achieved the same levels of reading fluency as they had in English, however; arguably as a result of limited exposure to the second language (Geva & Clifton, 1994).

Orchestration of reading strategies

The differences in the reading fluency results between both groups of French second language readers supported the need to examine students' knowledge of and perceived use of reading strategies. Think-aloud data revealed that high-performing readers in FI expressed knowledge of or use of reading strategies almost twice as many times ($n = 208$) in comparison to the at-risk reader group ($n = 121$). When asked more specifically about which strategies helped them read in French, answers from the at-risk FI group were typically limited to one or two strategies such as 'I know my ABCs in French and I just try to sound it out' (Owain, March, Grade 3). Moreover, units of analysis from at-risk students' think aloud transcripts were short and contained little elaboration even when prompting questions were posed, suggesting at-risk students' have limited knowledge of reading strategies and their use.

Excerpt 1
Researcher: What strategies help you read in French?
Lillian: Sounding out the words ... finding the letters in the words.
Researcher: Any other strategies you use to read words?
Lilian: No. (November, Grade 3)

Excerpt 2
Researcher: Did you use a lot of strategies to read this book or not a lot?
Owain: No.
Researcher: Why do you think you didn't use many strategies?
Owain: Because I kind of look at the words and just say them. (March, Grade 3)

Excerpt 3
Researcher: So what helps you understand when you read?
Allan: I don't know. (June, Grade 3)

Excerpt 4
Researcher: And why did you choose to chunk up the word here?
Owain: Because it's the quickest way.
Researcher: How do you know which strategy to use when?
Owain: I don't. I just pick one. (June, Grade 3)

Excerpt 5
Investigator: What helped you understand the story in this case?
Luke: Well, I have no idea. (June, Grade 3)

Answers to similar types of questions by high-performing second language students revealed that they were not only able to name, describe and indicate a wider use of strategies, but they were also more strategic by using strategies in combination with one another to ensure accomplishing the reading task.

Excerpt 1
Jessa: At first I didn't know what that [word] meant or that one meant.
Researcher: *Le soleil fait briller les crystaux de neige.* How did you figure it out?
Jessa: Crystaux sounds like crystal ... snow crystals! And then ... what does the sun do to snow crystals? It makes them brilliant. And what's brilliant in French ... briller. (June, Grade 3)

Excerpt 2
Researcher: What strategies were you using to read that book?
Marcelle: Stretching the word out and sounding it out and because in French and English there's a lot of words that sound exactly the same ... so I know that word. (November, Grade 3)

Excerpt 3
Researcher: What do you think it means, *Je ne voulais pas écraser les fleurs*?
Jessa: Couper, déchirer, écraser (she points to her teeth). They cut, your K9s tear and they mash.
Researcher: When did you learn about your teeth?
Jessa: In the last unit we did in science. (March, Grade 3)

When comparing both data sets, high-performing students had the ability to draw upon their strategies in an integrated way when facing reading challenges. They were strategic in their use of reading strategies and understood that the effectiveness of strategies is dependent on the particular reading situation. However, at-risk readers viewed reading strategies in isolation one from one another instead of seeing the relationships between them (Anderson, 1991; Cornaire, 1991; Grunderbeeck, 1994; Koda, 2005; Saint-Laurent *et al.*, 1995).

Types of reading strategies

Both at-risk and high-performing second language readers expressed knowledge of all five types of second language reading strategies: cognitive, memory, metacognitive, compensation, and socioaffective strategies (Oxford, 1990).

However, the data indicate that the degree to which these strategies were called upon varied between both groups of readers (see Table 8.1). For example, at-risk readers relied more heavily on cognitive strategies (69.4%) than all the other types combined, while their high-performing counterparts drew upon wider ranging types of strategies.

Table 8.1 Knowledge of and perceived use of strategies in terms of types

	Cognitive (%)	Metacognitive (%)	Memory (%)	Compensation (%)	Socio-affective (%)
At risk	69.4	4.95	18.2	4.1	3.3
High performing	52.9	15.4	24	6.25	1.4

Moreover, upon further analysis of the cognitive sub-categories, it was revealed that at-risk second language readers overwhelmingly used the following two lower-level cognitive strategies: breaking down the words into their parts and getting the idea quickly using pictures (69%). High-performing readers also drew upon these two cognitive strategies (42%), but used other cognitive strategies including deductive reasoning and transfer (15%), which at-risk readers never used (0%).

Role of metacognition

Data also revealed important differences between at-risk and high-performing FI readers in terms of their knowledge of and perceived use of metacognitive strategies; in particular, strategies used to ensure that the reading goal had been met (Table 8.1). High-performing readers reported using metacognitive strategies three times more (15.4%) than at-risk readers (4.95%). Transcript quotes further support the extent to which metacognitive strategies were being under-utilized by at-risk second language readers.

Excerpt 1
Researcher: How do you know that what you're reading is right?
Lilian: I don't.

Excerpt 2
Researcher: When you got to this word, how did you know you read it right?
Owain: I don't.
Researcher: Do you have any strategies to figure out if you said it right or not?
Owain: No, not really. (June, Grade 3)

Excerpt 3
Researcher: So how do you figure it out?
Lilian: Well sometimes I just look at the pictures. (March, Grade 3)

Excerpt 4
Researcher: How do you know if you got the words right or not?
Allan: I don't.
Researcher: So do you sometimes think, I wonder if I got that right or wrong?
Allan: Yeah you think about it mostly every time I don't know a word.
Researcher: What do you do when you're thinking about it?
Allan: Nothing. (June, Grade 3)

Beginning second language high-performing readers were much more likely to exhibit metacognitive knowledge about reading and were better able to describe their thinking and reading processes. Their answers were typically longer in length and were more descriptive.

Excerpt 1
Jessa: I said *maison* instead of *magasin*
Reseacher: And how did you figure it out?
Jessa: I saw the 'g'.
Researcher: What did you think when you saw the 'g'?
Jessa: That can't be *maison* ... that can't be *maison* ... *maison* does not have a 'g'. (March, Grade 3)

Excerpt 2
Researcher: So you sounded the word out?
Jessa: Yeah and asking – like you know how I stopped here and said it again.
Reseacher: So why did you do that, like went back and reread it?
Jessa: Because I didn't know quite what it was. I wanted to make sure I would know the word better. (June, Grade 3)

Excerpt 3
Researcher: So you weren't sure about this word.
Marcelle: Because if I say it really fast like Par-toit, then I'm like, that doesn't sound right because I went too fast. Maybe I should do it slower. So I'd be like par-t-out. (March, Grade 3)

Excerpt 4
Researcher: What helps you understand?
Gwen: You can look at the title ... and you know it's going to be about school, l'école. So let's say I start reading and I come up to école and I know it's about school and I said the zoo. We are going to the zoo. That would make no sense cause how the title is école and you're talking about the zoo. (June, Grade 3)

Excerpt 5
Heidi: I like reading in French. Sometimes if I get stuck on a word, I can read the sentence over again.
Researcher: How do you know if you need to read it over again?
Heidi: Because I feel it's wrong, like it doesn't make sense. Like it doesn't sound the same or feel the same.

Researcher: So how do you know if those French words are right?
Heidi: Because I feel like okay, it doesn't feel the way it feels when it's wrong. It feels the way it feels when it's right.
Researcher: So how do you know?
Heidi: Because I have that feeling. And I look at it. And I look at the spelling and I sounded it over again ... and it's like yeah, I know this word is right. (March, Grade 3)

Excerpt 6
Marcelle: Sometimes I know what the story is about, but sometimes I'm like okay, I didn't quite get that. I didn't quite get all the words. So then I'd look at the vocabulary and then I read it again. (March, Grade 3)

By using metacognition, these readers knew why they were reading and were able to reflect upon, monitor and evaluate their reading by integrating information in various ways. Conversely, poor readers lack or have inadequate cognitive and metacognitive strategies. They also have a harder time adapting their strategies to the reading task because their use of strategies is not as flexible as they are for strong, strategic readers (Geva & Clifton, 1994; Grabe, 2009; Saint-Laurent *et al.*, 1995).

Discussion

With regard to students' first and second language reading profiles, this study found that students entering a French second language program, having acquired some level of first language reading competency, were likely to retain a similar reading profile in French as they had in their first language. In other words, it could be expected that first language highly proficient readers would also be proficient high-performing readers in their second language. This supports other research conducted in FI contexts (Chamot & El-Dinary, 1999; Geva & Clifton, 1994; Macaro, 2001), which found that students who read with accuracy, with fluency and with comprehension in one language also do so in the other language. Similarly, children who experience difficulties in these areas in one language also experience similar reading challenges in their other language.

Although the number of participants was limited to eight children, this study points to a positive correlation between first and second language reading competency levels. As other studies have found, this study also suggests that certain measures used to predict English reading competency could be used to predict second language reading competency (Bournot-Trites, 2008; Erdos *et al.*, 2010; Genesee & Jared, 2008). These findings are important because they 'suggest that it is not necessary to wait until a hypothetical threshold of proficiency in the L2 is acquired before assessment of reading risk can be attempted' (MacCourbrey et al., 2004: 24). This, in turn, could facilitate the implementation of remedial reading support at the onset of second language acquisition without having to wait until a certain level of proficiency in the second language is attained (Genesee, 2007).

Regarding students' knowledge of and use of reading strategies, important differences were found when comparing at-risk and high-performing beginning second language learners. At-risk readers described using fewer strategies than their higher-performing peers and were drawing from a more limited pool of strategies. More specifically, when at-risk readers tried to remediate reading challenges, they were using the same few strategies, mostly targeting difficulties at the word level. At-risk second language readers were spending much of their processing time on bottom-up strategies such as decoding (i.e. breaking down the words into its parts). When taking Perfetti's bottleneck hypothesis[2] into consideration, this would imply that comprehension and, subsequently, the use of other types of strategies was compromised because too much energy was spent on trying to read French words (Raymond, 1988; Van Grunderbeeck, 1994). At-risk readers were also over-relying on looking at the pictures for meaning making. The overuse of a limited number of strategies would explain, to some extent, why other types of strategies, including the cognitive strategies of deductive reasoning and transferring, were rarely reported by at-risk readers.

The findings of this study also support the need to promote the development of metacognitive skills among at-risk readers, including strategies such as paying attention, self-evaluating and self-monitoring, which were seldom mentioned by these readers. As Paris et al. (1994: 796) noted, 'even when task goals are well defined and understood, children [beginning and less skilled readers] may fail to evoke deliberate plans. They may not be aware of potential actions that will achieve the goal ...'. It is therefore important to understand the strategies used by strong second language readers and share them with at-risk readers through explicit instruction. This can facilitate the exploitation of first and second language reading skills, abilities and experiences as well as facilitate metacognitive awareness (Koda, 2005; Chamot & O'Malley, 1994).

When students do not have sufficient reading strategies or lack automatized decoding and work recognition skills, they often times do not enjoy reading. This was the case for at least half of the at-risk readers. Known as the Matthew Effect, when reading tasks become laborious, it can lead to less motivation to undertake the tasks. Vocabulary development can slow down and as such, weak readers fall further and further behind their peers (Stanovich, 2004).

The data from this study were collected at the onset of second language acquisition, thus indicating that high-performing students were able to effectively exploit previously acquired knowledge, skills and abilities, likely from their strong first language reading backgrounds. The idea of viewing the first language as evidence of resourcefulness has been described in the cross-linguistic transfer literature as *preparedness for future learning*. Genesee (2006: 161) explained that, 'the learner's ability to generalize knowledge and abilities in the first language to second language literacy tasks is seen as a type of cross-language boot-strapping'. The students in this study had undergone three years of formal English literacy instruction, further suggesting that the high-performing students were taking advantage of the cumulative effects of first language reading, including the development of general knowledge, vocabulary, syntactic knowledge and comprehension abilities.

High-performing readers also had a more developed and deeper understanding of reading strategies that went beyond declarative knowledge. This explains to some extent why high-performing readers were reporting more metacognitive strategies. The three types of knowledge (declarative, procedural and conditional) are essential if readers are to become increasingly skilled and proficient. Declarative knowledge is manifested through one's belief statement about the task, its structure and characteristics, and its goals. It also includes readers' affirmations about their personal abilities to accomplish the task. Procedural knowledge is the ability to understand how to execute various actions or strategies. As was the case for this study's high-performing readers, their knowledge of declarative knowledge and procedural knowledge was supported by conditional knowledge; the ability to understand when to apply specific strategies and why they are valued in certain situations (Paris *et al.*, 1994).

Conclusion

This chapter reported on the findings from a two-year, longitudinal, ethnographic case study investigating second language students' reading development along with their knowledge of and use of reading strategies. The aim of this study was to compare at-risk and high-performing second language readers with respect to their knowledge of and perceived use of reading strategies in FI. Our analysis revealed patterns of reading development across both languages and important differences between ability levels (at-risk and high-performing readers) within this second language context. The major findings reveal that: (1) students followed similar reading profiles in both languages; (2) high-performing second language readers described using a greater number of reading strategies and deployed a greater amount of consolidated strategies when facing difficulties; (3) high-performing readers drew more evenly across a wider range of reading strategies including cognitive, metacognitive, memory, socio-affective and compensation strategies; and (4) some reading strategies were attributed more frequently to a specific group of readers. These findings have important implications for the teaching of reading in French second language contexts, particularly with regard to the diagnosis of difficulties and early intervention.

Notes

(1) The larger research project included 70 Grade 2 students who were transitioning from Grade 2 English into a Grade 3 French immersion entry point. The purpose of this larger research project was to describe the English and French reading profiles of students of varying academic abilities and to compare their knowledge and use of readings strategies across both languages.
(2) Perfetti's bottleneck hypothesis draws attention to the processing time required for reading. 'The more processing time consumed by decoding, the less processing space available for comprehension' (Raymond, 1988: 343).

References

Alderson, C. (2000) *Assessing Reading*. New York: Cambridge University Press.
Anderson, N.J. (1991) Individual differences in strategy use in second language reading and testing. *Modern Language Journal* 75, 460–472.
August, D. and Shanahan, T. (2006) *Developing Literacy in Second-Language Learners. Report of the National Literacy Panel on Language-Minority Children and Youth*. Mahwah, NJ: Lawrence Erlbaum Associates.
Bialystok, E. (2001) *Bilingualism in Development: Language, Literacy, & Cognition*. Cambridge: Cambridge University Press.
Bournot-Trites, M. (2008) Fostering reading acquisition in French immersion. Department of Language and Literacy Education, University of British Colombia, accessed 29 October 2012. http://literacyencyclopedia.ca/index.php?fa=items.show&topicId=240
Bruck, M. (1982) Language disabled children: Performance in an additive bilingual education program. *Applied Psycholinguistics* 3 (1), 45–60.
Canadian Parents for French (2006) *The State of French Second-Language Education in Canada*, accessed 1 November 2009. http://www.cpf.ca/eng/pdf/resources/reports/fsl/2006/pdfs/CPFAnnualE.pdf
Chamot, A. (2005) Language learning strategy instruction: Current issues and research. *Annual Review of Applied Linguistics* 25, 112–130.
Chamot, A. and El Dinary, P. (1999) Children's learning strategies in language immersion classrooms. *The Modern Language Journal* 83 (3), 319–338.

Chamot, A. and O'Malley, M. (1994) Language learner and learning strategies. In N. Ellis (ed.) *Implicit and Explicit Learning of Languages* (pp. 371–392). Boston, MA: Academic Press.
Clay, M. (2001) *Change Over Time in Children's Literacy Development*. Auckland: Heinemann.
Cornaire, C. (1991) *Le Point Sur...La Lecture en Didactique des Langues*. Montreal, QC: Centre Éducatif et Culturel Inc.
Cummins, J. (1983) *Bilingualism and Special Education: Issues in Assessment and Pedagogy*. Clevedon: Multilingual Matters.
Dressler, C. and Kamil, M. (2006) First- and second-language literacy. In D. August and T. Shanahan (eds) *Developing Literacy in Second-Language Learners. Report of the National Literacy Panel on Language-Minority Children and Youth* (pp. 197–238). Mahwah, NJ: Lawrence Erlbaum Associates Publishers.
Durgunoglu, A. (2002) Cross-linguistic transfer in literacy development and implications for language learning. *Annals of Dyslexia* 52, 189–204.
Erdos, C., Genesee, F., Savage, R. and Haigh, C. (2010) Individual differences in second language reading outcomes. *International Journal of Bilingualism* 15 (3), 3–25.
Fountas, I. and Pinnel, G. (2001) *Guided Readers and Writers*. Portsmouth, NH: Heinemann.
Garner, R. (1994) Metacognition and executive control. In R.B. Ruddell, M.R. Ruddell and H. Singer (eds) *Theoretical Models and Processes of Reading* (pp. 715–732). Newark, DE: International Reading Association.
Genesee, F. (1992) Second/foreign language immersion and at-risk English-speaking children. *Foreign Language Annals* 25 (3), 199–213.
Genesee, F. (2007) French immersion and at-risk students: A review of research evidence. *The Canadian Modern Language Review* 63 (5), 655–687.
Genesse, F., Geva, E., Dressler, C. and Kamil, M. (2006) Synthesis: Cross-linguistic relationships. In D. August and T. Shanahan (eds) *Developing Literacy in Second-Language Learners. Report of the National Literacy Panel on Language-Minority Children and Youth* (pp. 153–174). Mahwah, NJ: Lawrence Erlbaum Associates.
Genesee, F. and Jared, D. (2008) Literacy development in early French immersion programs. *Canadian Psychology* 49 (2), 140–147.
Genesee, F., Paradis, J. and Crago, M. (2004) *Dual Language Development and Disorders: A Handbook on Bilingualism and Second Language Learning*. Baltimore, MD: Brookes Publishing Co.
Geva, E. (2006) Learning to read in a second language: Research, implications, and recommendations for services. In R. Tremblay, R. Barr and R. Peters (eds) *Encyclopedia on Early Childhood Development* (pp. 1–12). Montreal, QC: Centre of Excellence for Early Childhood Development.
Geva, E. and Clifton, S. (1994) The development of first and second language reading skills in early French immersion. *The Canadian Modern language Review* 50 (4), 646–667.
Good, R.H., Kaminski, R.A., Shinn, M., Bratten, J., Laimon, L., Smith, S. and Flindt, N. (2004) *Technical Adequacy and Decision Making Utility of DIBELS* (Technical Report No. 7). Eugene, OR: University of Oregon.
Graham, S., Schwartz, S.S. and MacArthur, C.A. (1993) Knowledge of writing and the composing process, attitude toward writing, and self-efficacy for students with and without learning disabilities. *Journal of Learning Disabilities* 26 (4), 237–249.
Grabe, W. (2009) *Reading in a Second Language: Moving from Theory to Practice*. New York: Cambridge University Press.

Koda, K. (2005) *Insights Into Second Language Reading: A Cross-Linguistic Approach*. New York: Cambridge University Press.
Koda, K. (2008) Impacts of prior literacy experience on second-language learning to read. In K. Koda and A. Zehler (eds) *Learning to Read Across Languages* (pp. 68–96). New York: Routledge.
Keep, L. (1993) French immersion attrition: Implications for model building. Doctoral dissertation, The University of Alberta.
Macaro, E. (2001) *Learner Strategies in Second and Foreign Language Classrooms*. London: Continuum.
MacCourbrey, S., Wade-Woolley, L., Klinger, D. and Kirby, J. (2004) Early identification of at-risk L2 readers. *The Canadian Modern Language Review* 61 (1), 11–28.
Oxford, R. (1990) *Language Learning Strategies: What Every Teacher Should Now*. New York: Newbury House Publishers.
Paris, S., Lipson, M. and Wixson, K. (1994) Becoming a strategic reader. In R.B. Ruddell, M.R. Ruddell and H. Singer (eds) *Theoretical Models and Processes of Reading* (pp. 788–810). Newark, DE: International Reading Association.
Pinnel, G. and Scharer, P. (1987) *Teaching for Comprehension in Reading, Grades K-2*. New York: Scholastics Professional Books.
Raymond, P. (1988) Interference in second language reading. *The Canadian Modern Language Review* 44 (2), 343–349.
Rubin, J. (1987) Learner strategies: Theoretical assumption, research history. In A. Wenden and J. Rubin (eds) *Learner Strategies in Language Learning* (pp. 15–30). London: Prentice Hall International.
Saint-Laurent, L., Vézina, H. and Trépanier, M. (1995) Enseignement cooperative. In L. Saint-Laurent, J. Giasson, C. Simard, J. Dionne, É. Royer et collaborateurs (eds) *Programme d'Intervention Auprès des Élèves À Risque* (pp. 31–43). Montreal, QC: Gaetan Morin Editeur ltée.
Stanovich, K. (2004) Matthew effects in reading: Some consequences of individual differences in the acquisition of literacy. In R. Ruddell and N. Unrau (eds) *Theoretical Models and Processes of Reading* (5th edn) (pp. 454–516). Newark, DE: International Reading Association.
Skutnabb-Kangas, T. and Toukomaa, P. (1976) *Teaching Migrant Children's Mother Tongue and Learning the Language of the Host Country in the Context of the Socio-cultural Situation of the Migrant Family*. Helsinki: The Finnish National Commission for UNESCO.
Van Gelderen, A., Schoonen, R., De Glopper, K., Hulstijn, J., Snellings, P., Simis, A. and Stevenson, M. (2003) Roles of linguistic knowledge, metacognitive knowledge and processing speed in L3, L2 and L1 reading comprehension: A structural equation modeling approach. *The International Journal of Bilingualism* 7 (1), 7–25.
Van Grunderbeeck, N. (1994) *Les Difficultés en Lecture: Diagnostic et Pistes d'Intervention*. Boucherville, QC: Gaetan Morin Éditeur.
Wenden, A. (1987) Conceptual background and utility. In A. Wenden and J. Rubin (eds) *Learner Strategies in Language Learning* (pp. 3–13). London: Prentice Hall International.
Wise, N. and Chen, X. (2009) Early identificaiton and intervention for at-risk readers in French immersion. *What Works? Research into Practice*. Retrieved from: http://www.edu.gov.on.ca/rnh/literacynumeracy/inspire/research/at_risk_readers_en.pdf on May 24, 2013.

9 The Writing Processes of a Grade 7 French Immersion Student with Asperger Syndrome

Josée Le Bouthillier

Writing is an increasingly important skill in the 21st century with the heightened focus on literacy in Canadian curricula. Its importance as a valued skill is emphasized not only in one's native language but also in a second language (Hyland, 2007). This skill is equally essential at school, in the workplace, and in society at large (Graham & Perin, 2007).

At this point in time, in Canada, the early French immersion program is considered the most efficient program to learn a second language (Genesee, 2007). This program, however, has been deemed elitist and barriers exist to the inclusion of at-risk students (Arnett & Mady, 2010). Because of minimal research concerning at-risk students, parents tend to enrol their children in the regular program and educators often encourage students experiencing difficulties to drop the program (Genesee, 2007). Additionally, there is a lack of support for at-risk students (Rehorick *et al.*, 2006). However, despite these hurdles, there are at-risk students in French immersion.

Genesee (2007: 656) defines at-risk students broadly as: '(...) all these kinds of students – those with language, literacy, and academic difficulties or who are likely to experience such difficulties, whether they stem from what might be considered clinical factors (reading disability or language impairment) or from non-clinical factors (generally low levels of academic ability)'.

Many learning disabilities, disorders, and syndromes are encompassed in this definition. However, because there has been a considerable rise in the number of people diagnosed with autism spectrum disorder for reasons yet unclear and, because there is an imperative for the educational community to understand this disorder in order to respond to the needs of these students in schools, this study focuses on Asperger syndrome (AS), which falls under the broader umbrella of autism spectrum disorder. This disorder is described as a neurological-based developmental disability that affects the normal functioning of the brain (Leblanc et al., 2009). Research is scarce concerning school-aged writers with AS (Asaro & Saddler, 2009), even in first language writing.

Therefore, in an effort to contribute to the research about at-risk students in the early French immersion program, the aim of this case study is twofold: (1) to describe the cognitive writing processes of an Anglophone Grade 7 student with AS while writing a narrative in French and (2) to provide some teaching strategies for French immersion Language Arts (LA) teachers to support the development of writing as a response to this particular need.

Theoretical Framework and Literature Review

In order to describe the writing processes in French as a second language of a Grade 7 student with AS, it is essential to describe the cognitive processes at play when writing; thus, this study adopts a cognitive perspective.

A cognitive perspective

In terms of writing, Alamargot and Chanquoy (2001: 2) explain that '(...) text production can be defined as a finalised and complex activity, because it supposes to process, by the implementation of several mental processes, and with a general goal, to write in order to communicate, for example – a great amount of knowledge'. Thus, writing is viewed as any problem-solving activity where the writer needs to make use of at least four types of knowledge. These types of knowledge are domain knowledge – the conceptual content to be treated in the text; linguistic knowledge such as vocabulary and grammar rules; pragmatic knowledge – the necessary knowledge to adapt the content of the text for the audience as well as the form of the text; and procedural knowledge where the writer strategically uses and processes the three previous types of knowledge (Alamargot & Chanquoy, 2001).

Because of the complexity of the knowledge and the cognitive processes involved in writing, Hayes (2006) explains that these are easier to understand when represented by a framework. Since Hayes and Flower's writing model (1980) describing writing as a cognitive approach, different models have been proposed (e.g. Bereiter & Scardamalia, 1987; Kellogg, 1996, 2001). Each model adopts a different perspective by focusing on certain aspects of writing and, thus, all the models are important. Because of the focus of this chapter, Hayes and Flower's model will be used as a theoretical framework. The Hayes and Flower model describes the processes at play while writing a text.

Hayes and Flower's writing model (1980)

Hayes and Flower's model (1980) derives from think-aloud protocols during the writing of texts. The model consists of three main parts: the task environment, the writer's long-term memory and the writing processes. The task environment includes the instructions related to the task to be performed, namely, the topic, the audience and the motivating cues. These elements are exterior to the writer, but could influence his or her performance. The task environment also comprises the text produced so far. In the case of the writer's long-term memory, the knowledge of topic, the knowledge of audience and stored writing plans constitute this category. Therefore, referring back to the types of knowledge needed to write, the writer's long-term memory uses the domain knowledge for the knowledge of topic, the pragmatic knowledge for the knowledge of audience and the linguistic knowledge for the stored writing plans. Lastly, the writing is composed of three processes: (1) planning, which is subdivided into three sub-processes – generating, organising and goal setting; (2) translating, which consists of transforming the content plan prepared during the planning sub-process into a linguistic form; and (3) reviewing, which comprises the sub-processes of reading and editing. The 'monitor' component ensures the management and control of the three preceding processes by defining their order of activation.

Asperger syndrome

Since AS is a neurological-based developmental disability that affects the normal functioning of the brain (Leblanc *et al.*, 2009), this syndrome is likely to affect the cognitive processes at play while writing. Thus, in this section, the syndrome is described and links are made to the above-described writing model. Next, the literature about writers with AS is explored to identify their characteristics. Finally, the research questions are presented.

Characteristics of students with AS

AS is diagnosed according to the following criteria: a social impairment; a behaviour that includes activities and interests that are repetitive, patterned and focused; and an absence in delays both in language and in cognitive development (Griffin *et al.*, 2006). In a descriptive study of 40 children between the ages of 3 and 15, Church *et al.* (2000) further explained the characteristics of children with AS. Problem solving, planning, organization of thoughts, beginning and ending tasks, using pragmatic language, abstract and creative thinking, and taking a perspective were difficulties experienced by many of the children studied.

Linking the characteristics of students with AS and the writing model

With respect to Hayes and Flower's (1980) writing model, it is likely that the characteristics of AS will impact the cognitive processes at play during writing. Hayes and Flower view writing as a problem-solving activity, for example. During the planning process, writers develop a content plan that they 'translate' into linguistic form during the translating process. To achieve this, writers need to set themselves a goal to carry out their plan. This is problematic for a writer with AS, since the writing processes component of the model highlights the importance of thought organization within the planning sub-component of the processes to develop a content plan according to the writer's goal. In fact, Gould (1980) claims that planning is a fundamental component of writing and that expert writers devote two-thirds of their writing time to it. Moreover, writing in a second language adds a layer of difficulty and immersion students need three times the amount of time that first language writers need (Hall, 1993). Writing also demands pragmatic knowledge when the components of the task environment and the writer's long-term memory are accessed during writing. Also, perspective taking is important, especially in this study in which a student with AS wrote a narrative text. Narratives are embedded in the sociocultural fabric of life and they are used to make sense of experiences and relationships. As such, a writer needs to describe thoughts, emotions, actions and intentions as well as interpret them (Losh & Capps, 2003). Brown and Klein (2011), in their study comparing the narrative and expository writing of adults without disabilities to the writing of adults with AS, found that narrative was the most difficult genre for individuals with AS.

Writers with Asperger: What does the research say?

There is a dearth of research concerning students with AS in schools and, moreover, there are even fewer studies related to writing in school, and even fewer that examine a second language context. However, within the existing empirical research, it is well documented that students with AS generally struggle with writing (e.g. Dickerson *et al.*, 2007; Griffin *et al.*, 2006; Griswold *et al.*, 2002). It is important to specify though that one of the common findings regarding writing and individuals with AS is the high variability in their skills (e.g. Church *et al.*, 2000).

In their first language, writers with AS experience difficulty organizing their thoughts (Grisworld *et al.*, 2002), as well as starting and ending their thoughts (Church *et al.*, 2000). Organizing is an arduous task for writers with AS and their texts possess a weaker global coherence (Brown & Klein, 2011). Their texts lack a clear focus, present a distorted sense of audience and lack transition words. Also, students with AS are literal thinkers, thus idea development represents a challenge. This difficulty is compounded by the fact that writers with AS have limited interests (Myles *et al.*, 2003). Adding to the difficulties experienced by writers with AS is the tendency to avoid creating a plan to organize their ideas (Asaro-Saddler & Saddler, 2010). Because of their problems with the sociocultural and psychological elements of writing, texts written by students with AS are usually devoid of expression, in that the voice/tone of the texts tend to be neutral. Their sentences are usually short and lacking in complexity (Myles *et al.*, 2003). In addition, complex syntax poses problems. Overall, when compared with peers without AS, texts written by individuals with AS are generally of poorer quality (Brown & Klein, 2011).

Research concerning writers with AS is non-existent in the immersion context. However, there is research concerning at-risk students writing in second language contexts other than immersion, more precisely in English as a second language classes. First language writers with AS possess some characteristics similar to those of at-risk second language writers. For example, at-risk second language writers do not consider the overall structure of the text and have limited conceptions of the goals of writing and of audience. They also spend little time planning and revising (Leki *et al.*, 2008).

Research questions

Considering the scarcity of research regarding writers with AS writing in their first language and the non-existence of research in immersion, this study examines the following research questions:

(1) How is the profile of a Grade 7 immersion student with AS similar to native speakers with AS in a school setting?
(2) What are the cognitive processes at play during the writing of a French narrative text by a Grade 7 immersion student with AS?

Methodology

To address the research questions, a case study design, as it affords the opportunity for a detailed description (Merriam, 2009), was adopted. This study uses preliminary data from a larger ethnographic case study examining the writing development of Grade 7 at-risk writers and typically developing writers in a French immersion program. It borrows from a general applied qualitative research tradition in education and seeks findings that might contribute to instructional decisions that foster inclusiveness in French immersion and that might bring about change (Bogdan & Knopp Bilken, 2007).

Participants and sampling

This study focuses on Molly,[1] a Grade 7 student with AS in an early French immersion program. Molly attends Estey Middle School of 636 students in an urban area of New Brunswick. There are 25 students in Molly's class. There are two other students at-risk due to clinical factors and another four at-risk with non-clinical factors for a total of six at-risk writers. Mme Amélie is their French LA teacher as well as their homeroom teacher.

Mme Amélie has been teaching for 11 years. During her teacher education program, she had training in immersion teaching methodology. Mme Amélie also has a master's degree in educational administration. A few courses in her bachelor and master's programs focused on special education. In her 11-year career, she rarely attended any professional development related to inclusive practices, as they are not usually offered to immersion teachers. Despite the fact that Mme Amélie carefully scaffolds her writing instruction and uses evidence-based writing practices such as modelled writing, text analysis and peer and teacher conferences, Mme Amélie feels that her efforts are not successful with her clinically at-risk students. Molly is taking part fully in the regular classroom activities as she has no cognitive delays. The school's methods and resource teacher does not monitor her and there is no educational assistant in the classroom.

The selection of the school and the teacher was purposeful, based on the following criteria: (1) a middle school with an early French immersion program; (2) a middle school representative of middle schools in urban areas of this province; (3) a school within geographical proximity of the researcher; (4) a teacher trained in second language pedagogy; (5) a well-respected teacher with a good teaching record; and (6) a teacher with at least seven years of experience.

The sampling of at-risk students was also purposeful. For the purpose of this study, the researcher was looking for an intact class representative of immersion classrooms. The identification of at-risk writers was based on writing assessments and teachers' perceptions, not on clinical diagnoses.

Both the French and the English LA teachers conducted a formative writing assessment at the beginning of the school year to determine the needs of their students. To assess the texts, both teachers used the 6-traits provincial rubric (2). This is a 3-point scale rubric where student performance is evaluated as experiencing difficulty (ED), appropriate development (AD) and strong performance (SP) on the 6-traits of good writing: ideas, organisation, voice, word choice, sentence fluency and conventions. Molly obtained a general score of ED on both the English and French assessments, and she also scored ED for each individual trait. In addition, the researcher asked the current French and English LA teachers and the students' Grade 6 LA teacher to identify at-risk writers based on their perceptions. These three teachers all perceived Molly as one of the at-risk students within the class participating in the study.

Data collection

For the larger study, a total of four at-risk writers and, for purposes of comparison, four more-skilled writers were identified to be interviewed and to write two texts while thinking aloud.

In order to access Molly's writing processes, two think alouds were conducted. First, Molly wrote a story while thinking aloud and, four days later, Molly wrote a biography while thinking aloud. These two sessions were audio-recorded and, then, the think alouds were transcribed. The narrative think aloud sessions lasted for 38 minutes and 30 seconds. Also, during these sessions, a short interview was conducted (approximately 12 minutes) with Molly about instructional practices perceived helpful to her writing development.

To create Molly's profile, classroom observations were conducted as well as informal teacher interviews with Mme Amélie. The purpose of the researcher's first entry into the classroom, on the second day of school, was to get to know the students and to establish herself as part of the classroom environment, so that the students feel comfortable with her. The first entry consisted of four days for one-hour periods during French immersion LA for a total of four hours. When Mme Amélie started the first French unit, the researcher made a second entry in the classroom consisting of 18 days, with 1-hour visits per day. These were wide-scope classroom observations in order for the researcher to familiarize herself with the context of her study and to identify elements of the classroom activity such as instructional writing practices, teacher–student relationships, student–student relationships and, once the at-risk writers were identified, preliminary observations of individual students. Also, during class time, the researcher circulated, helped the students and interacted with them. In order to collect background information about the students, the parents of the participating students filled in a questionnaire. In addition, artefacts such as written texts, worksheets and lesson plans were collected.

Procedure

At the beginning of the individual think-aloud session with Molly, the researcher restated the purpose of the larger study: To understand how students in French immersion learn to write. Thereafter, she explained the think-aloud protocol to Molly and modelled the procedure. After each explanation, she asked Molly if she had any questions or concerns. Molly selected a topic from eight writing prompts that were accompanied by illustrations. These prompts were developed based on the researcher's observations related to the interests of the students participating in the study and were used as a springboard to writing a short story. Fifteen lines followed the illustration where the students needed to write a short study while thinking aloud. The researcher indicated to the students that they were to express themselves in the language(s) in which they were thinking, thus, for Molly either in French or in English. The researcher provided draft paper and linguistic resources, and suggested that they were to be used for planning and revising.

The audio-recorded data were transcribed by the researcher and analyzed by continually comparing them to the theoretical framework, the Hayes and Flower (1980) writing model.

Data Analysis

Findings

With regard to Question 1 – How is the profile of a Grade 7 immersion student with AS similar to native speakers with Asperger? – the data collected were compared to the clinical profile of a first language individual with AS. Molly's profile is presented in the following two paragraphs.

Molly is easily recognizable by a sweater adorned with a wolf, which she often wears. This 12-year-old French immersion student, like her peers with AS, is passionate, to the point of obsession, about a subject. In Molly's case, she absolutely loves animals, but more specifically wolves. In addition to her sweater, she owns many books about wolves and she knows a considerable number of facts about them (classroom observations). Generally withdrawn with her teacher and her peers, Molly becomes an avid talker when the conversation revolves around animals. In fact, she can be overly talkative about this topic and her conversation resembles more of a monologue to her interlocutors. She misses social cues when others try to redirect the conversation or try to take a talking turn. When animals are the focus of a conversation, Molly has the tendency to interrupt others (classroom observations and student interview).

Molly's mother tongue is English, but her parents enrolled her in the French immersion program because they value bilingualism and they wanted Molly to understand French culture and interact with French language speakers (parents' questionnaire). Molly likes school and is somewhat interested in writing in French and in English, depending on the topic. She is greatly interested in writing if the topic concerns animals (student interview). Despite liking school, Molly suffers from anxiety, a condition commonly associated with AS (teacher interview). In class, she is usually withdrawn. She puts her head down on her desk and her face is partly covered by her long brown hair. In order to deal with the sensory stimuli and her anxiety, Molly draws. She appears disengaged from the classroom. During work time, Molly dutifully places two or three words on a sheet and resumes drawing. Although Molly does not actively pursue relationships with her classmates, she interacts with them during small-group work designed by the teacher. In the whole class setting, Molly does not participate or share her ideas. Molly is more than able to express herself orally in French, but she struggles with writing and reading (classroom observations). Thus, in summary, it appears that the learning profile of a student with AS is the same, regardless of the language of instruction.

In order to address Question 2, Molly's cognitive writing processes are compared with Hayes and Flower's (1980) writing model. Also, her writing processes are studied as they relate to her profile.

Language usage

One of the instructions regarding the think aloud was that Molly had to use the language she was thinking in while writing. During the inaugural session, Molly only verbalised in French with the exception of when she slipped in an English word that she did not know or could not think of in French.

Topic selection

While the researcher explained the think-aloud procedure, Molly noticed some of the different writing prompts to choose from. One of the illustrations was a women dressed as a super hero dog. As soon as the think-aloud session started, Molly indicated that she had seen the prompt she would like to use, the one with the super hero dog because she found it funny. However, she did look at the other topics, but reaffirmed that she wanted the super hero dog topic. Molly chose her subject within 40 seconds.

Planning

Molly devoted 30 minutes and 46 seconds of her 38 minutes and 38 seconds total writing time to the planning component of the writing process. Her first action was to note that the person dressed up as a dog in the image did not have pants. This description was followed by an indication that Molly did not know what to write about: 'I don't know what to write... about'. (Three-second pause.) 'That is the only thing'.[2] When asked what was going on in her head, she stated: 'A lot of ideas'. The researcher asked how she would put these ideas on paper and she cued Molly by pointing at the draft paper. Molly ignored the cue and started generating ideas orally without using any writing or planning strategies. She did not plan on paper during the duration of her planning time. At no point did she consider the task environment except for the topic selection and the generation or goal setting for her writing. During that planning time, Molly generated 16 different big ideas for her story, many of which reminded her of personal experiences involving animals. She engaged in seven personal stories, three of them lengthy. Molly devoted 14 minutes and 10 seconds of her total 30 minutes and 46 seconds to planning, which represented roughly 45% of her planning time. Although these stories represented divergent thinking on Molly's part, they had little to do with her topic. For example, she explained that she often plays kangaroo with her younger siblings and that her grandmother had a mean dog that hated humans but loved cats. During all three of the lengthy stories, the researcher cued Molly to return to the task and all cues were ignored. Actually, for the third story, Molly interrupted the researcher cuing her, to start developing one of her big ideas to tell her personal story. At the end of the seventh personal story, a short one, Molly was cued again and she responded by expressing her difficulty with writing. Also, seven times, Molly engaged in the description of the illustration used as a prompt. Those descriptions were usually brief, the longest one being 1 minute and 54 seconds and the shortest one 7 seconds. Four times, the prompt created difficulty for Molly and was a barrier to her creativity despite being reminded that the prompt was a springboard for the story and she should not be limited by it. For example, Molly would have liked for the action to take place outside. In the illustration, the door was open to the outside, but the outside was not visible. Molly stated that she could not write a story that would take place outside because of the black. At two other points, to solve the dilemma,

Molly drew on the illustration to add what she thought was missing. In addition, Molly described some facts about dogs in two instances for a total of 47 seconds of planning time. Twice she mentioned that she had difficulty with topic selection and with spelling. Molly was cued 11 times in total to start putting her ideas down, and she ignored all except the last cue. In fact, she partially ignored the last cue, because the researcher stated: 'You can use this draft paper to organise your thoughts'. Molly proceeded to write without using the draft paper. The last 1 minute and 13 seconds of her planning time was spent developing her big idea orally.

Translating

Molly devoted 4 minutes and 48 seconds of her 38 minutes and 38 seconds total writing time to the translating process where she transposed her ideas in a linguistic form. She wrote 10 lines consisting of 4 sentences and 81 words. The four sentences were complex; two of these sentences were run on. Molly mainly used basic coordinating conjunctions like 'and' and 'but'. However, she did use 'therefore', 'when' and 'so that', once each. Her letter formation was clear, though she left large spaces between most words. The ideas, although basic, were presented in a logical, chronological order and were understandable to a sympathetic reader. Sentence construction, grammar, vocabulary and spelling represented areas of difficulty.

Molly's translating process was interrupted five times for a total of 35 seconds. She stated that she was not good with introductions; she asked if she had to use all the lines on the paper; she commented that one of her sentences was long; and finally, she explained that she used English words at times, because she did not know the specific vocabulary. In one other instance, Molly wondered about the little black spots on the paper that resulted from the photocopying. Twice during her translating process, Molly interacted with the component 'text already produced' of the task environment. Once she hesitated with the spelling of the word 'pour', erased it and spelled it correctly, and once she commented on the length of her sentence without re-reading it, but rather referred to the physical appearance of the sentence. While writing, Molly translated her exact oral ideas to written form.

Reviewing

Molly did not revise her text, despite being cued by the researcher. For the last 2 minutes and 16 seconds of the think aloud, she voiced that revising is extremely difficult for her: 'Beforehand, when I was younger, the teacher indicated where my mistakes were. Now, I have to look for them myself by using the dictionary. I can't do that, because I have no idea what are my mistakes'. Molly expressed many times that spelling was her main difficulty as well as choosing a topic. However, she explained that teacher–student conferences word banks related to the text to be written were helpful to her.

Discussion

Molly's profile in a second language classroom is highly congruent with students with AS in regular classrooms. Her interests are limited and she engages in repetitive behaviour such as drawing (Myles *et al.*, 2003). Social interactions are difficult for her within the classroom (Griffin *et al.*, 2006). Although Molly is withdrawn during most of the classroom activities, she becomes hyperverbal and she talks in long monologues when animals are the topic of conversation. Communication rules represent an area of difficulty and she has a tendency to interrupt or talk over her interlocutors when animals are discussed (Church *et al.*, 2000). Thus, as the analysis of the data relating to the second question demonstrates, the characteristics that Molly shares with her peers with AS in regular classrooms influence her ability to write.

Molly had difficulty with problem solving (Church *et al.*, 2000) and at no time during her think aloud did she set goals for her writing. Although she interacted with the task environment in regard to her topic, she never considered the audience or the motivating cues. In addition, she did not rely on her memory for knowledge of audience and stored writing plans. Therefore, it seems that pragmatic and linguistic knowledge posed problems in her case.

Planning is the main area of difficulty for students in their first language with AS (Brown & Klein, 2011) and that difficulty is also present while writing in a second language as evidenced by Molly's think aloud. Within the planning component, Molly stayed at the generating sub-component and, during the writing of a narrative text, she did not manage to use the organizing and goal setting sub-components. However, her processes could be different when writing in another genre, since narratives represent a particular challenge for writers with AS (Losh & Capps, 2003).

Also, there is evidence of literal thinking (Myles *et al.*, 2003). Molly, despite being cued that the illustration prompt was only a springboard to her story writing, limited her ideas to what the illustration represented exactly. In fact, when the illustration did not correspond to her ideas, she drew the elements that were missing. Idea development and attention are challenges for students with AS; Molly had a tendency to engage in divergent thinking and to tell personal stories.

In terms of the text produced by Molly, it exhibits many characteristics of first language texts written by students with AS. Her text possesses a weak global coherence; it is devoid of expression; her sentences are short;

and the text mechanics lack complexity. Thus, the overall quality of Molly's text is poor (Myles et al., 2003).

While writing, Molly engaged in a knowledge-telling strategy (Bereiter & Scardamalia, 1986). She did not reorganise the conceptual content and her text maintained the characteristics of an oral production. Except for the instance when Molly corrected the spelling of the word 'pour', she never interacted with the text in progress, a component of the task environment of Hayes and Flower's model (1980).

In addition, Molly did not engage in the reviewing process as she stated that it was too hard for her. There is nothing concerning this process in the literature about writers with AS. However, revising is identified as a challenge in the literature for at-risk writers both in first and second languages (Leki et al., 2008).

Conclusion

Although generalization is not possible from this case study, because there are similarities with previous studies about AS, some pertinent classroom implications can be suggested. Prior to considering the implications, two cautionary remarks are important. Because of the high variability in the writing skills of students with AS, teachers need to carefully observe these students in order to choose appropriate interventions (Griswold et al., 2002). Also, because students with AS usually react negatively to change (Griffin et al., 2006), it is important to implement interventions one at a time and to allow ample practice time, so that the behaviour becomes routine. Since these students struggle to transfer a skill to other contexts, practice time within different contexts is essential. Keeping these points in mind, the following are pedagogical suggestions for immersion teachers with student(s) with AS:

(1) Students with AS have difficulty with verbal cues. Therefore, very explicit teaching and directions are needed. It would help if teachers broke down the bigger task and explained it one step at a time. The student would then do the step, before his or her teacher explains the next one.
(2) Related to the first suggestion, written cue cards with instructions are useful. For example, teachers could write the steps of the planning process on a card. Another card could describe the steps for reviewing. These would be distributed to the student with AS at appropriate intervals.
(3) Students with AS have difficulty identifying the important information in written cues. If the writing task is described in written form, teachers should highlight the important information.

(4) With respect to planning, students with AS usually possess good visual–spatial skills. Graphic organizers are a useful strategy.
(5) For planning and idea development, since students with AS are usually concrete learners, concrete ways of organizing ideas, such as Post-It notes, can be an effective intervention.

Though this particular case study confirmed that the learning needs of the student with AS in French immersion paralleled the needs found in students with AS in the first language classroom, it also suggests that a second language context needs greater awareness of how these needs fit with the goals of the classroom. In Molly's case, when she spoke about her experience in the second language classroom, it was clear that she viewed her difficulties through the lens of deficits in her proficiency, rather than recognizing the limited supports that have typically existed for students in this position. For example, she struggled with spelling in both English and French, which made it difficult to apply language learning strategies, such as sounding out words or using a dictionary. Thus, for students with a profile like Molly's, it is clear that the use of supports that target their challenges in relation to language learning strategies is critical. Unfortunately, research in this area is currently limited and in need of additional attention.

Also, given Molly's problems with planning during the writing process, it is important to recognize that by the time she put pen to paper, she was exhausted. As shown in the literature review, such challenges have been found in students with AS in first language contexts. As Hall (1993) reminds us, students in immersion generally have fewer tools at their disposal to problem solve, and in the case of Molly, this means that she had fewer workarounds in the classroom to overcome exhaustion and get to work.

As the population of students with AS continues to grow, it is clear that schools need to be more aware of how best to respond to those needs in the classroom. There is an urgent need for research on this issue in French immersion if the goal of inclusivity is to be achieved.

Notes

(1) All names in this study are pseudonyms.
(2) All student quotes are translations of the researcher.

References

Alamargot, D. and Chanquoy, L. (2001) *Through the Models of Writing*. Dordrecht: Kluwer Academic Publishers.
Arnett, K. and Mady, C. (2010) A critically conscious examination of special education within FSL and its relevance to FSL teacher education programs. *Canadian Journal of Applied Linguistics* 13 (1), 19–36.

Asaro, K. and Saddler, B. (2009) Effects of planning instruction on a young writer with Asperger syndrome. *Intervention in School and Clinic* 44, 268–275.
Asaro-Saddler, K. and Saddler, B. (2010) Planning instruction and self-regulation training: Effects on writers with autism spectrum disorders. *Exceptional Children* 77 (1), 107–124.
Bereiter, C. and Scardamalia, M. (1987) *The Psychology of Written Composition*. Hillsdale, NJ: Lawrence Erlbaum Associates.
Bogdan, R. and Knopp Biklen, S. (2007) *Qualitative Research for Education* (5th edn). Boston, MA: Pearson Education.
Brown, H. and Klein, P. (2011) Writing, Asperger syndrome and theory of the mind. *Journal of Autism & Developmental Disorders* 41, 1464–1474.
Church, C., Alisanski, S. and Amanullah, S. (2000) The social, behavioural, and academic experiences of children with Asperger Syndrome. *Focus on Autism and Other Developmental Disabilities* 15 (1), 12–20.
Dickerson Mayes, S. and Calhoun, S. (2007) Learning, attention, writing, and processing speed in typical children and children with ADHD, autism, anxiety, depression, and oppositional-defiant disorder. *Child Neuropsychology* 13, 469–493.
Genesee, F. (2007) French immersion and at-risk students. *The Canadian Modern Language Review/La revue canadienne des langues vivantes* 63 (5), 655–688.
Gould, J. (1980) Experiments on composing letter: Some facts, some myths, and some observations. In L. Gregg and E. Steinberg (eds) *Cognitive Processes in Writing* (pp. 97–127). Hillsdale, NJ: Lawrence Erlbaum Associate.
Graham, S. and Perin, D. (2007) A meta-analysis of writing instruction for adolescent students. *Journal of Educational Psychology* 99 (3), 445–476.
Griffin, H., Griffin, L., Fitch, C., Albera, V. and Gingras, H. (2006) Educational interventions for individual with Asperger Syndrome. *Intervention in School and Clinic* 41 (3), 150–155.
Griswold, D., Barnhill, G., Myles, B., Hagiwara, T. and Simpson, R. (2002) Asperger Syndrome and academic achievement. *Focus on Autism and Other Developmental Disabilities* 17 (2), 94–102.
Hall, K. (1993) Process writing in French immersion. *The Canadian Modern Language Review/La revue canadienne des langues vivantes* 49 (2), 255–274.
Hayes, J. (2006) New directions in writing theory. In C. MacArthur, S. Graham and J. Fitzgerald (eds) *Handbook of Writing Research* (pp. 28–40). New York: The Guilford Press.
Hayes, J. and Flower, L. (1980) Identifying the organisation of writing processes. In L. Gregg and E. Steinberg (eds) *Cognitive Processes in Writing* (pp. 3–30). Hillsdale, NJ: Lawrence Erlbaum Associate.
Hyland, K. (2007) *Second Language Writing* (4th edn). Cambridge: Cambridge University Press.
Kellogg, R. (2008) Training writing skills: A cognitive developmental perspective. *Journal of Writing Research* 1 (1), 1–26.
Leblanc, L., Richardson, W. and Burns, K. (2009) Autism spectrum disorder and the inclusive classroom: Effective training to enhance knowledge of ASD and evidence-based practices. *Teacher Education and Special Education* 32 (3), 166–179.
Leki, I., Cumming, A. and Silva, T. (2008) *A Synthesis of Research on Second Language Writing in English*. New York: Routledge.
Losh, M. and Capps, L. (2003) Narrative ability in high-functioning children with autism or Asperger's Syndrome. *Journal of Autism and Developmental Disorders* 33 (3), 239–251.

Merriam, S. (2009) *Qualitative Research. A Guide to Design and Implementation*. San Francisco, CA: Jossey-Bass.

Myles, B., Huggins, A., Rome-Lake, M., Hagiwara, T., Barnhill, G. and Griswold, D. (2003) Written language profile of children and youth with Asperger syndrome: From research to practice. *Education and Training in Developmental Disabilities* 38, 362–369.

Rehorick, S., Dicks, J., Kristmanson, P. and Cogswell, F. (2006) *Quality learning in French second language in New Brunswick: A brief to the Department of Education*. Fredericton, New Brunswick. www.unbf.ca/L2/Research/current/ documents/ FSLStudyUNBreport_complete.pdf

Part 4

The Revival, Maintenance and Growth of Aboriginal Languages in Canada

10 A Fair Country? Consideration of Canada's Debt to Indigenous Language Renewal

Donna-Lee Smith, Josephine Peck and Donald Taylor

John Ralston Saul (2008: 3) opens *A Fair Country* with: 'We are a metis civilization. What we are today has been inspired as much by four centuries of life with the indigenous civilizations as by four centuries of immigration'.

If indeed, as Ralston Saul would have us believe, Canada is a 'Metis civilization' and we have been 'inspired' not only by the results of our open-door immigration policy, but equally by our civilizations of Indigenous forefathers, can we extrapolate that 'we', the collective who are part of the dominant culture, 'owe' much to the First Peoples? If so, what is it that we 'owe' them in terms of Indigenous language and culture – what is our responsibility?

Here, we examine the status of Indigenous languages in general across Canada, and the future of the Mi'kmaq language in particular, to explore the need to stabilize at-risk Indigenous languages – and we might want to examine what our role has been, and should be, concerning the fate of Indigenous languages. There are three sections to our exploration and examination: (1) a heartfelt *rant* driven by our collective experience concerning the status of Indigenous languages across Canada; (2) the *challenges* associated with developing a scientifically controlled environment in order to empirically test the implications of using the heritage language as a vehicle for formal education in a real-world Indigenous community; and (3) the experimental *results* that represent the voices of Mi'kmaq children in Eskasoni (a Mi'kmaq community sitting on the shores of the Bras d'Or Lake of Cape Breton, Nova Scotia, chosen for its committed program to the stabilization and rejuvenation of the Mi'kmaq language).

The Rant

We are a civilization that opens its arms to the diversity of its immigrants – and closes its eyes to the cultures of its First Peoples; a pluralistic civilization that celebrates our diverse 'face' – and ignores the third-world conditions of many of our Indigenous citizens; a civilization lauded for being first in the world to adopt a multicultural policy – and ultimately, a civilization that has failed to protect the languages of our First Nations, Inuit and Metis peoples (Harper, 2008).

In his argument about our debt to Indigenous peoples, Ralston Saul reminds us that Canada owes its early wealth to the trade between Europeans and First Peoples, and we learn of the early Europeans who married into powerful Indigenous families and thrived. He cites Champlain as saying, 'Our young men will marry your daughters, and we shall be one people' (11). But instead, the Metis nation was born; and Indigenous languages and cultures were decimated across our fair country.

We were once a land of 65 languages spoken by First Nations, Inuit and Metis peoples (see UNESCO, 2011). Today, only three remain viable: Inuktitut, Cree and Ojibwa. Some died from cultural genocide, but most from cultural, political and/or economic marginalization and/or hegemony (see UNESCO, 2011). Others will, over time, go the way of the polar bear – drowning in a sea of political waffling.

We seem, as a nation, to care about the impending doom of the polar bear; we seem to understand that once it is gone, there is no going back – no Jurassic Park waiting in the wings. We certainly make less fuss about our disappearing Indigenous languages – they are just not symbolic, cute or furry. Yet, their demise is as catastrophic to cultural diversity as the demise of the polar bear will be to fauna diversity. Linguistically speaking, the well-muscled languages of commerce, English, French and Mandarin (for example) are bullying the fragile languages of Cree, Inuktitut and Ojibway (for example) into economic submission. This begs the question: if Indigenous languages carry no economic capital, what is their value? In our search for an answer, it bears keeping in mind that Inuktitut is about 8000 years old – an immensely rich, complex oral language, and that English, by comparison, is the new kid on the block.

When we examine our polyglot, immigrant-based country, we have to question what difference the loss of sophisticated, ancient languages would make; examine the difference to Canadians in this fast-paced, make-a-buck world; examine reasons for not letting languages die their natural death; and examine the needs of the Indigenous children who may be better served by learning the language of commerce. Part of the answer lies in the realization that Indigenous languages are as crucial to our earth, to our humanity and to our understanding, as is the polar bear. Part of the problem lies in the realization that anyone reading this homily has long been warming seats in the choir loft.

Those of us in the field of linguistics and Aboriginal education are all too familiar with Canada's role in cultural and linguistic genocide; we know that there is not an Indigenous culture, language or person in our fair country who has not been victimized by this genocide; we know about the legacy of the residential school system; we know about the disconnect and we hear the rumblings of the emergent movement across the land, 'Idle No More'. Systematic in all layers of government, education and society since early contact, the racism that instigated and perpetuates cultural genocide has irretrievably decimated Indigenous languages. Cree, Inuktitut and Ojibway are currently the only lived languages, but they too, over the coming generations, may well be reduced to learned languages.

One language that has been all but destroyed is Mi'kmaq, spoken along the east coast of North America for about 6000 years. Despite the early European contact, the legacy of the residential school system, the decline of intergenerational transfer of language, and the proximity of English in all communities, Mi'kmaq has survived into the 21st century. Until a few decades ago, Mi'kmaq was a lived language, but it is now reduced to a learned language. Fewer people speak it fluently; the Elders, as in all nations, are the keepers of the language; and when an Elder dies, the loss to the community is akin to a book being burned in Alexandria.

According to UNESCO's *Atlas of the World's Languages in Danger* (2009), 'More than 200 languages have become extinct around the world over the last three generations'. UNESCO recognizes the importance of intergenerational transfer of language and rates levels of endangerment as the following: 'Vulnerable: Most children speak the language, but it may be restricted to certain domains (e.g. home); Definitely endangered: Children no longer learn the language as their mother tongue in the home; Severely endangered: Language is spoken by grandparents and older generations; while the parent generation may understand it, they do not speak it to children or among themselves. Critically endangered: The youngest speakers are grandparents and older, and they speak the language partially and infrequently' (see UNESCO, 2011).

UNESCO lists the Mi'kmaq language as 'Vulnerable', but it may be more accurately listed as 'Definitely Endangered'; it is akin to Mohawk, labeled as 'Definitely Endangered'. In the Mohawk communities of Quebec, children learn their heritage language if their parents enroll them in the Mohawk immersion school, but the majority of parents opt to have their children educated in English or French. In Mi'kmaq communities in Nova Scotia, most parents opt to enroll their children in the English schools – and there are many communities that do not offer an immersion Mi'kmaq option.

The *Cambridge Handbook of Endangered Languages* (Austin & Sallabank, 2011) lists four main causes of language endangerment: (1) famine and disease; (2) genocide; (3) political repression; and (4) cultural/political/economic marginalization and hegemony. All of Canada's Indigenous peoples have suffered from all four causes; for example: (1) *Famine*: In the 1930s, there was widespread starvation among Inuit and Cree in Quebec; historically, diseases such as TB, measles, influenza and small pox were common across Canada – today, the rates of TB and diabetes are epidemic. (2) *Genocide*: In the 1800s, the Beothuk, an Indigenous nation in Newfoundland, was decimated by Europeans, although not all experts agree with the term genocide. (3) *Political repression*: In 1953, Inuit families were forcibly resettled in Resolute Bay and Grise Fiord; from 1876 (Indian Act) to 1996, Indigenous children were forced to relocate and attend church-run residential schools: ethnocide and cultural genocide. (4) *Cultural, political and economic marginalization and hegemony*: Resulting from colonization – and the fact that there is no economic power linked to Indigenous languages and culture. The latter is the 'most common cause of language endangerment' (Austin & Sallabank, 2011).

Mi'kmaq, like all Indigenous languages in Canada, has been affected by all four causes of language endangerment. The effects of language loss on the First Peoples of Canada are immeasurable. And the impact on any of us if we were stolen from our family, denied the right to speak our language, learn our culture or raise our children according to our customs is unimaginable.

Our friend and colleague, Josephine Peck once said: 'How can our children express their world view if they no longer have their language?' A Mi'kmaq Elder, Josephine lives in Wagmatcook, Cape Breton; she comfortably wears both the moccasin and the running shoe; is fluently bilingual; immersed in her culture and language; receiver of the Governor General's Award for Excellence; former teacher and principal; and is currently teaching culture and language at both the community and university levels.

For over 15 years, the authors have worked on various projects concerning the status and preservation of the Mi'kmaq language. In the late 1990s, Peck and Smith delivered McGill University's Certificate in Aboriginal Languages in Education, and in 2000, they wrote a recommendation report for the preservation of the Mi'kmaq language. Currently, Peck, Smith and Taylor are completing a five-year longitudinal language research project.

Josephine Peck's personal story is of interest to our discussion in that it speaks to the value of intergenerational transfer of language and culture. She is a gifted storyteller, and what is included here is a mere summation.

Josephine says that it is thanks to her parents that she was not taken away to a residential school when she was five. She remembers the Indian agent coming to the end of the lane leading to her family's home; he was a man her father knew through trade. When the agent stepped onto the edge of the family's plot, Josephine's father emerged from the doorway of their home with his shotgun in hand. Aiming at the Indian agent, (so the story goes) he yelled, 'The next step you take, take it backwards!'. So, Josephine stayed home with her parents and extended family and continued to learn the Mi'kmaq ways and language until she was nine. By then, many of her friends and cousins were attending the Indian day school in Waycogmah, and she asked if she could go too.

Josephine attended the school and thrived. She loved being with her friends; the students were not punished if they spoke their mother tongue; and the nuns were kind, some of whom even tried to speak Mi'kmaq. Josephine received a solid academic training and went on to St Xavier University for a Senior Diploma in Education, a Bachelor of Social Work and a Master's in Literacy; she ended her long teaching career by becoming the principal of the school in Wagmatcook. Her eldest daughter is principal of the school in Waycogmah and received a national award for her administrative skills in 2011.

Yet, even with all of Josephine's commitment to the Mi'kmaq language and culture, there has been erosion in the intergenerational transfer within her own family: her children are bilingual, but her grandchildren are less so; they understand the heritage language when she speaks to them, but they are not conversant in Mi'kmaq. Like many Indigenous languages across Canada, Mi'kmaq suffered from the Indian Act policies that the Canadian government put in place, including a primary one: Indigenous women lost their Indian status when they married non-Indigenous men; as a result, many families moved off the reserves. When this discriminatory, sexist policy was rescinded through Bill C-31 and the families moved back onto the reserves, many of the children had lost their heritage language. Was this cultural genocide wrapped in benevolent policy reversal? The ever-pervasive English television, radio, movies, music and internet ensured even less Mi'kmaq was heard in the communities.

While Josephine Peck's story speaks to academic success, in that many students suffered emotional and physical abuse while attending these schools. Rita Joe, the renowned Mi'kmaq poet, attended Shubenacadie Indian residential school, infamous for its abuse of students – and suffered throughout her years there. Arguably, Joe's most famous poem, 'I Lost my Talk' is an eloquent reminder of the damage that loss of language inflicts.

In an interview with CBC shortly before her death, Joe said, 'I was brainwashed. "You're no good," I was told every day at Shubie [residential school]'. While many Indigenous people are concerned about the loss of their languages, they are also concerned about the economic welfare and future of their children, leaving many families opting to have their children educated in English or French – opting for the power of the colonialists' languages. If this is the choice that families and communities make, who does care about language loss? Who in Canada (or the world) does care other than the remaining (relatively few) speakers, and linguists? Peter Ladefoged (1992) argued that 'language death is a natural part of the process of human cultural development, and that languages die because communities stop speaking them for their own reasons'. However, according to UNESCO, many factors have led to the demise of the Aboriginal peoples' languages – and few if any were due to their 'own reasons'. Ladefoged (1992) further argues 'that linguists should simply document and describe languages scientifically, but not seek to interfere with the processes of language loss'. But ask any member of any Indigenous community whether they wish their children and grandchildren to be fluent in their heritage language, and the answer will be a resounding 'yes'. And the 'yes' will be as heartfelt even for communities who have lost virtually all contact with their Indigenous language – because, as the United Nations Forum on Indigenous Issues states (2008: 1), 'when an indigenous language is lost, so too is traditional knowledge on how to maintain the world's biological diversity and address climate change and other environmental challenges'.

The intergenerational transference of language best ensures the life of a language, but this transfer was intentionally broken through the legacy of the residential school system – Canada's 100-year-long answer to the 'Indian problem'. Ironically, the dominant culture now plays a constructive role in the preservation of Indigenous languages. Ironic, because the majority of Canadians live within driving distance of the United States; are more familiar with Turks and Caicos than Kuujjuaq; have a romantic vision of the Arctic – the land of the polar bear and the midnight sun; have never set foot on a reserve; and have no knowledge about Indigenous peoples other than what the media tell them. And most importantly, the majority would not see a connection between language loss, healthy communities and capable, problem-solving citizens – or recognize that the dominant culture has a responsibility. This is not the least ironic because English and French are the languages of the colonizers.

There is a hint of hope from the broader literature detailing studies of immersion programs in minority languages; for example, Spanish or Arabic in the American school system. But the difference is that Spanish and Arabic are minority languages only in this situation – outside of America, they are spoken by millions, while Indigenous languages like Mi'kmaq are minority languages not only in Canada – but in the rest of the world as well. Minority languages are unique; they are fragile; and they do not have the benefits, the status and the power of the world's dominant languages. In Canada, Anglophones may go to school in French, and Francophones may go to school in English; both are powerful languages spoken by millions around the world; both have political, economic and cultural support.

There are three steps to rescuing or stabilizing at-risk languages: documentation, revitalization and maintenance. Is it possible for Indigenous peoples to rescue or stabilize their languages without political, economic and cultural support? Is the investment viable? Who is going to make the investment? Do speakers of minority languages have the political, economic and cultural status and support to encourage the speakers of the dominant languages to care enough to rescue languages that carry no economic power?

Ask Aboriginal people about their dreams for their children and grandchildren and they speak with one voice: we want our heritage language and culture to be strong and we also want the opportunity for our future generations to engage in the mainstream culture and language. Ask anyone singing in the choir and they will give the same answer.

One of the main reasons why Aboriginal parents and caregivers may not choose to enroll their children in heritage languages programs and schools is the fear that their children will not have competent skills in the dominant language – and, feeling forced to choose between the heritage and the dominant languages, they opt for the latter. But there is a growing body of research showing that learning in the heritage language does not detract from acquiring competent literacy skills in the dominant language.

The Challenges

To further explore the hypothesis that learning in the heritage language does not detract from acquiring competent literacy skills in the dominant language, we delineated the challenges of creating a scientifically controlled environment in a real-world Indigenous community; and we posed two empirical questions: (1) Can instruction through the Indigenous language play a constructive role in revitalizing languages? (2) Is learning in the heritage language in the best interest of children?

To begin addressing these questions, we build on the longitudinal study by Taylor and Wright (2003), 'Do aboriginal students benefit from education in their heritage language? Results from a ten-year program of research in Nunavik'. We also look at the longitudinal study by Usborne *et al.* (2011), 'Learning Through an Aboriginal Language: The Impact on Students' English and Aboriginal Language Skills'. The latter looked at early results from language testing in 2008/2009.

Our next task was to locate language tests, testers and groups of Mi'kmaq children. The language tests used in the project were adapted from those used in a longitudinal study of language skills conducted by the Kativik school board in Nunavik, Quebec. The original set was used to assess the Inuktitut, English and French skills of Inuit students, and was developed jointly by McGill University's Professor Donald Taylor, his colleague Stephen Wright and a team of Inuit, Francophone and Anglophone educators affiliated with the Kativik school board.

The original set of tests was adapted for the current research project, undertaken by the project researchers, Josephine Peck and Donna-Lee Smith, and by a Mi'kmaq curriculum committee to ensure that the tests specifically met the requirements of assessing Mi'kmaq students for language acquisition. The content of the tests was reviewed by a Mi'kmaq language panel in Wagmatcook for both linguistic and cultural accuracy; and through a careful procedure of translation and back-translation, identical tests were developed in both languages. Overall, the tests were expected to be difficult, allowing room for the students to improve across grades.

Eight tasks designed to assess general language competencies and specific language skills comprised the tests. These tasks included colors, shapes, counting, numbers, body parts, alphabet, animals and story comprehension. The tests were culturally and linguistically adapted, age appropriate – and visually appealing.

The tests were administered in the spring of 2010 and 2011 by trained, bilingual testers. The sessions were conducted outside of the classroom one-on-one with each student, with each session taking approximately 30 minutes. Reports from the testers indicate that the students enjoyed participating in the test sessions.

We chose to administer our tests in Eskisoni, Cape Breton, a community with a large number of Mi'kmaq speakers; a community where Mi'kmaq is heard in the homes and in the streets; a community where parents are concerned about their children's futures and the future of the Mi'kmaq culture and language; a community where parents can opt to send their children to the English regular program with Mi'kmaq as a subject, or to the Mi'kmaq immersion program where learning is through the Mi'kmaq language. Our goal was to perform an in-depth comparison of the Mi'kmaq and English language skills across grades of students attending these programs. We chose two groups of Mi'kmaq children whose intellectual and social backgrounds

Table 10.1 Number of students tested in Eskasoni (2010 and 2011)

Year	Grade	Immersion	Regular
2010	Kindergarten	43	28
	Primary	38	44
	Grade 1	23	48
	Grade 2	26	54
2011	Primary	43	40
	Grade 1	37	65
	Grade 2	16	39
	Grade 3	25	58

were similar; this scenario allowed us to observe an in-place control group of Mi'kmaq children in the regular program and the experimental children in the immersion program (Table 10.1).

The Results

After administering the battery of tests in the spring of 2010 and 2011, we focused our statistical analyses on comparisons between Mi'kmaq students in the immersion program and students in the regular program in terms of performance in both the Mi'kmaq language and English. We begin with the 2010 results from the tests in Mi'kmaq; Figure 10.1 presents a

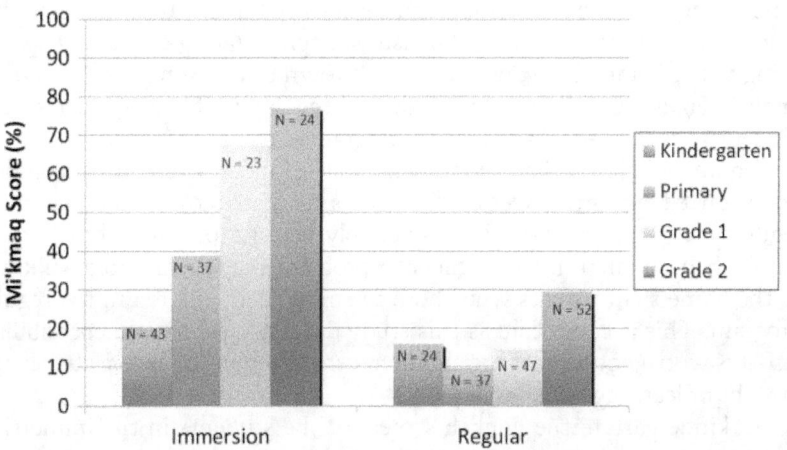

Figure 10.1 Total *Mi'kmaq* language scores in Eskasoni (2010)

breakdown of the scores from kindergarten to Grade 2, across the immersion and the regular programs.

As we can see, the students in the immersion program had substantially higher Mi'kmaq scores over the four grades than did the students in the regular program. While this would be expected, it is interesting to note that the children in the immersion program in kindergarten had only slightly, and non-significant, higher Mi'kmaq scores compared to the students in the regular program – an attestation to the strength of the Mi'kmaq language in Eskasoni. In other words, young children across the community had similar language skills from learning the language at home and hearing it in the streets.

In Primary Year 2, the difference between the two groups was much greater, where the students in the immersion program had higher scores than did the students in the regular program, 38.55% compared to 9.65%. While the kindergarten scores revealed that the language is, to a certain degree, a lived language, the Primary scores indicated that the children's language skills benefited from in-class learning.

In Grade 1, the students in the immersion program also had much higher scores than did the students in the regular program, 67.24% compared to 14.22%. The same was true for Grade 2, where the immersion students had very high Mi'kmaq scores, 76.90% compared to 29.47%. This is a clear indication that the language that the children learn in the regular program is not equivalent to that of the children in the immersion program.

To compare overall language acquisition, we administered the same tests to the same children in both the regular and immersion programs, but this time in English – the dominant language of Cape Breton. Television, movies, radio and computers are all in English; shopping, eating out, doing sports, going to the library, in Sydney the closest town to Eskasoni, would all be in English. Figure 10.2 shows a breakdown of the English language scores from kindergarten to Grade 2 across both programs.

Figure 10.2 shows that, the students in the kindergarten immersion program started out with lower English scores compared to the students in the regular program, 33.46–48.29% – possibly because parents who chose to enroll their children in the immersion program may speak more Mi'kmaq in the home than parents who chose to enroll their children in the regular program. This is conjecture as this study did not look into this possibility; also it is worth noting that the children were tested in the spring after many months of learning in Mi'kmaq.

In kindergarten, the English scores for the students in the immersion program were still lower than those of the students in the regular program, 47.45% compared to 67.22%. Perhaps parents concerned about their children's English language acquisition might think it is time to switch

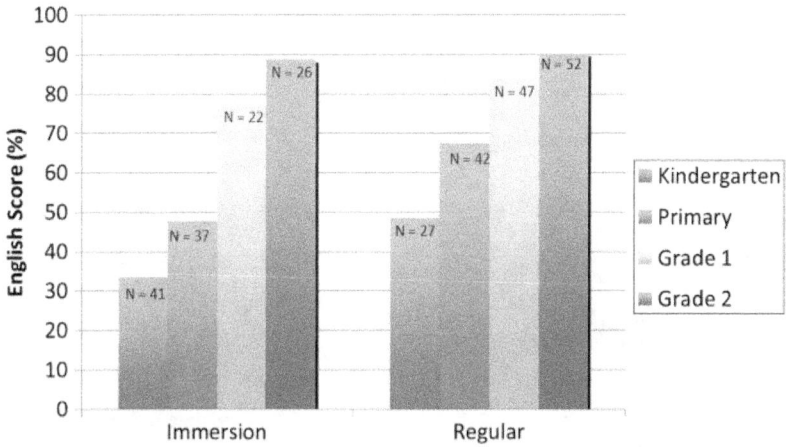

Figure 10.2 Total *English* language scores in Eskasoni (2010)

programs, but if they hold on until the end of Grade 1, they will see that the numbers speak for themselves: the gap between the students in the two programs narrowed. The scores for the students in the immersion program were only slightly lower than the English scores of the students in the regular program, 76.67% compared to 83.67%. This is an indication that the students are starting to transfer their literacy skills learned in Mi'kmaq to the dominant language, English.

In Grade 2, the English scores for the immersion students were almost identical to those of the students in the regular stream, 88.60% compared to 90.00%. We were thrilled by this result; here was solid data showing that the students in the immersion program not only met expectations in terms of their Mi'kmaq acquisition, but by Grade 2, they were doing just as well in English.

We conducted the same tests in 2011 – running the same set of tests with the same set of students as they moved up a grade. We begin with the Mi'kmaq language scores – from kindergarten to Grade 3 across both language programs.

Figure 10.3 shows that the results of the tests in 2011 were similar to those in 2010: the students in the immersion program had strikingly higher Mi'kmaq scores over the four grades than the students in the regular program.

In kindergarten, the students in the immersion program already had much higher Mi'kmaq scores compared to the students in the regular program, 31.17% compared to 8.65%. In Grade 1, this difference was even

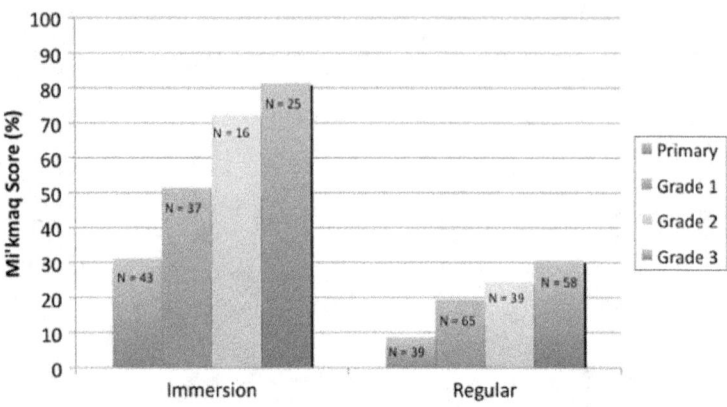

Figure 10.3 Total *Mi'kmaq* language scores in Eskasoni (2011)

greater, with the students in the immersion program achieving higher scores than the students in the regular program, 51.43% compared to 19.41%. In Grade 2, the students in the immersion program also had much higher scores than the students in the regular program, 72.28% compared to 24.45%. The same was true for Grade 3, where the immersion students had very impressive Mi'kmaq scores, much higher than the scores of the students in the regular program, 81.30% compared to 30.60%.

Next, the English language skills of the students were analyzed; Figure 10.4 shows the scores by grade across the two programs. As expected,

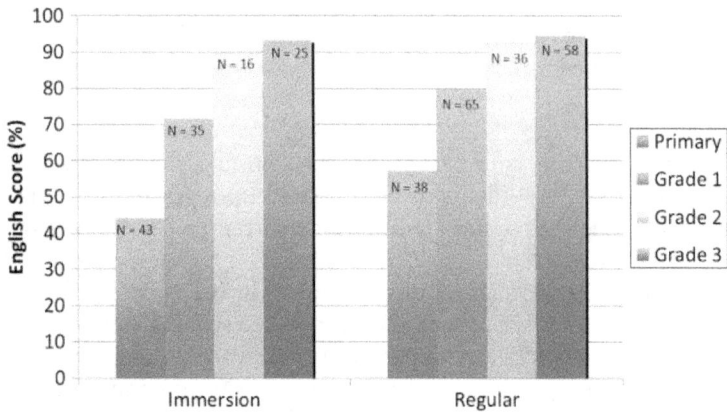

Figure 10.4 Total *English* language scores in Eskasoni (2011)

the students in the kindergarten immersion program started out with lower English scores compared to the students in the regular program, 44.01% compared to 57.11%. But by Grade 1, the English scores for the students in the immersion program were only slightly lower than those for the students in the regular program, 71.57% compared to 79.75%, and by Grade 2, the gap was even less, 89.84% compared to 92.72%. Finally, in Grade 3, the immersion students' English scores were almost identical to those of the students in the regular stream, 93.32% compared to 94.45%.

As in 2010, the students in the Mi'kmaq immersion program in 2011 learned much more Mi'kmaq than the students in the regular program, and they did just as well in English. These hard data irrefutably show that learning in Mi'kmaq is not detrimental to learning a second language (dominant) language and is consistent with other studies such as Wright *et al.* (2000) in Subtractive bilingualism and the survival of the Inuit language: Heritage- versus second-language education. Ostensibly, learning in any heritage language would not be detrimental to gaining strong literacy skills in any dominant language; caveat notwithstanding: the immersion program must go beyond teaching just the oral language and must give the children a strong base in academic language skills. It is these oral and academic skills that will be transferred to the dominant language when the children transfer into the regular stream; in our collective experience we have not seen a program in Canada where the heritage immersion program runs from kindergarten through to Grade 12; most schools transfer their students out of the immersion program by Grade 4 at the latest. If the immersion program has not given the students strong academic skills to transfer to the regular program, learning in the dominant language will falter, and the heritage language program will be blamed.

While it may be expected that the students in the Mi'kmaq immersion program would be much stronger in Mi'kmaq compared to the students in the regular program, what was an *unexpected* result was that the students in the immersion program had Mi'kmaq skills at similar levels to their English skills. What was an *exciting* result was that their English skills were just as strong as those of the students in primarily English language classrooms. Even though the immersion students spent almost all day in Mi'kmaq, they ended up being just as strong in English as their peers in the regular stream. These results can assure parents that having their children learn through the heritage language does not detract from their learning the dominant language as found for many languages, Indigenous and otherwise. The strength of the students' skills in English is an attestation to the prevalence of the dominant language in Mi'kmaq communities in Cape Breton – and would not necessarily be the case in communities where the heritage language is the lived language. For example, in Inuit villages in Northern Quebec, Inuktitut is the dominant, lived language; French and English are the second, learned languages.

The importance of the findings is clear: an increase in ability in one language does not decrease ability in another language. Further evidence is given by Wright *et al.* (2000) that when the ability in one language increases, it transfers to the other language, so there is a benefit to both languages.

While there is no doubt that including Mi'kmaq as a language of instruction in Mi'kmaq schools is an effective method of improving skills in the Mi'kmaq language – and this is an important tool for revitalizing and growing the language – the task of teaching minority languages such as Mi'kmaq in schools is not a trivial dilemma. With the break in the intergenerational transfer of language – the legacy of the residential school system – there are fewer fluent speakers and even fewer university-trained speakers and teachers. In reality, it tends to be older ladies, Elders, who are the keepers of languages; and as knowledgeable and as fluent as they are, without formal education or teaching experience, passing on the language in a school setting often becomes a major challenge. However, what is encouraging in Eskasoni is that there are a significant number of young people who are learning to 'live' the language – and who are enrolling their children in the immersion programs.

The Indigenous peoples of Canada have the will to document, revitalize and maintain our Indigenous languages. The question lies in whether the governments have the political will to pay their 'debt' to our Indigenous forefathers. While we offer reasonable accommodation to our immigrants who are encouraged to celebrate their cultures and languages according to Canada's multicultural policy, we offer little such celebration to Indigenous peoples – asking assimilation of them instead. Yes, we are a 'Metis civilization', and it is worth noting that compared with the total Canadian population, the Aboriginal population is likely to continue its faster growth. The average annual rate increase for the Aboriginal population (1.8%) was projected to be more than double the rate projected for the total population of Canada (0.7%) (Growth of Aboriginal Population, Statistics Canada). The 'face' of Canada is changing and as a nation, we need to change our response to heritage language acquisition.

The answer to why Indigenous languages must be saved may not be easy, but one thing is clear: to not do so is systemic discrimination; to not do so speaks ill of Canada and its multicultural policy; and to not do so 'will hasten the extinction of the language itself' (Taylor, 2009). Our research, and that of our peers, is not unique in the body of literature on at-risk Indigenous languages; however, the data support the work being done in this field, and what we have looked at is an Indigenous language that after hundreds of years of contact with a dominant language is still alive – even if marginally. This is a testament to the determination of communities like Eskasoni not to see their languages die – despite the discrimination, the lack of funding, the pervasive use of English and the loss of Elders. This chapter is for the parents who fear that immersion programs mean poor skills in the dominant language – and it is for all of us who recognize the intrinsic value of Indigenous languages and the diversity they bring to our fair country – a diversity that is as necessary as the polar bear.

Acknowledgement

The research was supported by funds from the Mi'kmaq Kina'matnewey for Josephine Peck, Donna-Lee Smith and Esther Usborne, and funds from the Social Sciences and Humanities Research Council for Donald Taylor. We wish to thank Esther Usborne for her contributions to the compilation and analysis data that constitute the basis of this chapter.

References

Austin, P.K. and Sallabank, J. (eds) (2011) *The Cambridge Handbook of Endangered Language*. London: University of London.

Harper, S. (2008) *The prepared text of the apology Prime Minister Stephen Harper delivered in the House of Commons*, accessed 6 February 2013. http://www.canada.com/windsorstar/html

Joe, R. Interview, accessed 13 December 2012. http://wwwcbc.ca/news/arts/books/story/2007/03/22/rita-joe.html

Ladefoged, P. (1992) Another view of endangered languages. *Language* 68 (4), 809–811.

Ralston Saul, J. (2008) *A Fair Country*. Toronto: Viking.

Smith, D-L., Peck, J. and Taylor, D.M. (2011) Mi'kmaw immersion really works! An evidence-based analysis. L'nui'sultinej Conference, St. Xavier University, Antigonish, Nova Scotia.

Statistics Canada (2005) *Growth of aboriginal population*, accessed 8 February 2013. http://www.statcan.gc.ca/pub/91-547-x/2005001/4072106-eng.htm

Taylor, D.M. and Wright, S.C. (2003) Do aboriginal students benefit from education in their heritage language? Results from a ten-year program of research in Nunavik. *The Canadian Journal of Native Studies* XXIII (1), 1–24.

United Nations Education, Science and Cultural Organization (2009) New Edition of the UNESCO Atlas of the World's Languages in Danger, Accessed 6 February 2013. www.unesco.org/culture/languages-atlas

Usborne, E., Peck, J., Smith, D-L. and Taylor, D.M. (2009) *Learning Through an Aboriginal Language: The Impact on Students' English and Aboriginal Language Skills*. Mi'kmaq Kina'matnewey Report.

Usborne, E., Peck, J., Smith, D-L. and Taylor, D.M. (2011) Learning through an Aboriginal language: The impact on students' English and Aboriginal language skills. *Canadian Journal of Education* 34 (4), 200–215.

Wright, S.C., Taylor, D.M. and Macarthur, J. (2000) Subtractive bilingualism and the survival of the Inuit language: Heritage- versus second-language education. *Journal of Educational Psychology* 92 (1), 63–84.

Wright, S.C. & Taylor, D.M. (2010) Justice in Aboriginal language policy and practices: Fighting institutional discrimination and linguicide. In D.R. Bobocel, A.C. Kay, M.P. Zanna and J.M. Olson (eds) *The Psychology of Justice and Legitimacy* (pp. 273–298). New York: Psychology Press.

11 First Nations, Métis and Inuit K-12 Language Programming: What Works?

Carmen Gillies and Marie Battiste

The growing Indigenous youth population, the huge education gaps between Indigenous and non-Indigenous peoples and their implications for the future of Canada have sparked national policy discussions. Over the last decade, the Council of Ministers of Education, Canada (CMEC), issued *Learn Canada 2020* (2010), outlining the CMEC's current priorities in public education for building a vibrant knowledge-based economy in Canada, including enhancing Aboriginal student successes.[1] The CMEC astutely recognizes that success can only be achieved through addressing inclusivity and minority languages. In Saskatchewan, where nearly 13% of the population is Aboriginal, the Ministry of Education has also stressed the relationship between Aboriginal student success and language restoration. Consequently, in 2005, the Saskatchewan Ministry of Education contracted the Aboriginal Education Research Centre at the University of Saskatchewan to identify literature that assists in illuminating best practices in implementing First Nations and Métis language programming into Saskatchewan schools. This chapter presents a portion of that report, drawing particular attention to five areas that support success in the development of Indigenous language strategies for K-12 learners.[2]

While the three chapters presented in this section combine to offer a preliminary discussion of the interrelationship between the socio-historic realities of colonization, government policies aimed at assimilation, the erosion of languages and the current issues affecting Indigenous peoples' language revitalization, it is important to acknowledge these integral power dynamics and their continual effects on Indigenous languages. Although all languages change and evolve over time naturally, Indigenous languages have suffered immeasurable losses from common enemies – colonization and official governmental policies and practices supporting only official languages.

Imposed assimilative education through official language instruction, such as Indian residential schools in Canada, has had a significant traumatic effect on Indigenous peoples' languages, disrupting the intergenerational transmission of language within Indigenous communities (Fishman, 2006). This disruption has caused Indigenous languages to decline rapidly, leading to Indigenous language revitalization and self-determination movements for at least 30 years that have initiated bilingual programs with increased movement toward immersion programs. The recovery of Indigenous languages, though, has been a difficult process as hegemony and power dominate as issues for Indigenous peoples. In 2008, Canadian Prime Minister Stephen Harper apologized to Aboriginal peoples for forcing them to attend Canada's residential schools and for the known excesses of the residential school system, acknowledging that the system was meant to 'kill the Indian in the child'. While the apology and subsequent funds awarded to victims of residential schools are part of the Harper government strategy to address Aboriginal reconciliation issues, Indigenous languages remain necessary and vital aspects of the future of Aboriginal peoples (Ireland, 2009; Littlebear, 2009). Yet, recognizably, few Indigenous language programs exist in Canadian provincial schools (Skutnabb-Kangas & Phillipson, 2005). Over two decades ago, the Assembly of First Nations (1990) reported a variance of between 52 and 73 Indigenous languages existing in Canada, some with only a few speakers. By the mid-1990s, the number of Aboriginal languages was reduced to 54 (Norton & Fettes, 1995). According to 2006 statistics, however, the number of Indigenous language speakers has increased, not due to regular home usage but due to second language instruction (Norris, 2007). This finding is likely the result of First Nations schools that have implemented language programming. Through treaties, Canada's federal government is responsible for the funding and jurisdiction of First Nations schooling; however, since 1973, First Nations have assumed greater control over their schools, giving prominence to the recovery of languages. Although some provincial and territorial schools offer language programs and classes, the recovery of Aboriginal languages has not been replicated to the same extent in these systems (Baloy, 2011).

While many schools have experimented with different language programming approaches, research indicates that K-12 Indigenous language classes in blocked time slots do not contribute significantly to acquisition or retention (Charles, 2005; Hermes, 2009; McIvor, 2009). Rather, immersion programs have been documented as being the most successful for Indigenous language learning, as an important vehicle for language renewal, maintenance and transmission (Blair & Laboucan, 2006; Greymorning, 1997; Kipp, 2009; Maracle, 2002; Orr et al., 2005; Sock & Paul-Gould, 2012).

For example, research has found that students who attend Indigenous language immersion schools from kindergarten to Grade 3 have higher chances of becoming fluent in both Indigenous and dominant languages, leading to increased academic success and increased self-esteem (Cummins, 2001b; Eichstaedt, 2006; Epstein, 2009; Skutnabb-Kangas & Phillipson, 2005; Sock & Paul-Gould, 2012; Taylor & Wright, 2003; Thomas & Collier, 2002; Usborne *et al.*, 2011). Significantly, links have also been made between K-3 Indigenous language immersion programs and decreased rates of youth suicide (Hallet *et al.*, 2007). Current scholarship on Indigenous language programs offer critical information regarding how governments, schools and communities can work collaboratively to create innovative and successful K-12 Indigenous language initiatives. This chapter is thus organized around five essential areas of Indigenous language programming across education systems: sustainable funding; community support and influence; language status and prestige; teacher certification and training; and Indigenous pedagogy.

K-12 Indigenous Language Programs: What Works?

Sustainable funding

Perhaps most significant to any language recovery effort will be the government's priorities as designated in legislation, policy and funding support. New Zealand, the United States, Finland, Greenland and Australia have initiated such government legislation, supporting commitments to Indigenous language funding. In Canada, two territories, the Northwest Territories and Nunavut, have legislation that includes Indigenous languages in addition to the two official Canadian languages. The provinces and Yukon include Indigenous language instruction in some content areas of the curriculum. The need for consistent, long term and adequate funding for Indigenous language program success is emphasized throughout the literature (Blair & Laboucan, 2006; Canadian Heritage, 2005; Moore & Hennessy, 2006; Neganegijig & Breunig, 2007; Spolsky, 2002; Toulouse, 2003; Wetzel, 2006). Systematic infrastructure of classrooms, trained instructors, new curricula and material resources create additional costs for schools that require more than regular programming, as successful international K-12 programs have shown. For example, Te Reo in New Zealand and Ke Kula Laiapuni Rainbow School in Hawaii have government financial support, backed by government legislation (Johansen, 2004). The current level of governmental funding for Indigenous language protection in Canada has been described as 'not adequate to meet even the most basic needs for language planning or programming' (Canadian Heritage, 2005c: 86). For instance, funding for French language programming in Yukon K-12 schools is several times higher than that for Indigenous languages (Moore & Hennessy, 2006c: 126) and in provinces such as Saskatchewan the statistics are similar (Canadian Heritage, 2005c: 63). There is a clear need for governments, and other agencies, to support Indigenous K-12 language programming through legislation and financial investment. Research has also indicated that when local Indigenous peoples determine how adequate funding is allocated, programs are more effective (Martinez & Strong, 2005; Bell & Marlow, 2009).

Community support and influence

In almost all instances where there are successful Indigenous language programs, a core group of committed individuals have led and facilitated the projects (Johansen, 2004; Stelómethet Gardner, 2004). Members of such groups have been diverse in age and language abilities, including Indigenous community members, parents, Elders, teachers, policy makers, linguists and other language preservation and restoration experts (Breinig, 2006). Such leaders have demonstrated 'good organizational abilities and sensitivity to both individual differences and collective needs' (Grenoble, 2009c: 64). For example, in Canada, Mohawk language activist Dorothy Lazore has been inspired by Maori Ko Hunga Reo and Kura Kaupapa School, becoming a major catalyst for Mohawk language immersion schools in Quebec as well as a major player in most Canadian immersion programs (Freeman *et al.*, 1995).

Establishing goals shared by core group members that reflect the social and historical context of the community and language has also been identified as critical in successful programming (Maracle, 2002; Taylor & Wright, 2003). Grenoble (2009c: 64) suggested that the creation of shared goals requires an honest inventory of the state of the language and resources, including 'the number of speakers, with an assessment of their levels of knowledge of the language and of their commitment to learning and/or using the language'. Community-based interviews, surveys and the use of scales have assisted in determining the stage of language loss (Bauman, 1980; Canadian Heritage, 2005; Fishman, 1991; Taylor & Wright, 2003). Research has also confirmed that linguists can play pivotal roles in Indigenous language programming through producing grammatical frameworks, language materials and dictionaries, promoting the language and applying for agency funding (Breinig, 2006; Pheasant-Williams, 2003; Rice, 2009). Yet, research has also stressed that outsiders to the community must recognize that 'language shift is the result of a history of colonization, unequal power relations, and other imbalances' (Grenoble, 2009c: 61). According to Speas (2009: 35), 'It is clear to all who work on endangered languages that only community-based projects have any hope of success, and [outsiders] must be willing to do those things that communities decide they need, rather than telling communities what is needed'.

Unlike other heritage language programs, Indigenous language programs demand innovative, community-linked influence due to language endangerment, Indigenous rights to sovereignty and the need for local Indigenous guidance (Benally & Viri, 2005; Graham, 2005; Morgan, 2005; Suina, 2004). For example, Maori immersion programs in New Zealand and the Hawaiian Puna Leo immersion programs are often cited as the most successful and influential in the literature, making them excellent examples of how success in K-12 schools can result from grassroots community influence (Harrison & Papa, 2005; Johnson & Johnson, 2002; Kepa & Manu'atu, 2006; Mita, 2007). It is important to note, though, that while community involvement implicates the inclusion of parents, extended family and Elders (Blair & Laboucan, 2006; Johansen, 2004; McIvor, 2005; Roy & Morgan, 2008; Smith & Peck, 2004), not all community members may share similar beliefs concerning language programming (Grenoble, 2009). It is therefore important to provide community members with a forum to vocalize opinions, concerns and ideas (Kroskrity, 2009), to validate and make community involvement a priority.

Language status and prestige

Cummins (2001a) has consistently argued that language programing is about power relations. Languages viewed as prestigious, or of high value, by Indigenous and dominant communities, are more likely to be preserved and revitalized (Johansen, 2004; McCarty, 2003; Peter, 2007). Although oppressive colonizing policies banning Indigenous languages have been lifted in some countries, Eurocentric attitudes and stigmas attached to speaking Indigenous languages remain (Peter, 2007; Roy & Morgan, 2008; Spolsky, 2002). In addition, pervasive governmental efforts at assimilation through current school systems lead many in Canada to believe that English is superior and learning Indigenous languages will set children back (Brandt & Ayoungman, 1989). Such beliefs have prevented parents, community members, students, teachers, school staff and others from participating in and committing their full support to Indigenous language programming (Blair & Laboucan, 2006; McCarty et al., 2006; McLeod, 2003; Roy & Morgan, 2008). For example, there is evidence that Indigenous language teachers are negatively affected when parents, colleagues, administrators and the broader community undervalue the languages of instruction, leading to decreased home usage and limited program success (Spolsky, 2002; Suina, 2004). Beliefs in the inferiority of Indigenous languages have also caused students to feel shame when learning languages (Daniels-Fiss, 2008; Goodfellow, 2003). Sock and Paul-Gould (2012) have illustrated, however, that immersion students' tested successes in comprehension and fluency in English after at least four years of Mi'kmaw immersion programming have improved the attitudes of English stream parents and teachers, increasing local administrators' support for Mi'kmaw immersion programming.

While Indigenous immersion programs have led to increased academic success, it is important to highlight that abilities in standard English literacy continue to be connected with access to power (McCarty *et al.*, 2006) and come with material benefits that are not associated with Indigenous language abilities (Epstein, 2009). Research suggests that program planners must build partnerships with key agencies and governments in ways that strengthen perceptions and offer concrete benefits, such as employment and education opportunities, that come from learning an Indigenous language (Canadian Heritage, 2005c: 75). Lafortune (2000) contends that positive-language image marketing is an essential ingredient in reversing language loss trends in Native American communities as it results in consciousness shifts. A wide variety of language prestige enhancers and documented positive research results is needed to boost the will of stakeholders in making programs possible and sustainable.

Teacher certification and training

Research has emphasized an urgent need to increase teacher certification and Indigenous language instruction training opportunities (Blair & Laboucan, 2006; Greymorning, 1997; Johansen, 2004; Johnston & Johnson, 2002; Kipp, 2009; Maracle, 2002; McIvor, 2005; Morgan, 2005; Roy & Morgan, 2008; Smith & Peck, 2004; Suina, 2004). The lack of certification in Indigenous language instruction has often left administrators with two choices: hire fluent speakers of the target language who have little training or no formal teaching certification or hire teachers who are formally certified in language instruction but are not fluent in the target language. Additionally, not all Indigenous languages have a written orthography and many are primarily oral based. Consequently, teachers' skill levels with their own ancestral language may vary in terms of speaking and especially writing fluency in the Indigenous language (Charles, 2005c: 108).

Although school districts usually require teacher certification, the literature indicates that some have opted to forego this requirement due to the shortage of certified Indigenous language teachers. For instance, one committee hired four teachers with 'the language ability, cultural knowledge and commitment' but without teaching certificates (Graham, 2005c: 324). To compensate for the lack of training, the school district provided professional development opportunities throughout the year. Other schools, such as in British Columbia, have hired certified teachers not fluent in the language of instruction, who then work with linguistically and culturally fluent Elders (McIvor, 2005c: 12). A similar example occurred at the Sealaska Heritage Institute when two Haida language teachers with minimal fluency were hired and then studied with Elders (Breinig, 2006c: 114). Hinton (2003: 79) explained that non-fluent teachers work effectively with 'elderly fluent community speakers in the community'. The idea to learn from Elders emerged from the Master Apprentice Language Learning Programs (MALLPs) founded in California in 1983, where a single Elder is assigned to a student to establish a core group of speakers and instructors (Johansen, 2004: 579). MALLP uses several language learning approaches and theories, including input hypothesis, total physical response (TPR), linguistic elicitation, communicative competence in a modified form and ethnographic research in cases of endangered languages (Hinton, 2002).

Other institutions have elected to develop teaching certificate programs (Moore, 2003; Morgan, 2005; Stelómethet Gardner, 2004). For example, the first Mohawk immersion teacher program was established in 1985 in Kahnawake territory (Maracle, 2002). A teacher on the staff at the immersion school developed the curriculum and taught the course. Nine students were selected to attend the 10-month, full-day immersion course. Smith and Peck (2004) described another program initiated by the Wagmatcook, First Nation of Nova Scotia and McGill University. The Certificate in Indigenous Literacy Education provides teacher training to fill the need for teachers in the K-2 immersion program for K-2 and Mi'kmaq language classes offered to Grades 3-12. Research on the effectiveness of the initiative indicates that nearly all participants, including children, grandparents and Elders were positive about the outcomes (Sock & Paul-Gould, 2012). The certificate is based on the Cree as the Language of Instruction Program, developed by teachers of the James Bay Cree School Board in Quebec. When designing Indigenous language teacher training programs, research has demonstrated that it is important to consider the context and needs of students, including financial support and student housing (Breuning, 2007; Maracle, 2002; Suina, 2004).

According to Eichstaedt (2006), all of the successful immersion programs in American schools were partnered with a university. University partners and research scholars can, '[h]elp tribal communities with training and technical expertise in a number of areas to support the initiatives'

(Eichstaedt, 2006c: 30). Skutnabb-Kangas and Phillipson (2005: 7) provided a comprehensive list of the ways in which universities can 'promote the survival of Indigenous languages and ... protect the linguistic human rights of Indigenous Peoples'. Although universities can contribute to Indigenous language acquisition and retention in multiple ways, numerous studies suggest that universities best contribute through augmenting and providing teacher certification programs and conducting needed research (Blair & Laboucan, 2006; Moore, 2003; Morgan, 2005; Roy & Morgan, 2008; Smith & Peck, 2004; Suina, 2004).

Indigenous pedagogy

Research has demonstrated a need for K-12 Indigenous language pedagogical approaches including curricula, resources and assessment methods situated within Indigenous paradigms (Graham, 2005; Hermes *et al.*, 2012; Kepa & Manu'atu, 2006; Romero-Little, 2006). Indigenous knowledges constantly respond to the flux in which they are situated and thus caution has been advised before oversimplifying or 'mystifying' Indigenous knowledge systems through pedagogy (Battiste, 2002). Indigenous pedagogy, therefore, represents ways of knowing and learning attached to the collective connection to Indigenous worldviews, to particular locations where knowledge is fostered, shared and created (Battiste, 2002). Furthermore, unlike western languages, spirituality is central within Indigenous epistemologies, embedded in languages, and thus should be reflected in pedagogy (Johnson & Johnson, 2002; McLeod, 2000; Moore, 2003; Spolsky, 2002). As such, successful Indigenous language programming must connect with community.

While it may be necessary to create a curriculum that meets provincial standards, Meek and Messing (2007) cautioned against systematically translating English curriculum resources into Indigenous language curricula and resources. Such activity has contributed to low rates of long-term success, and to cultural mistakes or blunders (Graham, 2005; Stelómethet Gardner, 2004). For example, Borden (2010) emphasized that Mi'kmaw[3] speakers have grammar structures and ways of expressing ideas that are different from English mother tongue speakers. For Mi'kmaq, context matters, such as counting makes sense only in regard to what is being counted, and space and shape are additional elements that English often ignores. Thus, the translation of English into Indigenous languages or Indigenous languages into English is often difficult, if not impossible. Since Indigenous language programming has had a short span of focused support compared to English or French in Canada, however, First Nations, Métis and Inuit language curricula and resources continue to be inadequate in most schools. Consequently, teachers spend much of their time making materials for their daily work. To counter the lack of developed resources, research has highlighted a need to enlarge learning opportunities through acknowledging and utilizing local community resources including Elders, individuals, events, ceremonies and locations (Holm & Holm, 1995; McIvor, 2005; Suina, 2004). McIvor (2005c: 11), however, cautioned teachers not to 'drown out the Elders' and other community resources through tokenizing their involvement.

In addition to a need for curricula and resources, research has indicated that Indigenous language teachers should avoid using standard western pedagogical techniques, such as teaching students to memorize words due to the variance in dialects and the verb-based nature of Indigenous languages (Berlin, 2000; Pheasant Williams, 2007). Rather, students need to hear more examples, visualize examples, and use oral repetition as it is possible to spend an entire class or more studying one Indigenous word or phrase to develop an awareness of the greater meaning of each sound (Roy & Morgan, 2008c: 241). Additionally, because Indigenous languages are primarily oral languages, Maracle (2002) encouraged teachers to spend more time developing students' oral skills and to be aware of students' varying dialects before developing reading and writing skills. Because Indigenous languages are holistic and relational (Pheasant Williams, 2007), McLeod (2003: 118) suggested that language pedagogy should be 'based on four domains of human development: mental, physical, spiritual, and emotional'. McLeod (2003) further stressed the importance of Indigenous pedagogical practices such as using stories to validate students' experiences, acknowledging students' linguistic background and cultural history and emphasizing the importance and purpose of Indigenous languages.

Research has indicated that safe learning environments, where language use is modeled, encouraged, and celebrated, have led students to emerge as leaders in Indigenous language transmission (Daniels-Fiss, 2008; McLeod, 2003; Roy & Morgan, 2008). For example, research of early childhood education Indigenous immersion programs has stressed a need to keep language programs simple, to not over-stimulate students (McIvor, 2005) and to provide healthy food and adequate facilities (Maracle 2002). Learning outside of the classroom has also been identified as integral to pedagogical effectiveness throughout grade levels (Sims, 2009; Toulouse, 2003), through 'language events' (Morgan, 2005), summer immersion courses, culture camps, student exchanges (Blair & Laboucan, 2006), land-based learning (Neganegijig & Breunig, 2007), websites (Moore & Hennessy, 2006) and broadcasting (David, 2004).

Within Indigenous paradigms, academic achievement is but one measurement of educational success. Indigenous nations have used performance and observation-based assessments, more congruent with Indigenous learning, that complement program objectives in culturally responsive ways (Borgia, 2009; Peter et al., 2003). Success has also been measured according to qualitative indicators such as increased student self-esteem and confidence (Sock & Paul-Gould, 2012; Taylor & Wright, 2003). Maracle (2002) has suggested assessment strategies such as providing student self-evaluations, videotaping student presentations and developing fluency-level pre-tests to place students in appropriate classes regardless of age. McLeod (2003) recommended that students' journals reflect upon and evaluate personal comfort levels in language usage.

Responding to limited pedagogical supports, Indigenous language teachers have been encouraged to share curricula, resources and assessment strategies, and to work collaboratively (Maracle, 2002; McLeod, 2003). Teachers alone, however, cannot and should not be held responsible for developing the resources needed to create and implement effective Indigenous language programs. Schools, governments and universities must be accountable to support Indigenous language teachers with additional resources and specialists. This is especially true for immersion programs where, unlike English streamed classes, one teacher typically must provide instruction across diverse subject areas including physical education, music and health (Sock & Paul-Gould, 2012).

Conclusion

Indigenous learning is situated within communities that value holistic, lifelong, experiential, community-based, and spiritually grounded knowledge, rooted in Indigenous languages. What we found in this literature review was that these principles of learning infiltrated through Indigenous language programs and ultimately held what worked. Researchers caution that K-12 school contexts can be incongruent with Indigenous language learning contexts. Recognizing the role of communities and parents in creating and maintaining languages has been important to the survival and revitalization of Indigenous languages. While a paucity of research exists on Indigenous languages, and program development will be shaped by community contexts and the needs of schools, students and provincial and territory ministries, this literature review highlighted five key areas that can strengthen K-12 Indigenous language programs. Immersion programming is most significant to Indigenous language learning, and the literature reviewed suggests that a framework guided by the five areas identified in this chapter can be used to guide commitments to effective and generative K-12 Indigenous language programming.

Notes

(1) First Nations, Métis and Inuit are designated Aboriginal groups recognized in the Canadian Constitution. This chapter uses 'Aboriginal' when the literature represents Indigenous peoples of Canada, and uses Indigenous as a more inclusive term in international contexts.
(2) Numerous studies have been conducted to assess the state of Aboriginal languages in Canada, and how best to implement language initiatives. Two comprehensive documents are *Towards a New Beginning: A Foundational Report for a Strategy to Revitalize First Nation, Inuit, and Métis Languages and Cultures*, by the Task Force on Aboriginal Languages and Cultures (Canadian Heritage, 2005) and The Western and Northern Canadian Protocol's *The Common Curriculum Framework for Aboriginal Language and Culture Programs: Kindergarten to Grade Twelve* (Western Canadian Protocol [WCP], 2000).
(3) Mi'kmaw is the singular of Mi'kmaq and can be used as an adjective.

References

Assembly of First Nations (1990) *Towards Linguistic Justice for First Nations*. Ottawa: Assembly of First Nations.
Baloy, N. (2011) 'We can't feel our language': Making places in the city for Aboriginal language revitalization. *American Indian Quarterly* 35 (4), 515–548.
Battiste, M. (2002) *Indigenous Knowledge and Pedagogy in First Nations Education: A Literature Review with Recommendations*. Ottawa: Indian and Northern Affairs Canada.
Battiste, M. (2005) *State of Aboriginal learning. A background paper for the national dialogue on Aboriginal learning*, accessed 6 February 2013. Ottawa: Canadian Council on Learning. www.ccl-cca.ca/pdfs/AbLKC/StateOfAboriginalLearning.pdf
Bell, L. and Marlow, P. (2009) Visibility, healing and resistance: Voices from the 2005 Dena'ina language institute. *Journal of American Indian Education* 48 (1), 1–18.
Benally, A. and Viri, D. (2005) Diné Bizaad [Navajo Language] at a crossroads: Extinction or renewal? *Bilingual Research Journal* 1 (29), 85–108.
Berlin, L.N. (2000) The benefits of second language acquisition and teaching for Indigenous language educators. *Journal of American Indian Education* 39 (3), 1–24.
Blair, H. and Laboucan, B.J. (2006) The Alberta language initiative and the implications for Indigenous languages. *Canadian Journal of Native Education* 29 (2), 206–214.
Borden, L.L. (2010) Transforming mathematics education for Mi'kmaw students through *Mawikinutimatimk*. PhD thesis, University of New Brunswick.
Borgia, M. (2009) Modifying assessment tools for Ganöhsesge:kha: A Seneca culture-language school. In J. Reyhner and L. Lockard (eds) *Indigenous Language Revitalization, Encouragement, Guidance & Lessons Learned* (pp. 191–210). Flagstaff, AZ: University of Northern Arizona.
Brandt, E.A. and Ayoungman, V. (1989) Language renewal: Dispelling the myths, planning for the future. *Canadian Journal of Native Education* 16 (2), 42–77.
Breinig, J. (2006) Alaskan Haida stories of language growth and regeneration. *American Indian Quarterly* 30 (1), 110–118.
Canadian Heritage (2005) *Towards a new beginning: A foundational report for a strategy to revitalize First Nation, Inuit and Métis languages and cultures*, accessed 6 February 2013. www.afn.ca/uploads/files/education2/towardanewbeginning.pdf

Cappon, P. (2007) Measuring success in First Nations, Inuit and Métis learning. *Policy Options*, accessed 6 February 2013. http://www.ccl-cca.ca/NR/rdonlyres/0D0A5FA7-1191-43D9-A46D-F13D7C9BECAB/0/Cappon_PolicyOptions.pdf

Charles, W. (2005) Qaneryaramta Egmiucia: Continuing our language. *Anthropology and Education Quarterly* 36 (1), 107–111.

CMEC (2010) *Learn Canada 2020*, accessed 6 February 2013. http://www.cmec.ca/278/Press-Releases/Canada%27s-Ministers-of-Education-Advance-Learn-Canada-2020-Priorities.html?id_article=265

Cummins, J. (2001a) Identity and empowerment. In J. Cummins (ed.) *Negotiating Identities: Education for Empowerment in a Diverse Society* (2nd edn) (pp. 1–26). Los Angeles, CA: Association for Bilingual Education.

Cummins, J. (2001b) Bilingual children's mother tongue: Why is it important for education? *Sprogforum* 7 (19), 15–20.

Daniels-Fiss, B. (2008) Learning to be Nehiyaw (Cree) through language. *Diaspora, Indigenous, and Minority Education* 2 (3), 233–245.

David, J. (2004) *Aboriginal Language Broadcasting in Canada: An Overview and Recommendations to the Task Force on Indigenous Languages and Cultures Final Report*. Ottawa: Debwe Communications Inc.

Eichstaedt, P. (2006) A matter of survival. *Diverse Issues in Higher Education* 23 (19), 28–31.

Epstein, R. (2009) *The Languages We Speak: Aboriginal Learners and English as an Additive Language: A Literature Review of Promising Approaches and Practices–Full Report*. Winnipeg: Manitoba Education, Citizenship, and Youth.

Fishman, J.A. (1991) *Reversing Language Shift: Theoretical and Empirical Foundations of Assistance to Threatened Languages*. Clevedon: Multilingual Matters.

Fishman, J.A. (2006) Language policy and language shift. In T. Ricento (ed.) *An Introduction to Language Policy: Theory and Method* (pp. 311–328). Malden, MA: Blackwell.

Freeman, K., Stairs, A., Corbiere, E. and Lazore, D. (1995) Ojibwe, Mohawk, and Inuktitut alive and well? Issues of identity, ownership and change. *Bilingual Research Journal* 19 (1), 39–69.

Goodfellow, A. (2003) The development of 'new' languages in Native American communities. *American Indian Culture and Research Journal* 27 (2), 41–59.

Graham, B. (2005) The development of Aboriginal language programs: A journey towards understanding. *Canadian Journal of Education* 28 (3), 318–338.

Grenoble, L. (2009) Linguistic cages and the limits of linguists. In J. Reyhner and L. Lockard (eds) *Indigenous Language Revitalization: Encouragement, Guidance & Lessons Learned* (pp. 61–69). Flagstaff, AZ: Northern Arizona University.

Greymorning, S. (1997) Going beyond words: The Arapaho immersion program. In J. Reyhner (ed.) *Teaching Indigenous Languages* (pp. 22–30). Flagstaff, AZ: Northern Arizona University.

Hallet, D., Chandler, M. and Lalonde, C. (2007) Aboriginal language knowledge and youth suicide. *Cognitive Development* 22 (4), 329–399.

Harrison, B. and Papa, R. (2005) The development of an Indigenous knowledge program in a New Zealand Maori-Language immersion school. *Anthropology and Education Quarterly* 36 (1), 57–72.

Hermes, M. (2005) 'Ma'iingan is just a misspelling of the word wolf': A case for teaching culture through language. *Anthropology and Education Quarterly* 36 (1), 43–56.

Hermes, M., Bang, M. and Martin, A. (2012) Designing Indigenous language revitalization. *Harvard Educational Review* 82 (3), 381–402.

Hinton, L. (2002) *How to Keep Your Language Alive: A Commonsense Approach to One-On-One Language Learning.* Berkeley, CA: Heydey Books.
Hinton, L. (2003) How to teach when the teacher isn't fluent. In J. Reyhner, O. Trujillo, R.L. Carrasco and L. Lockard (eds) *Nurturing Native Languages* (pp. 79–92). Flagstaff, AZ: Northern Arizona University.
Holm, A. and Holm, W. (1995) Navajo language education: Retrospect and prospect. *The Bilingual Research Journal* 19 (1), 141–167.
Ireland, B. (2009) *Moving from the head to the heart: Addressing the 'Indian's Canada's problem' in reclaiming the learning spirit: Aboriginal learners in education,* accessed 6 February 2013. Aboriginal Learning Knowledge Centre. www.ccl-cca.ca/pdfs/ablkc/AboriginalLearnersEdu_en.pdf
Johansen, B.E. (2004) Back from the (nearly) dead: Reviving Indigenous languages across North America. *American Indian Quarterly* 28 (3/4), 566–582.
Johnston, B. and Johnson, K.A. (2002) Preschool immersion education for Indigenous languages: A survey of resources. *Canadian Journal of Native Education* 26 (2), 107–124.
Kepa, M. and Manu'atu, L. (2006) Indigenous Maori and Tongan perspectives on the role of Tongan language and culture in the community and in the university in Aotearoa-New Zealand. *American Indian Quarterly* 30 (1/2), 11–29.
Kipp, D. (2009) Encouragement, guidance and lessons learned: 21 years in the trenches of Indigenous language revitalization. In J. Reyhner and L. Lockard (eds) *Indigenous Language Revitalization: Encouragement, Guidance & Lessons Learned* (pp. 1–9). Flagstaff, AZ: Northern Arizona University.
Kirkness, V.J. (2000) The preservation and use of our languages: Respecting the natural order of the creator. In B. Burnaby and Reyhner, J. (eds) *Indigenous Languages Across the Community* (pp. 17–23). Flagstaff, AZ: Northern Arizona University.
Kroskrity, P.V. (2009) Language renewal as sites of language ideological struggle: The need for 'ideological clarification'. In J. Reyhner and L. Lockard (eds) *Indigenous Language Revitalization: Encouragement, Guidance & Lessons Learned* (pp. 71–83). Flagstaff, AZ: Northern Arizona University.
Lafortune, R. (2000) *Native Languages as World Languages: A Vision for Assessing and Sharing Information about Native Languages Across Grant Making Sectors and Native Country.* Minneapolis, MN: Grotto Foundation, Inc.
Littlebear, L. (2009) *Naturalizing Indigenous knowledge: Synthesis paper,* accessed 6 February 2013. Aboriginal learning Knowledge Centre. www.ccl-cca.ca/pdfs/ablkc/naturalizeIndigenous_en.pdf
Maracle, J. (2002) Adult Mohawk language immersion programming. *Journal of Education* 37 (3), 387–403.
Martinez, C. and Strong, G. (2005) *Recognizing the Importance of Native Language: A Funding Model for Native Language Revitalization.* Minneapolis, MN: Grotto Foundation, Inc.
McCarty, T. (2003) Revitalizing Indigenous languages in homogenizing times. *Comparative Education* 39 (2), 147–163.
McCarty, T.L., Romero, M.E. and Zepeda, O. (2006) Reclaiming the gift: Indigenous youth counter-narratives on Native language loss and revitalization. *American Indian Quarterly* 30 (1/2), 28–48.
McIvor, O. (2005) The contribution of Indigenous heritage language immersion programs to healthy early childhood development. In J. Whitehead (ed.) *Research Connections Canada: Supporting Children and Families* (Vol. 12) (pp. 5–20). Ottawa: Canadian Child Care Federation.

McIvor, O. (2009) *Strategies for Indigenous language revitalization and maintenance,* accessed 6 February 2013. Canadian Language and Literacy Research Network. http://literacyencyclopedia.ca/index.php?fa=items.show&topicId=265

McLeod, Y. (2003) Change makers: Empowering ourselves thro' the education and culture of Indigenous languages. *Canadian Journal of Native Education* 27 (1), 108–126.

Meek B. and Messing, J. (2007) Framing Indigenous languages as secondary to matrix languages. *Anthropology and Education Quarterly* 38 (2), 99–118.

Mita, D.M. (2007) Māori language revitalization: A vision for the future. *Journal of Native Education* 30 (1), 101–107.

Moore, P.J. (2003) Lessons on the land: The role of Kaska elders in a university language course. *Canadian Journal of Native Education* 27 (1), 127–139.

Moore, P. and Hennessy, K. (2006) New technologies and contested ideologies: The Tagish first voices project. *American Indian Quarterly* 30 (1/2), 119–137.

Morgan, M. (2005) Redefining the Ojibwe classroom: Indigenous language programs within large research universities. *Anthropology and Education Quarterly* 3 (1), 96–103.

Neganegijig, T. and Breunig, M. (2007) Native language education: An inquiry into what is and what could be. *Canadian Journal of Native Education* 30 (2), 305–321.

Norris, M.J. (2007) Aboriginal languages in Canada: Emerging trends and perspectives on second language acquisition. *Canadian Social Trends* 83, 19–27.

Norton, R. and Fettes, M. (1994) *Taking Back the Talk: A Specialized Review on Aboriginal Language and Literacy.* A research study prepared for RCAP. Ottawa: Canada Communications Group.

Orr, J., Tompkins, J. and Murray Orr, A. (2005) Successes of the Mi'kmaq immersion program in one community. Unpublished research study, St. Francis Xavier University.

Peter, L. (2007) 'Our beloved Cherokee': A naturalistic study of Cherokee preschool language immersion. *Anthropology and Education Quarterly* 38 (4), 323–342.

Peter, L., Christie, E., Cochran, M., Dunn, D., Elk, L., Fields, E., Fields, J., Hirata-Edds, T., Huchaby, A., Raymond, R., Shade, H., Sly, G., Wickliffe, G. and Yamamoto, A. (2003) Assessing the impact of total immersion on Cherokee language revitalization: A culturally responsive, participatory approach. In J. Reyhner, O. Trujillo, R.L. Carrasco and L. Locard (eds) *Nurturing Native Languages* (pp. 7–23). Flagstaff, AZ: Northern Arizona University.

Pheasant Williams, S. (2003) The development of Ojibway language materials, *Canadian Journal of Native Education* 27 (1), 79–83.

Rice, K. (2009) Must there be two solitudes? Language activists and linguists working together. In J. Reyhner and L. Lockard (eds) *Indigenous Language Revitalization: Encouragement, Guidance & Lessons Learned* (pp. 37–59). Flagstaff, AZ: Northern Arizona University.

Romero-Little, M.E. (2006) Honoring our own: Rethinking Indigenous languages and literacy. *Anthropology and Education Quarterly* 37 (4), 399–402.

Roy, H. and Morgan, M.J. (2008) Indigenous languages and research universities: Reconciling worldviews and ideologies. *Canadian Journal of Native Education* 31 (1), 232–247.

Sims, C.P. (2005) Tribal languages and the challenges of revitalization. *Anthropology and Education Quarterly* 36 (1), 104–106.

Skutnabb-Kangas, T. and Phillipson, R. (2005) *Education through the medium of the mother-tongue: The single most important means for saving Indigenous languages,* accessed 6 February 2013. Rationales and Strategies drawn from a Symposium on Immersion Education for First Nations. Fredericton, NB: St. Thomas University and Assembly of First Nations. http://www.educatorsforimmersion.org/LI_pdf/rationals.pdf

Smith, A. (2009) *Indigenous Peoples and Boarding Schools: A Comparative Study,* accessed 6 February 2013. A Report prepared for the Secretariat of the United Nations Permanent Forum on Indigenous Issues. www.un.org/esa/socdev/unpfii/documents/E_C_19_2009_crp1.pdf

Smith, D.L. and Peck, J. (2004) Wksitnuow Wejkwapniaqewa—Mi'kmaq: A voice from the people of the dawn. *McGill Journal of Education* 39 (3), 342–353.

Sock, S. and Paul-Gould, S. (2012) Student achievement, fluency, and identity: An in-depth study of the Mi'kmaq immersion program in one community. MEd thesis, St. Francis Xavier University.

Speas, M. (2009) Someone else's language: On the role of linguists in language revitalization. In J. Reyhner and L. Lockard (eds) *Indigenous Language Revitalization, Encouragement, Guidance & Lessons Learned,* accessed 6 February 2013. Flagstaff, AZ: University of Northern Arizona. http://jan.ucc.nau.edu/~jar/ILR/

Spolsky, B. (2002) Prospects for the survival of the Navajo language: A reconsideration. *Anthropology and Education Quarterly* 33 (2), 139–162.

Statistics Canada (2008) *Indigenous Peoples in Canada in 2006: Inuit, Métis and First Nations, 2006 Census.* Ottawa: Statistics Canada.

Stelómethet Gardner, E.B. (2004) Tset Hikwstexw te Sqwelteltset: We hold our language high. *Canadian Journal of Native Education* 28 (1/2), 130–148.

Suina, J.H. (2004) Native language teachers in a struggle for language and cultural survival. *Anthropology and Education Quarterly* 35 (3), 281–302.

Taylor, D. and Wright, S. (2003) Do Aboriginal students benefit from education in their heritage language? Results from a ten-year program of research in Nunavik. *The Canadian Journal of Native Studies* 22 (1), 1–24.

Thomas, W.P. and Collier, V.P. (2002) *A national study of school effectiveness for language minority students' long-term academic achievement,* accessed 6 February 2013. Fairfax, VI: George Mason University/Center for Research on Education, Diversity & Excellence. www.usc.edu/dept/education/CMMR/CollierThomasExReport.pdf

Toulouse, I.B. (2003) Transference of concepts from Ojibwe into English contexts. *Canadian Journal of Native Education* 27 (1), 84–88.

Usborne, E., Peck, J., Smith, D.L. and Taylor, D. (2011) Learning through an Aboriginal language: The impact on students' English and Aboriginal language skills. *Canadian Journal of Education* 34 (4), 200–215.

Western Canadian Protocol (2000) *The common curriculum framework for Aboriginal language and culture programs: Kindergarten to Grade 12,* accessed 6 February 2013. http://education.alberta.ca/media/929730/abor.pdf

Wetzel, C. (2006) Neshnabemwen renaissance: Local and national Potawatomi language revitalization efforts. *American Indian Quarterly* 30 (1/2), 61–87.

12 How Have Aboriginal North Americans Responded to Writing Systems in Their Own Languages?

Barbara Burnaby

Contact between Aboriginal North Americans and Europeans from 1500 to the present has piqued the intellectual and practical curiosities of both Aboriginal peoples and Europeans on this continent, with many results. Despite numerous tragic injustices, conflicts and misunderstandings over the centuries among European newcomers, Aboriginal inhabitants and their respective descendants, a myriad of creative outcomes have evolved from the contact between them, not least being the unique forms and practices of literacy in North American Indigenous languages. Reliable information about Aboriginal language literacy is largely scattered, even buried, in various kinds of documents, mostly written by non-Aboriginal people. However, in recent decades, the research on literacy among Aboriginal people has diversified, and Aboriginal writers have contributed their specific views on the topic of literacy in their environment.

This chapter reviews the literature on Aboriginal literacy in North America to explore Aboriginal perspectives on literacy in their languages from direct and indirect documentation. Because the literature is fragmentary at best and, until recently, largely recorded only from Euro-North Americans' points of view, a thematic approach has been taken in this chapter to indicate possible trends throughout the complex history of North America since 1500.

Defining Literacy in the North American Aboriginal Context

Ideological conditions tempering values attached to literacy

As context for understanding Aboriginal language literacies, we must constantly keep in mind the hugely varied, constantly changing paradigms of literacy brought by Europeans from the 1500s. The content in this chapter is embedded in a broad history of literacy events and flow of practices that we can only sketch here.

Around the time of the earliest contacts between Europeans and North American Aboriginal peoples, the Council of Trent (1545–1564) was encouraging the use of vernacular languages in religious instruction to permit direct access by common believers to the written religious word (e.g. Bragdon, 2000: 180; Greenfield, 2000: 204–206). English spelling in England was not standardized until between about 1650 and 1750, and Noah Webster's famous American-English dictionary began its influential life in 1783. In the five centuries since 1500, the proportions of literates and the levels of usage of literacy in Aboriginal North American languages have been, in many situations, probably at a comparable level to those of European language literacy among all but the elite of European and Euro-North American society (e.g. Greenfield, 2000; McGrath, 1984). From 1800, the link between formal schooling and literacy firmed up, with compulsory education more or less the norm in North America by about the mid-20th century. Geographic isolation meant that some Aboriginal groups were among the last to get formal, government-supported schooling and, when they did, it was clouded by the imposition of residential schooling and general repression of Aboriginal languages.

Also, around the mid-20th century, various debates arose in North America and Europe about the nature of literacy. One component of the debates viewed alphabetic literacy (rather than syllabic or ideographic) as the ideal (e.g. Bloomfield, 1933; Pike, 1947), indeed as one of the factors or even *the* most important factor distinguishing Western industrialized societies from primitive ones (e.g. Lévi-Strauss, 1964; Olson, 1977). The latter proposition, characterized as The Great Divide, was hotly contested, notably by Street (1984) and Scribner and Cole (1981), who argued that literacy is a multifaceted social phenomenon which cannot be linked causally to the specific psychological abilities of individuals or overall societal development.

Meanwhile, the North American bubble of confidence that literacy, thanks to public education, was virtually universal on the continent was burst in the 1980s. Major economic developments revealed that literacy, at least literacy up to certain standards of proficiency supposedly needed by many employers, was neither universal nor even adequately present (e.g. Deslauriers, 1990; Economic Council of Canada, 1990). Various large-scale national and international studies (e.g. Kirsch & Mosenthal, 1993; National Center for Educational Statistics, 1998; Statistics Canada, 1991) found that the level of formal schooling was not as tightly correlated with demonstrable literacy skill as many people had previously supposed. North American Aboriginal people have been singled out as particularly low on measures of both English language literacy skills and formal educational achievement (e.g. Hughes, 1990: 6–10; McCarty & Watahomigie, 1998: 73). Finally, a fascinating, highly challenging debate has arisen about the status of certain kinds of oral testimony by Aboriginal peoples in Canadian courts. The central issue is the validity of oral traditions in the face of Western legal systems heavily invested in the value of the written record. The acceptance of Aboriginal oral traditions and histories in legal actions has been much debated and continues to affect judgements of profound importance to specific Aboriginal groups (von Gernet, 1996).

In sum, in order to study literacy among Aboriginal people in North America throughout their period of contact with European newcomers, one must account for the fluid and complex nature not only of the manifestations of reading and writing, but also of the concepts and powers accompanying them. The preceding discussion suggests some reasons why literacy is often associated with specific sets of values, such as belonging to a superior culture; having various skills useful in religious development; being able to take part in all aspects of citizenship by acting in accordance with written law; or being a desirable employee. The ideologies that attach such values to literacy are rarely explicit in documents describing Aboriginal literacies. Makers of documents choose what to write about and what to exclude, interpreting situations according to their emic perspectives. Therefore, the record we have to draw from to appreciate the experiences of literacy among Aboriginal peoples needs to be approached with great caution.

Themes Related to Literacy Among Aboriginal Peoples

A preeminent scholar of Aboriginal literacy, Walker (1981, 1996) points out the variety of roles played by Aboriginals and Europeans in initiating writing systems for Aboriginal languages; the complexity of Aboriginal language situations; the continuing viability and development of many Aboriginal languages and their literacies despite highly adverse conditions and lack of mainstream support; and the unique choices made by Aboriginal peoples to use literacy as opposed to other media for communications.

In this chapter, these overviews from Walker's studies form a backbone and a backdrop to the discussion of themes emerging as the research and discussion about literacies in Aboriginal languages grow. The themes outlined in the following sections are offered as an extension of previous work, including Walker's, with an emphasis on newer work. These themes illustrate clusters of ideas I have found about the phenomena of literacy in Aboriginal languages and particularly how Aboriginal peoples have responded to models of literacy brought by Europeans. It must be kept in mind that information about Aboriginal literacies only exists because someone happened to document them; therefore, they cannot be seen as an indication of frequency or distribution of real activity. Specifically, we can get a sense of the kinds of activities that *may* characterize Aboriginal literacy but we cannot rule out the possibility that some things did take place just because they have not been mentioned. Also, from a literature that has effectively *described* a rich array of orthographies that have been developed, the themes here focus less on *what* was created and more on *who* was involved and *how* the systems were used. In this chapter, space only permits a few examples from a large literature.

Theme 1: Who took responsibility and the initiative to create and develop Aboriginal language literacy?

Most of the original work in creating writing systems for Aboriginal languages in North America was done by European newcomers and later by Euro-North Americans (Goddard, 1996; Mithun, 1996). However, the size and nature of the role of Aboriginal people in the origination and development of writing systems for Aboriginal languages is less certain because they were not necessarily in a position or culturally disposed to record their activities in the forms available today. Some Aboriginal people who became literate in a European language went on to develop writing systems to record information in their own languages. A significant part was also played by Aboriginal people who adapted writing systems devised by Europeans for Aboriginal languages. Also, at least two writing systems were developed by Aboriginal people who were apparently not previously literate in any language (i.e. Sequoia and Uyakoq).

Mostly, it was missionaries and other Euro-North Americans who developed the first writing systems for Aboriginal languages, or at least they left the best records. Clearly, many such newcomers achieved great feats of language learning and linguistic analysis to create and develop writing systems for Aboriginal languages. However, the vast amount of innovative and extension work on Aboriginal literacy must have involved large numbers of devoted, perceptive and hard-working mother tongue speakers of Aboriginal languages, many of whom have not been suitably credited in the public record.

Mithun (1996: 56) notes that, among Aboriginal researchers, some have become academics themselves, pursuing advanced degrees in linguistics and anthropology, some have worked in collaboration with linguists, and some have worked independently.

Theme 2: Spread (and decline) of Aboriginal writing systems

A crucial indication of the ways in which Aboriginal peoples responded to the invention of writing systems for their languages by Europeans or by members of their own communities comes mainly from numerous accounts of the success stories (e.g. Bragdon, 2000; Greenfield, 2000; Shearwood, 1986).

These records of highly positive responses to new writing systems in Aboriginal communities strongly indicate not only the interest in Aboriginal communities for the technology (and perhaps its intended purposes) but also their readiness to learn and use it. However, taking these documents as an indication of universal Aboriginal reactions is risky. First, the record may well be biased in favour of the inventions and their inventors. It would not be surprising if the creators and promulgators of new writing systems recorded and disseminated such evident successes in terms of the numbers of new readers. In fact, these enthusiastic accounts may have served as indirect evidence of the effectiveness of the work to convert Aboriginal peoples to Christianity. Analysing the documentation for negative cases and long-term impact is more challenging than recognizing initial successes. In some cases, Aboriginal communities rejected the written forms of their languages (McCarty & Watahomigie, 1998), and in others, both Aboriginals and non-Aboriginals feared certain impacts of literacy on the population (Greenfield, 2000).

At least three major reasons have been proposed for the decline or demise of Aboriginal language writing system use: (1) the precipitous decline and in some cases, extinction of the languages themselves (Burnaby & Beaujot, 1986; Krauss, 1991); (2) the highly controversial role of residential and/or compulsory schooling delivered in English (McCarty & Watahomigie, 1998); and (3) the advent of technologies, such as the telephone, which sometimes replaced the written language as a form of communication (Burnaby & MacKenzie, 1985).

Overall, there is no doubt that a number of writing systems for Aboriginal languages, when initially introduced, were embraced with enthusiasm and community participation, but that some others were refused. Mostly, the impact of the introduction of Aboriginal language writing is undocumented.

Theme 3: Range of uses of Aboriginal literacies

To fully appreciate Aboriginal literacies, we must address the uses of Aboriginal literacies and the extent to which they became an important medium in community life. Documenting the *practice* of a literacy in a community in all its institutions over time rather than just describing its *artefacts* (written/printed materials) is challenging. The records available are relatively few and necessarily reflect the values of the recorder as to whether the glass is half empty or half full.

Goody (1977, as cited by Bragdon, 2000: 281) notes that a written language in previously non-literate communities has provided for a codification and regulation, enabling, for example, work in the judiciary and in census taking. Further, missionaries, both by describing the languages themselves and by introducing vernacular literacy, contributed to new communicative practices. Thus, Europeans introduced (imposed?) norms of form and substance of communication not only between Aboriginals and non-Aboriginals but also among Aboriginals themselves.

McGrath (1984: 27) summarizes the range of literature in Inuktitut, developed over time, as the Bible, the Book of Common Prayer, and the hymnals; translations by missionaries of secular works; original, practical works by non-Inuit; schoolbooks; and original works by Inuit authors. She contrasts such developments of and motivations for Inuktitut literacy under the missionaries with the kinds of literacy and numeracy learned by the Inuit who, from the 18th century on, changed their economic patterns to get access to the local, European-initiated businesses of whaling and fur trading (McGrath, 1984: 6–7). Special mention is made in the literature of the value to the Inuit of being able to write letters in Inuktitut, especially to their children who were sent away to residential schools.

Finally, some emphasize the point that literacy in most Aboriginal languages is a skill and a role for specialists rather than an expectation for the whole population. Indeed, this scribal profession has been the norm in many societies worldwide at least until the modern era. Both Burnaby and Mackenzie (1985: 71) and Valentine (1995: 101) describe literacy use in northern Algonquian communities where the language is still flourishing. In these communities, a large proportion of the population practiced a passive use of reading through decoding to sound a few well-known religious texts. However, in these communities, 'a number of specialist occupations required higher literacy skills, for example, in the store or the band office, as the lay reader in church services, to read and write letters, to teach syllabics in school or to write notices in syllabics for the school and nurses.

Theme 4: How Aboriginal language literacies were taught and learned

The spread of many writing systems for Aboriginal languages tended to result from individuals teaching the writing system to one another with minimal support from the originators of the system (Greenfield, 2000). In addition, sometimes, teachers from the Aboriginal communities would lead schools where the language was the medium of instruction (e.g. Bragdon, 2000). In some cases, Aboriginal literacy was taught through collaborations between the Aboriginal community and missionaries, for example, in the Mohawk nation (Hart, 2000). Following such initiatives in the 1600s and 1700s, there were numerous reports of various kinds of spontaneous and regular, long-term and short-term approaches to teaching Aboriginal literacies by Aboriginal and non-Aboriginal missionaries and school teachers.

However, with the growth of compulsory schooling in the late 19th and early 20th centuries, Aboriginal languages and literacy in Aboriginal languages played differing roles in schooling for Aboriginal children, and were frequently banned through draconian English-only policies. After WWII, 'there were movements in Canada and the United States intended to include and develop Aboriginal languages through literacy teaching in schools (Walker, 1984). There is evidence from the late 20th century suggesting that community practices of Aboriginal literacy teaching and learning continue despite formal classes in schools (e.g. Kirkness & Bowman, 1992; McGrath, 1984).

Theme 5: Levels of Aboriginal literacy actually attained

Clearly, the functions of Aboriginal literacy in general were and are much more restricted than those of English or French in current Canadian society. In most cases, reading material is scarce, and what exists is not very demanding and/or critical in terms of the need to get information from it. The most difficult Aboriginal language literacy tasks of (1) getting new information from previously unseen text and (2) of writing for others to read have not been required of the general population of speakers. Often, a few community specialists, if anyone, undertake this work.

Reportedly, in the late 17th century, a Massachutt writing system was being used by 30% of the colony, following its introduction around 1650 (Bragdon, 2000). In the 19th century, 25–90% of the Cherokee nation was reported to be literate, and the literacy rate within the Cherokee population was said to be highest within the traditional, full-blood communities (Silver & Miller, 1997: 198). In a survey of the Ojibwe, Oji-Cree (Severn Ojibwe) and Cree communities in northwestern Ontario, where traditional language fluency is quite high, Ningewance (1992–1993) found a higher reading and writing rate among adults than students, but nearly all of the self-reported data revealed literacy rates below 50%.

In 1991, Statistics Canada collected self-report data for the Aboriginal Peoples Survey (APS). The APS contained questions (not asked of other Canadians) concerning: how many read Aboriginal languages (36.2%); who taught them – parents (54%), grandparents (32%), elders (25%), school teachers (39%) or someone else (24%); what reading materials do speakers of Aboriginal languages read (40% newspapers, 36% newsletters and 28% magazines); how many write Aboriginal languages (25.5%); who taught them – parents (54%), grandparents (29%), elders (23%), school teachers (44%) or someone else (22%) (Statistics Canada, 1993: Table 2.1).

A number of challenging issues arise from this kind of documentation. First, specific problems exist around how the figures were arrived at. Special attention to existing records to tease out the sources of such information would be useful. Second, in Aboriginal communities currently, new studies on the levels of fluency in Aboriginal literacies are needed to take into account the teaching of Aboriginal languages as part of school programs. Finally, such studies are potentially complicated by the fact that many contemporary programs in schools are aimed at teaching Aboriginal languages as second languages to children who do not speak them but know them only passively. When school programs teach literacy in a language that has little or no function in the community, it can be difficult to provide children with the motivation and the practice in reading to become fluent readers in the sense that schoolchildren are expected to become fluent in English.

Theme 6: Aboriginal literacy and identity

Whatever the day-to-day functions and levels of reading and writing skills in Aboriginal languages may be or have been, there is no negative and a considerable amount of positive evidence that the very existence of literacies in Aboriginal languages has conveyed significant meaning to speakers of those languages beyond the literal ideas expressed by the language. Some notes in the literature credit spiritual agencies as the force behind Aboriginal literacy learning. At least two inventors of unique syllabic scripts for Yupik in Alaska credit divine intervention with their work. Nichols, writing about the Cree syllabary (1996: 601), notes that it has been given an Indigenous origin in Cree legend, and some have seen its sources in quill and beadwork designs.

Aboriginal identity appears to be especially strongly tied to orthographies that are distinctly different from the Roman alphabetic system of most European languages. Although there were attempts during the 19th century to get the Mi'kmaq to use a Roman orthography, rather than a previous hieroglyphic writing system, in order supposedly to permit greater access to the scriptures, the use of Roman writing in Mi'kmaq did not develop substantially until the first few decades of the 20th century, and even then there was continued loyalty to the hieroglyphic religious materials (Greenfield, 2000: 204–207).

In these days of growing globalization, much ink is being spilt concerning the value and role of minority languages, including the relationships between their speakers and those of more powerful languages. Evidence indicates the importance of Aboriginal literacies to the identity of Aboriginal peoples (including bilinguals and those who do not speak their ancestral languages), and should be taken into account in broader discussions regarding the maintenance or revival of Aboriginal languages themselves.

Theme 7: Relationship between Aboriginal language literacies and oral tradition

Some authors emphasize the degree to which Aboriginal people integrated literacy in their languages into their previous and ongoing oral traditions. For example, Battiste (1985) describes how the various forms of literacy in Mi'kmaq introduced by Europeans were adopted quickly and effectively because they could be interpreted through the pre-contact cultural norms of communication and experience with transmission of meaning through pictographs, wampum1 and other visual means. She discusses how the values and purposes of the Mi'kmaq literacy taught by European priests were adopted into family, community and spiritual life on the Mi'kmaqs' own terms. Forced assimilation to English in the 20th century through compulsory schooling threatened Mi'kmaq linguistic and cultural survival, whereas previous European initiatives regarding literacy in Mi'kmaq had been culturally reinforcing. Greenfield (2000) also points to evidence of how religious meaning permeated the hieroglyphs used by the French missionaries and supported communication between them and the Mi'kmaq.

Walker (1984) reviews a broad range of literacy and related practices among the Cherokee, the Passamaquoddy, the Innu and the Mi'kmaq, and concludes:

It seems that there was among the far northeastern Algonquians an oral tradition and a persistent and pervasive stress on accuracy in the transmission of oral texts. This accounts for the use of mnemonic devices, either wampum, birchbark, Le Clerq's ideograms, or Ventomile's Roman alphabet. But these were not perceived as visual representations of speech. They were only catalysts for accurate recitation of sacred texts. (Walker, 1984: 50)

Overall, an analysis of the impact and development of literacies in Aboriginal languages in North America seems to indicate: (1) that Aboriginal people extended their communicative practices through literacy that included functions and forms modelled on European usage; but (2) that such inclusions were largely of their own choosing; and (3) that further developments were in directions that fitted in with their existing needs or cultural forms of communication.

Theme 8: Issues of standardization

In the past five decades, issues of the standardization of Aboriginal writing systems have come to the fore. Reaching and enforcing a consensus about spelling seems to engender tension among speakers universally. From the work of many scholars in this area (e.g. McCarty & Watahomigie, 1998), it appears that the identification of the users with their writing system comes into play when standardization is attempted. The Inuit have a remarkable history not only in taking to literacy when Europeans supplied them with models but also by developing it for their own purposes. McGrath (1984) wished for the standardization of Inuit writing systems in part to unite the circumpolar Inuit community. An important step towards such a unified orthography took place in 1976, representing an unprecedented agreement among the Intuit not only to have one standard system of representing the sounds of the language across all dialects but also to organize it could be directly converted between syllabics and Roman letters. Shearwood (1998) recounts how the infrastructure for self-government in the new Territory of Nunavut (formed in 1999) was made possible in part through the 1976 agreement. He describes sociodemographic links between orthographic practices and groups within the community as a result of the ways in which the different generations felt the need to convey and/or change the written language to fit its new status as a territorial official language.

MacKenzie's experience in working with the Cree of the east coast of James Bay reinforces a number of the patterns regarding standardization in the Inuit case. Like many Inuit, the Cree had been using a syllabic system, based on Evans' work, since the middle of the 19th century. Somewhat analogously to the contentious features in Inuktitut that Shearwood (1998) noticed in his research, MacKenzie documents a decade of discussion with the Cree about writing system standardization.

Theme 9: Definition of literacy(ies) revisited

'Debate is ongoing over the existence of any *pre-contact writing systems* for an Aboriginal North American language. Academic study of visual symbols and symbol systems created by Aboriginal peoples has largely been conducted separately from that of the oral languages, notably stemming from the extensive work of Mallery (1886, 1893). Across this definitional divide between pictures and writing, the research and description of writing systems for Aboriginal languages have tended to concentrate on writing systems which evolved on the basis of European models, on their artefacts in terms of publications rather than on their use in daily life, and on their technology as good representations of the sound or morphology systems of the language.

However, in recent years, the focus of a number of studies of literacy in Aboriginal languages in North America has been on the ways in which Aboriginal peoples have incorporated their own communicative patterns, including the use of their unique visual systems, to meet their own communication needs. Scholarship is beginning to show how Aboriginal peoples have been far from passive in this area by taking leadership roles in creating and developing new systems, and have, through practice, moulded systems to best suit their own purposes. A few have also raised the topic of the role played by Aboriginal visual as well as oral communication systems in the evolution of Aboriginal literacy.

Basso and Anderson (1977) opened up the discussion of the meaning and function of the visual systems created by Aboriginal peoples in their study of the symbols of Silas John in Apache. They showed how these symbols relate to Apache language and religious culture in multiple ways, and concluded that: we must acknowledge the possibility that several structurally distinct forms of writing were developed by North America's Indian cultures. Concomitantly, we must be prepared to abandon traditional ideas of typological similarity and simplicity among these systems in favour of those that take variation and complexity into further account (Basso & Anderson, 1977: 101). From the consideration of the study of Aboriginal language literacies here, one might expect that more argument following the linguistic relativity tradition might ensue with respect to the relationship between Aboriginal and Western forms of written/visual communication.

Theme 10: Current perspectives on practice in Aboriginal literacies

Today, it is crucial that we take stock of the evolution of literacies in Aboriginal languages and critically examine its results in the current context. One crucial factor is that Aboriginal languages in North America are now massively affected by the shift to English and French, and thus there is, understandably, also a shift in the roles, uses and values of literacies in Aboriginal languages. The effect is that there is more diversity than ever before in factors affecting Aboriginal literacy at the local level. Another overarching condition is the form of the modern, national state and the impact of globalization. Enmeshed in this context are the values and priorities of the mainstream, of minority groups, and of individual communities. The highest levels of government, as holders of the most evident power and resources, have, to some extent, recognized the validity of Aboriginal claims for recognition and maintenance of Aboriginal languages in their communities and beyond. It is necessary, then, to take into account global actions (and nonaction) from the top down *in addition to* local initiatives (and dilemmas) to meet the unique Aboriginal literacy needs inherent at the community level.

In this layered mosaic of needs and interests, discussions of Aboriginal literacy tend to divide into two almost entirely separate streams, one regarding literacy in Aboriginal languages and the other concerned only with Aboriginal peoples' acquisition of literacy in mainstream languages. In many cases, especially when only literacy in the mainstream language is being considered, the quality of the argument would benefit if the authors were to take heed of factors relating to both or all of the languages relevant. General solutions in global discussions seem to avoid as much as possible mentioning the actual language of literacy, but instead discuss literacy in an abstract way.

More recently, a number of articles by Aboriginal scholars and practitioners and a full issue of the *Canadian Journal of Native Education* (27: 1) have been devoted to Aboriginal literacy. The focus is on literacy in mainstream languages while acknowledging the importance of literacy in Aboriginal languages as appropriate in each context. All the authors hone in on the importance of *how* the literacy is taught rather than on the specifics of *what* is taught (Antone, 2003).

A number of scholars (e.g. Antone *et al.*, 2003) reiterate the importance of the reality of Aboriginal patterns of communication in general and literacy in particular. The present climate of opinion has a strong place within the larger movement of recent years to support and revitalize minority languages worldwide.

Conclusions

From this review of broad and complex scholarship, it is not possible to draw new conclusions. Nonetheless, it is clear that Aboriginal people in North America have been far from passive in their responses to the literacy models that Europeans brought with them. Aboriginal people assessed what they were offered and often accepted it in some form or another; made new initiatives where they saw the need; and moulded all the new forms to suit their own communication needs and practices. For a long time, documentation and analysis of such events appeared to be mainly focused on what Euro-North Americans saw, interpreted, intended and understood. However, in recent decades, Aboriginal perspectives have entered the literature on Aboriginal literacy, especially from Aboriginal authors directly. Now that Aboriginal individuals are becoming increasingly involved in practising Aboriginal literacy and doing research on it, one can expect even more light to be shed on the Aboriginal side of the phenomenon as well as more Aboriginal control over new developments in the medium.

Under the various themes in the previous sections, implications can be drawn for further study and practical applications, such as the scope of functions likely to be effective in Aboriginal literacy, strategies for teaching and learning that are worth pursuing, the proper role of literacy specialists within communities, factors involved in the standardization of writing systems, and so on. The tendency for research to include sociolinguistics and discourse, as well as phonological and grammatical studies, is now established and promises to support further initiatives to balance Euro-North American perspectives with those of Aboriginal peoples.

Note

Wampum beads are made from shells.

References

Antone, E. (2003) Culturally framing Aboriginal literacy and learning. *Canadian Journal of Native Education* 27 (1), 7–15.

Antone, E., Blair, H. and Archibald, J. (2003) Editorial: Advancing Aboriginal languages and literacy. *Canadian Journal of Native Education* 27 (1), 1–6.

Basso, K.H. and Anderson, N. (1977) A Western Apache writing system: The symbols of Silas John. In J.A. Fishman (ed.) *Advances in the Creation and Revision of Writing Systems* (pp. 77–104). The Hague, Paris: Mouton.

Battiste, M. (1985) Micmac literacy and cognitive assimilation. In B. Burnaby (ed.) *Promoting Native Writing Systems in Canada* (pp. 7–18). Toronto: OISE Press.

Bloomfield, L. (1933) *Language*. New York: Holt.
Bragdon, K. (2000) Native languages spoken and written: Views from southern New England. In E.G. Gray and N. Fiering (eds) *The Language Encounter in the Americas, 1492–1800: A Collection of Essays* (pp. 173–188). New York, Oxford: Berghahn Books.
Burnaby, B. and MacKenzie, M. (1985) Reading and writing in Rupert House. In B. Burnaby (ed.) *Promoting Native Writing Systems in Canada* (pp. 57–81). Toronto: OISE Press.
Burnaby, B. and Beaujot, R. (1986) *The Use of Aboriginal Languages in Canada: An Analysis of the 1981 Census*. Ottawa: Department of the Secretary of State.
DesLauriers, R.C. (1990) *The Impact of Employee Illiteracy on Canadian Business*. Ottawa: Conference Board of Canada.
Economic Council of Canada (1990) *Good Jobs, Bad Jobs: Employment in the Service Economy*. Ottawa: Minister of Supply and Services Canada.
Goody, J. (1977) *The Domestication of the Savage Mind*. Cambridge: Cambridge University Press.
Greenfield, B. (2000) The Mi'kmaq hieroglyphic prayer book: Writing and Christianity in Maritime Canada, 1675–1921. In E.G. Gray and N. Fiering (eds) *The Language Encounter in the Americas, 1492–1800: A Collection of Essays* (pp. 189–211). New York, Oxford: Berghahn Books.
Hart, W.B. (2000) Mohawk schoolmasters and catechists in mid-eighteenth-century Iroquoia: An experiment in fostering literacy and religious change. In E.G. Gray and N. Fiering (eds.) *The Language Encounter in the Americas, 1492–1800: A Collection of Essays* (pp. 230–257). New York, Oxford: Berghahn Books.
Hughes, K. (1990) *'You Took My Talk': Aboriginal Literacy and Empowerment*. Fourth Report of the Standing Committee on Aboriginal Affairs. Ottawa: House of Commons.
Kirkness, V.J. and Bowman, S.S. (1992) *First Nations and Schools: Triumphs and Struggles*. Toronto: Canadian Education Association.
Kirsch, I.S. and Mosenthal P. (1993) Interpreting the IEA Reading Literacy scales. In M. Binkley, K. Rust and M. Winglee (eds) *Methodological Issues in Comparative Educational Studies: The Case of the IEA Reading Literacy Study*. (pp. 135–192).Washington, DC: National Center for Educational Statistics, US Department of Education.
Krauss, M. (1973) Eskimo-Aleut. In T. Sebeok (ed.) *Trends in Linguistics*. The Hague: Mouton.
Krauss, M. (1991) The world's languages in crisis. *Language* 68 (1), 4–10.
Lévi-Strauss, C. (1964) *Le cru et le cuit*. Paris: Librairie Plon.
MacKenzie, M. (1985) Spelling reform among the James Bay Cree. In B. Burnaby (ed.) *Promoting Native Writing Systems in Canada* (pp. 49–55). Toronto: OISE Press.
Mallery, G. (1886) *Pictographs of the North American Indians: A Preliminary Paper*. Bureau of American Ethnology Annual Report 4. Washington, DC: Smithsonian Institution.
'Mallery, G. (1893) *Picture-writing of the American Indians*. Bureau of American Ethnology Annual Report 10. Washington, DC: Smithsonian Institution.
McCarty, T.L. and Watahomigie, L.J. (1998) Language and literacy in American Indian and Alaska Native communities. In B. Pérez (ed.) *Sociocultural Contexts of Language and Literacy* (pp. 69–98). Mahwah, NJ: Lawrence Erlbaum.
McGrath, R. (1984) *Canadian Inuit Literature: The Development of a Tradition*. Canadian Ethnology Service Paper No. 94, Mercury Series. Ottawa: National Museum of Man.
Mithun, M. (1996) The description of Native languages of North America: Boas and after. In W.C. Sturdevant (ed.) *Handbook of North American Indians* (Vol. 17) (pp. 43–63). Washington, DC: Smithsonian Institution.

National Center for Educational Statistics (1998) *Literacy in OECD Countries: Technical Report on the First International Adult Literacy Survey*. Washington, DC: US Department of Education.

Nichols, J.D. (1996) The Cree syllabary. In P.T. Daniels and W. Bright (eds) *The World's Writing Systems* (pp. 599–611). Oxford: Oxford University Press.

Ningewance, P. (1992–1993) *Dreaming in a Strange Language: A Report on the Native Language Development Project, Sioux Lookout District, 1992–83, Phase One*. Toronto: Ministry of Education and Training.

Olson, D.R. (1977) From utterance to text: The bias of language in speech and writing. *Harvard Educational Review* 47 (3), 257–281.

Pike, K.L. (1947) *Phonemics: A Technique for Reducing Languages to Writing*. Ann Arbor, MI: University of Michigan Press.

Scribner, S. and Cole, M. (1981) *The Psychology of Literacy*. Cambridge, MA and London: Harvard University Press.

Shearwood, P. (1986) Secondary school writing in the Northwest Territories of Canada. Masters dissertation, Ontario Institute for Studies in Education, University of Toronto.

Shearwood, P. (1998) Literacy and social identity in a Nunavut community. Doctoral dissertation, Ontario Institute for Studies in Education, University of Toronto.

Silver, S. and Miller, W.R. (1997) *American Indian Languages: Cultural and Social Contexts*. Tucson, AZ: University of Arizona Press.

Statistics Canada (1991) *Adult Literacy in Canada: Results of a National Survey*. Ottawa: Statistics Canada.

Statistics Canada (1993) *Language, Tradition, Health, Lifestyle and Social Issues: 1991 Aboriginal Peoples Survey*. Catalogue Number 89-533. Ottawa: Statistics Canada.

Street, B. (1984) *Literacy In Theory and Practice*. Cambridge: Cambridge University Press.

Valentine, L.P. (1995) *Making It Their Own: Severn Ojibwe Communicative Practices*. Toronto: University of Toronto Press.

Walker, W. (1981) Native American writing systems. In C.A. Ferguson and S.B. Heath (eds) *Language in the USA* (pp. 145–174) Cambridge: Cambridge University Press.

Walker, W. (1984) Literacy, wampums, the Gudebuk, and how Indians in the far northeast read. *Anthropological Linguistics* 26 (1), 42–52.

Walker, W. (1996) Native writing systems. In W.C. Sturdevant (ed.) *Handbook of North American Indians* (Vol. 17) (pp. 158–184). Washington, DC: Smithsonian Institution.

Conclusion: Additional Conceptions of Second Language Education in Canada

Callie Mady and Katy Arnett

Though the original, traditional French immersion program of Canada has made a lasting contribution to our understanding of second language education across the world, it should not remain identified as 'the' language education program of Canada. To do so would deprive the world of important understandings of other conceptions of second language education that have been developed and expanded in the Great White North.

As the first section in this volume has aptly demonstrated, language education in Canada is not just about the study of one of the country's two official languages, by students who speak the other official language. The rising immigrant population in Canada has led to rising populations of students in language programs, who are adding English and French to the language they speak at home with their families. This language study is largely viewed as an important part of the development of the Canadian identity for new arrivals and their families (as shown by Carr, this volume) and that these multilingual students perform well when given the opportunity to add French to their language toolbox (as shown by Mady, this volume). Yet, questions remain about how best to support the students who come to Canada on a temporary basis for the purpose of developing skills in one of the two official languages (as shown by Garbati, this volume).

The second section of the volume has enabled us to better understand what is possible in terms of heritage language maintenance for immigrants. Immigration is impacting many countries besides Canada, and its influence on language traditions is immeasurable in some regards. As the three chapters in this section have shown, the right to access and pursue opportunities to initiate and/or maintain proficiency in their heritage languages is an important part of the transition to life in a new country. Collectively, we know how such programs can be used to support ties to the community (Guardado & Becker, this volume), their relationship to identity development (Noels, this volume) and how the position/placement of the language program within the larger Canadian context can shape its success (Duff & Li, this volume).

The third section of the volume did turn attention to the well-known French immersion program, but did so for a student population who has been historically excluded from the context – students with disabilities and language-related challenges. Shifts in views about disability and the rights of individuals to have access to opportunities has required French immersion programs to rethink how they support language development for *all* students in its programs, though there is still much work to do. First, there needs to be an examination of the philosophies and beliefs that inform ideas about second language education for students who struggle with language, just as much as there needs to be an examination of the implications of continuing to view immersion as an 'enrichment' program (as shown by Arnett, this volume). From a practical standpoint, we need to better understand how challenges with one's first language can inform the way we provide support in the process of developing proficiency in a second language. As shown in this volume, there are some starting points for students learning to read in another language (Bourgoin & Dicks, this volume) and for students developing their writing skills in the target language (Le Bouthillier, this volume).

Finally, Canada is also in a position to add to the conversation about how to revive and sustain the Indigenous languages of a country's original inhabitants. An ugly part of Canada's linguistic history, the decimation of Indigenous languages, has brought Canada's Aboriginal communities to a critical point in their efforts to keep their language traditions alive. The contributions in this section offer insights into the potential benefits of applying the features of the French immersion program to programming in an Aboriginal community (Smith *et al.*, this volume), understanding the features that must comprise Aboriginal language programs if they are to succeed in their efforts to spread the language (Gillies & Battiste, this volume) and the challenges that remain in trying to shape understandings of written language literacy within Aboriginal languages (Burnaby, this volume).

Taken in conjunction with the positive image presented by much of French immersion research, these chapters offer a broad picture of Canadian second language education. The contributions to this volume share attempts to improve second language education for all. Observation of this wider view offers the potential for a better understanding of second language education in Canada. However, beyond observation, this volume seeks to improve second language education and research in Canada and beyond.

Index

Aboriginal communities and languages
Apache, 194

Beothuk, 156

Cherokee, 190–192
Cree, 154–156, 175, 191–194

Eskasoni, 153, 161–167

Innu, 192
Inuit, 154, 156, 160, 165–6, 176, 189, 193
Inuktitut, 154–5, 160, 166, 189, 194

Kuujjuaq, 158

Maori, 172–3
Massachut, 190

Aboriginal language immersion programs, 155, 156, 158–167, 170–5, 177–8
Aboriginal literacy, oral tradition 186, 192
Aboriginal literacy, perspectives of, 184
Aboriginal literacy, standardization, 185–6, 193–4, 196
Aboriginal literacy, written, 159, 163
Alberta, 55–68, 95
Allophone, 35, 71, 103
Anglophone, 3, 5, 17, 22, 90–96, 104, 136, 159
Asperger Syndrome (see Autism Spectrum Disorder)
Attitude, 6–18, 41–48, 72–76, 87, 94, 96, 112

Métis, 153–154, 166, 169, 176
Mi'kmaq, 153–167, 175–6, 192
Mi'kmaw, 174, 176
Mohawk, 155, 172, 175, 190

Nunavik, 160

Ojibwe (Ojibway), 154–5, 191
Oji-Cree, 191

Passamaquoddy, 192
Puna Leo, 173

Sequoia, 187

Uyakoq, 187

Yupik, 191

Autism Spectrum Disorder, 135–50

British Columbia, 22–35, 55–69

Cape Breton, 153, 156, 160, 162, 165
Chinese language, 72, 81, 87–97
Community involvement, 173
Community support, 171–2
Core French, 3–19, 38–50
Cree (see Aboriginal languages)

English language learner (see allophone)
English speakers (see anglophone)
Exemptions, 28, 103–115

Index

Family, 45, 46, 48, 55–68, 72, 77, 78, 87, 92, 93, 173, 192
First Nations, 154, 169–178
Francophone, 3, 4, 22, 88, 90, 159–60
French immersion, 25, 33, 39, 91, 96, 103–115, 118–132, 135–149
French speakers (see Francophones)
Funding, language programs, 89, 91, 108, 112, 167, 170–2

German language, 71–84
Grassroots programs, 55–68, 173

Heritage languages, 5, 18, 19, 34, 71–84, 199
Heritage language programs, K-12-based, 87–96, 153–167, 173
Heritage language programs, community-based, 55–68

Identity, 13, 191–2, 22–25, 30, 32, 35, 55–68, 71–84, 87, 93, 95–6, 191–2
Immigrants (see newcomers)
Immigrant language programs (see newcomer language programs)
Inclusion, 17–8, 27, 34, 49, 103–115, 135, 173, 193
Indigenous languages (see Aboriginal languages)
Intensive French programs, 22–35

Language awareness, 3–18
Language loss, 57, 87, 158, 172, 174
Language proficiency, 40–2, 46, 66, 68, 73, 82, 87, 89, 92, 93, 103, 106, 119, 148, 186
Language status, 3, 25, 32, 83, 88, 90, 92, 104, 153, 156, 157, 159, 171, 173, 193
Language strategies, 6, 9–18, 40, 119, 120–132, 147, 148, 169, 196
Learning Disabilities, 103–115, 118–132, 135–149
Literacy, written language, 4, 9, 12, 26, 40, 89–96

Manitoba, 4, 104, 109
Mi'kmaq language (see Aboriginal languages)
Minority languages
Minority language programs, 81, 90, 158, 166, 169, 192, 195

Motivation, general, 41, 48, 68, 93, 95, 130, 189, 191
Motivation, integrative, 6–16
Motivation, orientations, 71–84
Multilingualism, 5, 17–9, 24, 47, 68, 91–96

New Brunswick, 4, 104, 108, 109, 140
Newcomers, 55, 184, 186–7
Newfoundland & Labrador, 26, 104, 108, 110, 156
Northwest Territories, 4, 104, 171
Nova Scotia, 4, 104, 108, 109, 110, 111, 153, 156, 175
Nunavut, 4, 104, 171, 193

Ontario, 4, 5, 18, 38, 39, 42, 47, 49, 104, 108, 110, 191

Parent Support of English language study, 159
Parent Support of French language study, 5, 17, 23, 24, 25, 30, 31, 33–5, 39, 112–114, 143
Parent Support of heritage language study, 56, 59–69, 82, 92, 155–7, 159, 160, 162, 165, 167–178
Pedagogy, 23, 40, 68, 84, 103, 118, 140, 147, 171, 176–9
Prince Edward Island, 4, 104

Reading difficulties, 118–132
Reading strategies, 118–132
Residential Schools, 155–158, 166, 170, 185, 188
Residents, permanent, 38
Residents, temporary, 39, 49

Self-determination theory, 71, 75, 76, 79
Social capital, 23, 24, 30, 35
Spanish language, 29, 30, 45, 55–68, 72, 91, 158, 159

Teacher certification, 171, 174, 176
Transfers, 103–115

Willingness to communicate, 6–18
Writing, 6–18, 31, 89, 92, 122, 135–149, 174, 177, 184–196

Yukon Territory, 104, 171, 172

For Product Safety Concerns and Information please contact our EU Authorised Representative:

Easy Access System Europe

Mustamäe tee 50

10621 Tallinn

Estonia

gpsr.requests@easproject.com

www.ingramcontent.com/pod-product-compliance
Lightning Source LLC
Chambersburg PA
CBHW070606300426
44113CB00010B/1420